Virtualization and Forensics

A Digital Forensic Investigator's Guide to Virtual Environments

Diane Barrett
Gregory Kipper

Technical Editor
Samuel Liles

ELSEVIER

AMSTERDAM • BOSTON • HEIDELBERG • LONDON
NEW YORK • OXFORD • PARIS • SAN DIEGO
SAN FRANCISCO • SINGAPORE • SYDNEY • TOKYO
Syngress is an imprint of Elsevier

SYNGRESS®

Syngress is an imprint of Elsevier.
30 Corporate Drive, Suite 400, Burlington, MA 01803, USA

This book is printed on acid-free paper.

Notices
Knowledge and best practice in this field are constantly changing. As new research and experience broaden our understanding, changes in research methods, professional practices, or medical treatment may become necessary.

Practitioners and researchers must always rely on their own experience and knowledge in evaluating and using any information, methods, compounds, or experiments described herein. In using such information or methods, they should be mindful of their own safety and the safety of others, including parties for whom they have a professional responsibility.

To the fullest extent of the law, neither the Publisher nor the authors, contributors, or editors, assume any liability for any injury and/or damage to persons or property as a matter of products liability, negligence or otherwise, or from any use or operation of any methods, products, instructions, or ideas contained in the material herein.

Library of Congress Cataloging-in-Publication Data
Application submitted

British Library Cataloguing-in-Publication Data
A catalogue record for this book is available from the British Library.

ISBN: 978-1-59749-557-8

Printed in the United States of America
10 11 12 13   5 4 3 2 1

Elsevier Inc., the author(s), and any person or firm involved in the writing, editing, or production (collectively "Makers") of this book ("the Work") do not guarantee or warrant the results to be obtained from the Work.

For information on rights, translations, and bulk sales, contact Matt Pedersen, Commercial Sales Director and Rights; e-mail m.pedersen@elsevier.com

For information on all Syngress publications,
visit our Web site at www.syngress.com

Typeset by: diacriTech, Chennai, India

Working together to grow
libraries in developing countries

www.elsevier.com | www.bookaid.org | www.sabre.org

ELSEVIER   BOOK AID International   Sabre Foundation

To my sister and best friend – Michele.

– Diane

To Azure, McCoy, and Grant – the best kids in the world!

– Greg

CONTENTS

Acknowledgments

Publishing a book takes the collaboration and teamwork of many individuals. We would like to acknowledge all those who supported us on this endeavor. Our thanks to Angelina Ward, Amber Schroader, Eric Cole, Jay Varda, Chris Romano, Paul Aronhime, George Fadeley, Chris Burns, Jim Jaeger, Tomas Castrejon, Marci Woolson, Leo Fox, Kelli O'Neill, Edward Haletky, and Richard Bares.

Diane would like to thank everyone whom she drove crazy while working on this project, especially her coauthor. Greg, thanks so much for all your input and hard work.

Specifically, Greg would like to thank Diane for her vision in choosing to take on this project and the privilege for allowing him to be a part of it.

INTRODUCTION

It often amazes me the impact certain technologies could have on society and how often organizations look at the functionality benefits but fail to realize the overall impact they could have long term. One area that is often overlooked is security. The reason why security is often viewed as expensive or as difficult to deploy is because it is often done in a reactive not proactive manner. We wait for problems to occur and try to implement solutions when it is too late in the process. If security was thought about from the beginning, there are usually cost-effective ways to make sure that the benefits of the new technology are used and organizations' information is properly protected. One area where this cycle is currently playing out is with virtualization and cloud security.

If you ask a forensic expert to perform analysis on a compromised system, this is a straightforward task, and you will notice the confidence in which he or she can implement the task. However, if you mention it is a completely virtualized environment, the confidence changes to fear very quickly. Virtualization is all around us, and with the continued push of reducing costs and moving to cloud computing, this trend only increases over the coming years; however, our ability to analyze these systems is still in its infancy even though the technology is quickly maturing.

In a traditional data center if one computer is compromised, a single system or business process is at risk. If you move to a virtualized environment, the entire paradigm shifts. Now if one virtual machine is compromised, the potential for guest escape and host compromised is potentially possible, and now a single compromise can be devastating to an organization. More importantly is how do you perform incident response. Having a compromise is a potential risk in any environment, but preventing reinfection is the key to security-minded organizations. At the heart of the eradication step in incident response is the forensic analysis, to better understand what happened and how it could be prevented.

Forensic analysis involves analyzing two key components of the system: memory and the hard drive. On a typical system, a memory dump could be performed to understand what has recently been written into memory and specific programs and libraries analyzed. Similar analysis can be performed on the hard drive, finding individual files that have been deleted and recovering the information. With the introduction of virtualization, all of this changes. Now the entire memory and hard drive of the virtualized environment reside in a single file in the memory or the hard drive. Traditional techniques do not scale, and security professionals are faced with a dilemma – How do we analyze the systems forensically since standard methods no longer work? Let me introduce a key piece of research and literature, *Virtualization and Forensics*.

If your organization is using virtualization in any capacity, always remember that being proactive is more cost effective than being reactive. The proactive method involves learning the methods in this book to train your staff, so when an incident occurs, they can quickly perform the forensics and minimize the damage to your systems.

For those who choose to ignore the importance of knowing how to perform forensics in a virtualized environment, you can always use the golden security rules of last resort: drink and pray (and not necessarily in that order).

– Dr. Eric Cole

ABOUT THE AUTHORS

Diane Barrett has been involved in the information technology (IT) industry for over 20 years. She spent 7 years in software development before continuing her career in technology by her involvement in education, network security, and digital forensics. She holds an MS in IT with an INFOSEC specialization and is currently working on a PhD with a specialization in information security. She has spent the last several years performing digital forensics in civil litigation cases and has published numerous works as both a primary and coauthor focusing on computer forensics and network security. These works include "Computer Forensics JumpStart" and "Computer Networking Illuminated." She has also been the featured speaker at many industry events.

Gregory Kipper has been involved in the field of IT security and information assurance over the past 16 years. He has spent the last 10 years of his career working in the field of digital forensics and the impacts emerging technologies have on crime and crime fighting. During that time, he has been the keynote speaker at select industry events and has published numerous papers in regards to the future and the impact of digital forensics. He is currently pursuing a master's in emerging technologies. He is also a published author in the field; his works include "Investigator's Guide to Steganography" and "Wireless Crime and Forensic Investigation."

Technical Editor

Samuel Liles (M.S.C.S) is an associate professor of IT at Purdue University Calumet. He is a senior faculty member in the Computer Information Technology department delivering operating systems, networking, and security curriculum with a focus on security and forensics. He provides consulting services to all levels of government. He has served in the military, held various positions in law enforcement, and worked as an IT consultant for over 15 years.

VIRTUALIZATION

HOW VIRTUALIZATION HAPPENS

INFORMATION IN THIS CHAPTER

- Physical Machines
- How Virtualization Works
- Hypervisors
- Main Categories of Virtualization
- Benefits of Virtualization
- Cost of Virtualization

Just about every technology magazine and article published today mentions virtualization or cloud computing. According to the research published by Gartner, Inc., 18 percent of server workloads in 2009 ran on virtualized servers; that share will grow to 28 percent this year (2010) and reach almost half by 2012 (Messmer, 2009). The survey statistics show that large enterprises have driven server virtualization over the last several years and that VMware holds the largest market share against a handful of competitors, including Microsoft, Citrix, Red Hat, and others. There are close to six million virtual machines (VMs) believed to be in use today. Gartner analysts predict that virtualization will be the default for the enterprise over the next few years.

Furthermore, a *Network World* article by Dubie (2010) states that the CIOs who participated in the survey put virtualization as a top priority for 2010. This is up from the third position in 2009, and cloud computing technologies shot up from sixteenth place to the second priority for CIOs. With more emphasis being placed on going green and power becoming more expensive, virtualization offers cost benefits by decreasing the number of physical machines required within an environment. A virtualized environment offers reduced support by making testing and maintenance easier.

On the client side, the capability to run multiple operating environments allows a machine to support applications and services for an operating environment other than the primary environment. This reduces upgrade costs and allows more uniformity in desktop environments. The worldwide hosted virtual desktop (HVD) market will accelerate through 2013 to reach 49 million units, up from more than 500,000 units in 2009, according to Gartner, Inc. Worldwide HVD revenue will grow from about $1.3 billion to $1.5 billion in 2009, which is less than 1 percent of the worldwide professional PC market, to $65.7 billion in 2013 (Gammage & Jump, 2009).

Virtualization is also found on mobile devices. For example, the Garnet VM can run native Palm operating system (OS) applications on several models of the Nokia Internet Tablet. As of December 2009, it supports over 30,000 applications. It is estimated that by 2012, more than half of all new smartphones shipped will include hardware virtualization support.

In the data center, approximately 16 percent of the workload is virtualized. Figure 1.1 shows data from a TechTarget Virtualization Decisions 2009 survey, which collected data from July 2009 to September 2009 with responses from more than 900 IT professionals worldwide (*Virtual Data Center E-Zine*, 2010).

These developments should be of interest to the digital forensic investigator for several reasons. First and foremost, computer forensics professionals will be required to detect and examine such environments. Virtual environments (VEs) are showing up from the desktop to the data center. In the case in which a virtual desktop is used, acquiring a dead drive image may produce

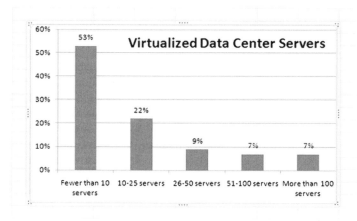

Figure 1.1 Data Center Virtualization Data

very little, if any, evidence. An increase in the use of VEs and applications that can be run from a Universal Serial Bus (USB) device means that any incriminating evidence may not be readily found, especially if the device itself is not recovered. As the use of virtual machine environments (VMEs) increases, computer attackers are becoming increasingly interested in detecting the presence of VMEs, both locally and across the network. The interest is fueled by those who want to spread malware, steal data, or conceal activities. As malicious code is released that makes use of its own VME, it becomes essential for antimalware researchers to find ways to detect the VME in order to protect against malware.

Physical Machines

For purposes of discussion, and to provide a solid contrast for the remainder of this book, we define a physical machine as a hardware-based device such as a PC or server. Specifically, the physical computer is running at the electronic, or machine, level as opposed to the logical level. Physical machines also operate with much more direct access to the hardware, whereas users of VEs will relate to the data they access and work with based on the name of the file. A physical environment is concerned where the data is physically located on the sectors of the disk.

How Virtualization Works

A VM is a software implementation of a computer that executes programs like a physical machine. In "Formal Requirements for Virtualizable Third Generation Architectures," Popek and Goldberg, who have defined conditions that may be tested to determine whether architecture can support a VM, describe it as "an efficient, isolated duplicate of a real machine." VMs have been in use for many years, and some would say we have come full circle. The fundamental concept of a VM revolves around a software application that behaves as if it were its own computer. This is the original job sharing mechanism prominent in mainframes. The VM application ("guest") runs its own self-contained OS on the actual ("host") machine. Put simply, a VM is a virtual computer running inside a physical computer. The virtual OS can range from a Windows environment to a Macintosh environment and is not limited to one per host machine. For example, you may have a Windows XP host machine with Linux and Windows 2003

Figure 1.2 Linux XP and Windows 2003 Virtual Machines Running on a Windows XP-Based Host

VMs. Figure 1.2 shows Linux XP and Windows 2003 server VMs running on a Windows XP host machine.

The explosion of x86 servers revived interest in virtualization. The primary driver was the potential for server consolidation. Virtualization allowed a single server to replace multiple dedicated servers with underutilized resources.

Popek and Goldberg explained virtualization through the idea of a virtual machine monitor (VMM). A VMM is a piece of software that has three essential characteristics. First, the VMM provides an environment for programs that is fundamentally identical to the environment on the physical machine; second, programs that run in this environment have very little speed degradation compared with the physical machine; and finally, the VMM has total control of system resources. However, the x86 architecture did not achieve the "classical virtualization" as defined by the Popek and Goldberg virtualization requirements, and binary translation of the guest kernel code was used instead. This is because x86 OSes are designed to run directly on the physical hardware and presume that they control the computer hardware. Virtualization of the x86 architecture has been accomplished through either full virtualization or paravirtualization. Both create the illusion of physical hardware to achieve

Note

To facilitate virtualization, a hypervisor is used. The hypervisor controls how a computer's processors and memory is accessed by the guest operating system. A hypervisor or VMM is a virtualization platform that provides more than one OS to run on a host computer at the same time.

the goal of OS independence from the hardware but present some trade-offs in performance and complexity. Creating this illusion is done by placing a virtualization layer under the OS to create and manage the VM. Full virtualization or paravirtualization will be discussed later in this chapter. Both Intel and AMD have now introduced architecture that supports classical virtualization.

For a very in-depth explanation of virtualization, there are several published papers explaining the highly technical details of how virtualization works. For example, Adams and Agesen (2006) from VMware have written "A Comparison of Software and Hardware Techniques for x86 Virtualization." The current associated link is in the reference section at the end of this chapter.

In a physically partitioned system, more than one OS can be hosted on the same machine. The most common example of this type of environment is a dual-boot system where Microsoft and Linux OSes coexist on the same system. Each of these partitions is being supported by a single OS. VM software products allow an entire stack of software to be encapsulated in a container called a VM. The encapsulation starts at the OS and runs all the way up to the application level. This type of technology has the capability to run more than one VM on a single physical computer provided that the computer has sufficient processing power, memory, and storage. Individual VMs are isolated from one another to provide a compartmentalized environment. Each VM contains its own environment just like a physical server and includes an OS, applications, and networking capabilities. The VMs are managed individually similar to a physical environment. Unlike a physically partitioned machine, VM products allow multiple OSes to exist on one partition.

Virtualizing Operating Systems

Virtualized OSes can be used in a variety of ways. These environments allow the user to play with questionable or malicious software in a sandbox-type environment. For example, VMs can

Figure 1.3 Virtualization Concepts

be used to see how different OSes react to an attack or a virus. It can give the user access to a Linux environment without having to dual boot the laptop or PC. Finally, it allows an investigator to mount a suspect environment to see the environment just as the suspect used it. This can be helpful in presenting cases to a judge or jury. Showing the environment can have a big impact, especially if it can convey the content in a manner that the judge and jury would understand. Booting up a machine that has a pornographic background gets the point across much faster and clearer in the courtroom and in litigation conferences. Figure 1.3 shows the concept behind virtualizing OSes.

Virtualizing Hardware Platforms

Hardware virtualization, sometimes called *platform* or *server virtualization*, is executed on a particular hardware platform by host software. Essentially, it hides the physical hardware. The host software that is actually a control program is called a *hypervisor*. The hypervisor creates a simulated computer environment for the guest software that could be anything from user applications to complete OSes. The guest software performs as if it were running directly on the physical hardware. However, access to physical resources such as network access and physical ports is usually managed at a more restrictive level than the processor and memory. Guests are often restricted from accessing specific peripheral devices. Managing network connections and external ports such as USB from inside the guest software can be challenging. Figure 1.4 shows the concept behind virtualizing hardware platforms.

Server Virtualization

Server virtualization is actually a subset of hardware virtualization. This concept is most prominently found in data centers. It is mostly relied on as a power-saving measure for enterprises in an effort to implement cost-effective data centers and utilize the increased hardware resource capability of servers. In server virtualization, many virtual servers are contained on one physical

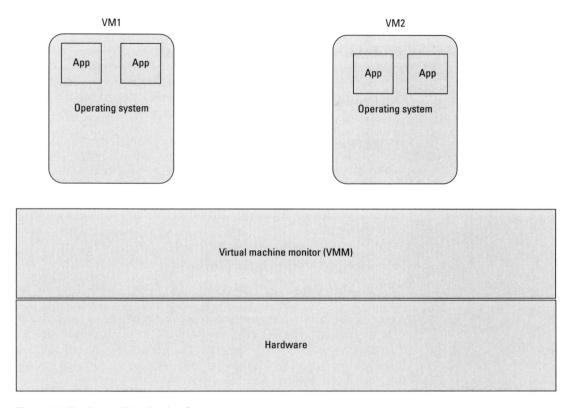

Figure 1.4 Hardware Virtualization Concepts

Note

A provided software platform is used to divide one physical server into multiple isolated VMs. The VMs are sometimes called *virtual private servers* (VPSes) or *virtual dedicated servers*, but depending on the virtualization vendor and platform, they can also be known as guests, instances, containers, or emulations. There are three popular approaches to server virtualization: the VM model, the paravirtual machine model, and virtualization at the OS layer.

server. This configuration is hidden to server users. To the user, the virtual servers appear exactly like physical servers.

Server virtualization has become part of an overall virtualization trend in enterprise environments, which also includes storage and network virtualization along with management solutions. Server virtualization can be used in many other enterprise scenarios including the elimination of server sprawl, more efficient use of server resources, improved server availability, and disaster recovery, as well as in testing and development. This trend is also part of the autonomic computing development, in which the server environment will be able to manage itself based on perceived activity. Chapter 11, "Visions of the Future: Virtualization and Cloud Computing," discusses the autonomic computing concept.

Hypervisors

In virtualization technology, a hypervisor is a software program that manages multiple OSes (or multiple instances of the same OS) on a single computer system. The hypervisor manages the system's processor, memory, and other resources to allocate what each OS requires.

Bare-Metal Hypervisor (Type 1)

Bare-metal or Type 1 hypervisors are hypervisors that install directly on top of the physical server. Basically, it is a thin OS that controls the hardware, handles resource scheduling, and monitors the guest. Type 1 native or bare-metal hypervisors are run directly on the hardware platform. The guest OS is not aware that it is not running on real hardware and does not require any modification, but it does require resources from the host.

The guest OS actually runs at the second level above the hardware. The hypervisor or VMM coordinates instructions between the guest and the host CPU. What that means is that the guest OS is controlled by the host system and the guest uses a virtual architecture, which is almost like the physical hardware. Type 1 hypervisors are typically the preferred approach to virtualization because they deal directly with the hardware, so higher virtualization efficiency is achieved. Some examples of the type of hypervisor are VMware ESX, Citrix XenServer, and Microsoft Hyper-V.

Embedded Hypervisor

A Type 1 hypervisor that supports the requirements of embedded system's development is an embedded hypervisor. Embedded hypervisors are designed into the hardware device itself. This is

Note

Hypervisors are designed for a particular processor architecture and may also be called *virtualization managers*.

similar to the way a computer basic input/output system (BIOS) works. The difference is that embedded hypervisors require additional steps such as formatting the machine storage for a particular product. Dell has been offering the VMware ESX3i hypervisor and the embedded Citrix XenServer hypervisor in the PowerEdgeTR805 and R905 models since mid-2008. In early 2009, LynuxWorks released an embedded hypervisor for high-assurance systems that runs on Intel Core 2 Duo processor-based systems. Some computer and server vendors ship new machines with embedded hypervisors.

The chips used in the embedded industry have less horsepower, the amount of memory they have is limited, and their use may be tied to a particular vendor, but they are popular because they can reduce attack exposure, minimize the number of drivers required, allow for boot up from VM images, and allow all virtual images to be stored on a single storage area network (SAN). Some of the compelling reasons for using embedded hypervisors are as follows:

- Support for multiple operating systems
- Secure encapsulation for any subsystem defined by the developer
- Failure of any subsystem cannot affect other subsystems
- Support for legacy embedded code
- Intellectual property protection from theft or misuse
- Migration of applications to multicore systems

The term embedded hypervisor is not restricted to just servers. For example, VMware and Citrix Systems have releases of a client-side Type 1 hypervisor that can be embedded. Embedded hypervisor technology can be used in systems to control automated machinery on a manufacturing floor or large medical devices. These hypervisors manage the underlying hardware differently from those offered for server virtualizations such as VMware, Citrix, and Microsoft, but the principle is the same. Another growing area for the use of embedded hypervisors is mobile devices. For example, in late 2008, Open Kernel Labs (OK Labs) released an embedded hypervisor named OKL4 that is used on the Qualcomm chipset inside a commercial Android-powered handset.

Hosted Hypervisor (Type 2)

A hosted or Type 2 hypervisor is software that runs on top of an already installed standard OS environment, such as Linux or Windows. The guest OS runs at the third level above the hardware. The hypervisor's control of resources is based on the resources presented by the underlying OS. The hypervisor merely runs as an application on the preconfigured OS, and the guest OS running on the hypervisor is the VM. The state of the guest OS is entirely encapsulated. Type 2 hypervisors are mainly used in systems where there is a need for a variety of input/output devices that can be supported by the host OS and in client systems where efficiency is less critical. Examples of this type of environment are Parallels Workstation, Microsoft Virtual Server, VMware Server, and VMware Workstation.

Main Categories of Virtualization

VMware was instrumental in resolving the challenges that the x86 architecture presented to virtualization. In 1998, VMware developed binary translation techniques that led to three alternative techniques for handling instructions in order to virtualize the CPU on the x86 architecture: full virtualization, paravirtualization, and hardware-assisted virtualization. Additionally, virtualization can be divided into categories such as native, OS, storage, and applications. Since these categories are very broad, it is helpful to distill them into specific categories to thoroughly understand the differences and the similarities between the different categories of virtualization.

Full Virtualization

Full virtualization is a virtualization technique used to provide a VME that completely simulates the underlying hardware. In this type of environment, any software capable of execution on the physical hardware can be run in the VM, and any OS supported by the underlying hardware can be run in each individual VM. Users can run multiple different guest OSes simultaneously. In full virtualization, the VM simulates enough hardware to allow an unmodified guest OS to be run in isolation. This is particularly helpful in a number of situations. For example, in OS development, experimental new code can be run at the same time as older versions, each in a separate VM. The hypervisor provides each VM with all the services of the physical system, including a virtual BIOS, virtual devices, and virtualized memory management. The guest OS is fully disengaged from the underlying hardware by the virtualization layer.

Full virtualization is achieved by using a combination of binary translation and direct execution. With full virtualization hypervisors, the physical CPU executes nonsensitive instructions at native speed; OS instructions are translated on the fly and cached for future use, and user level instructions run unmodified at native speed. Full virtualization offers the best isolation and security for VMs and simplifies migration and portability as the same guest OS instance can run on virtualized

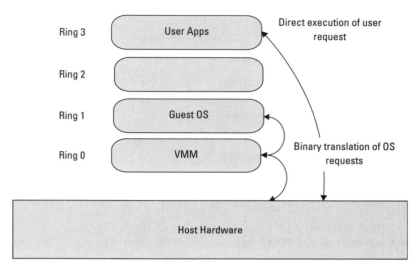

Figure 1.5 Full Virtualization Concepts

or native hardware. Figure 1.5 shows the concept behind full virtualization.

Paravirtualization

Paravirtualization involves modifying the OS kernel. The OS kernel acts as a bridge between the applications and the processing done at the hardware level. Paravirtualization replaces nonvirtualizable instructions with hypercalls that communicate directly with the virtualization layer hypervisor. A hypercall is based on the same concept as a system call. System calls are used by an application to request services from the OS and provide the interface between the application or process and the OS. Hypercalls work the same way, except the hypervisor is used. The hypervisor also provides hypercall interfaces for other kernel operations including memory management and interrupt handling.

In paravirtualization, after the host OS boots, the VM emulator is launched. Depending on the platform, the emulator uses either the VMLAUNCH (Intel) or the VMRUN (AMD) instruction to start execution of the VM. At that point, there are two copies of the OS in existence. The host is in a suspension mode, while the guest runs in an active state.

Although paravirtualization can introduce support issues in production environments because it requires deep OS kernel modifications, it is relatively easy compared with full virtualization. The open source Xen project is an example of paravirtualization. Figure 1.6 shows paravirtualization concepts.

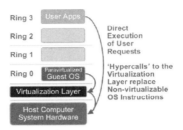

Figure 1.6 Paravirtualization Concepts

Hardware-Assisted Virtualization

Hardware-assisted virtualization is also called *native virtualization*, *accelerated virtualization*, or *hardware VM*, depending on the vendor. Hardware-assisted virtualization is a technology that allows for a CPU instruction set communication in which the VMM runs in a new root level mode below the OS kernel level. Support of this type of virtualization on Intel and AMD processors became available in 2006 but was first introduced on the IBM System/370 in 1972. In this type of virtualization, privileged and sensitive calls are set to automatically trap to the hypervisor. The binary translation used in full virtualization or the use of hypercalls in paravirtualization is no longer needed. Depending on the CPU manufacturer, the guest state is stored in either VM Control Structures (Intel) or VM Control Blocks (AMD). First-generation hardware-assisted technologies still lag behind in performance when compared to the full virtualization, but development of second-generation hardware-assisted technologies will improve virtualization performance while reducing memory overhead.

Figure 1.7 shows hardware-assisted virtualization concepts.

As a recap of the virtualization concepts discussed here, Table 1.1 is a comparison of the hardware virtualization types as listed in a white paper published by VMware titled "Understanding Full Virtualization, Paravirtualization, and Hardware Assist."

Alan Murphy of F5 published a white paper titled "Virtualization Defined – Eight Different Ways." Several of the eight methods of virtualization outlined in the paper will be discussed in the next several sections.

Operating System Virtualization

OS-level virtualization takes advantage of the low overhead of the OS-level architecture in an effort to efficiently use server resources. This provides low overhead while running many VMs

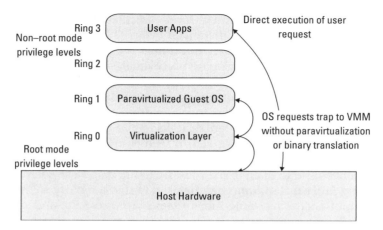

Figure 1.7 Hardware-Assisted Virtualization Concepts

Table 1.1 VMware's Summary Comparison of x86 Processor Virtualization Techniques

	Full Virtualization with Binary Translation	Hardware-Assisted Virtualization	OS-Assisted Virtualization and Paravirtualization
Technique	Binary Translation and Direct Execution	Exit to Root Mode on Privileged Instructions	Hypercalls
Guest Modification and Compatibility	Unmodified Guest OS and Excellent compatibility	Unmodified Guest OS and Excellent compatibility	Guest OS codified to issue Hypercalls, so it cannot run on Native Hardware or other Hypervisors Poor compatibility; Not available on Windows OSes
Performance	Good	Fair Current performance lags Binary Translation virtualization on various workloads but improves over time	Better in certain cases
Used By	VMware, Microsoft, Parallels	VMware, Microsoft, Parallels, Xen	VMware, Xen
Guest OS Hypervisor Independent?	Yes	Yes	XenLinux runs only on Xen Hypervisor VMI-Linux is Hypervisor agnostic

on a single physical server. In OS-level virtualization, the kernel allows for multiple isolated instances of an OS instead of just one. These instances are called *containers, VEs, VPSes,* or *jails*. They look and feel like a real server; however, it is an illusion. This technology is very similar to the chroot mechanism on a Unix or Linux OS. Here is how it works. Linux's directory system is built on a root directory very similar to the c: drive of a Windows OS. All directories are then created relative to the root directory. A chroot jail changes the visible root directory that the user sees, hence the name chroot. It is named after the chroot(2) system call, which is used to change the root of the file system as seen by the calling process. Programs can be used in this directory so that they cannot access or name files outside the directory, and the directory is called a *chroot jail*. The main benefit of a chroot jail is that the jail limits the portion of the file system; the daemon or background process can see to only the root directory of the jail. For example, if a server is compromised and the attacker uses it to modify files, the modification actually affects the chroot directory, not the actual root directory itself. This environment is used in testing and honeypotting.

The advantages to this form of virtualization are that it usually has little or no overhead. The programs in the virtual partition or "jail" use the OS's normal system call interface and do not need emulation or have to be run in an intermediate VM. This is in contrast to full virtualization and paravirtualization.

The disadvantage of OS-level virtualization is that it is not as flexible as other virtualization approaches. It can only host a guest OS that is the same as the host OS, although the use of different libraries and distributions are possible.

Application Server Virtualization

Application virtualization is also called *advanced load balancing* and has been around since load balancing came into being. Load balancing is a method that distributes the workload evenly across multiple devices such as servers, routers, and network cards. The concept behind application server virtualization is that access is provided to many different application services transparently. Figure 1.8 shows the concepts behind load balancing using Web servers.

As demonstrated in Figure 1.8, the firewall hosts a virtual interface accessible to the end user on the front end. On the back end, load balancing is done for a number of different servers and applications such as the Web servers shown. A virtual interface is exposed to the Internet as the actual Web server. The load balancing servers manage multiple Web servers or applications as a single instance.

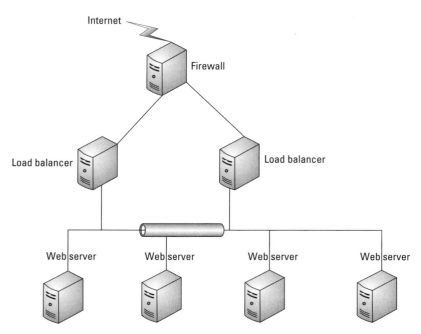

Figure 1.8 Load Balancing Concepts

This is referred to as one-to-many. One server is presented to the world, hiding the availability of multiple servers behind the firewall.

Application server virtualization works exactly the same way; only virtualization can be applied to just about any type of application architecture. This type of virtualization is common on Web server platforms and data center storage tiers.

Application Virtualization

Application virtualization is based on a concept different from virtualizing hardware with methods such as Type 1 and Type 2 virtualizations. In application virtualization, the virtualization concept involves a local device and an actual installed application in a remote location. Application virtualization is also called *thin client technology*. In this type of technology, the local device provides physical resources such as the CPU and random access memory that may be required to run the software, but nothing is installed locally on the device itself. The underlying principle is to have the application and OS separated, so the application is OS independent. In these implementations, although the user interface is transparent, the virtual application runs locally, and the application runs remotely. This technology is mostly deployed in corporate environments. Examples of this type of implementation are Microsoft terminal services, Citrix, and PanoLogic.

Network Virtualization

The concept of network or local area network virtualization involves virtualizing Internet Protocol (IP) routing, forwarding, and addressing schemes. Network virtualization provides a way to run multiple networks, each customized to a specific purpose, at the same time over a shared network using virtual IP management and segmentation, but it can be used in the opposite manner. In other words, network virtualization can be used to either merge multiple physical networks into one virtual network or logically segment a single physical network into multiple logical networks. Since this type of virtualization allows the interface to bring and teardown routing services, partitions can be created on the fly for one network without interrupting other services and routing tables on that same interface. This method splits up the available bandwidth into independent channels, so they can be assigned to a particular device in real time. Vendors such as Cisco and Nortel both have devices and implementations that support this type of virtualization.

Storage Virtualization

Storage virtualization is commonly used in SANs. In a SAN system, all the separate storage disks on the network are grouped and then merged in an array. Servers can then access the array as though it were a local storage device. SANs are made up of several components, such as disk arrays and switches. The storage space on each drive in a SAN is divided logically into storage blocks that can be assigned as a larger group spanning multiple physical drives. These storage blocks are managed as a single virtual storage device called a *storage pool*.

According to IBM, there are five types of storage virtualization:

- Disk drive virtualization takes place when the firmware abstracts the physical cylinder, head, and sector into a single logical block address.
- Storage system partitioning occurs when the storage system creates multiple partitions from a single storage resource.
- Block virtualization happens when the software abstracts multiple disk arrays into a single storage resource.
- Tape virtualization occurs as the software abstracts both tape drives and tape media onto a single disk resource.
- File virtualization is the creation of an abstraction layer between the file servers and the clients who access those file servers.

Storage virtualization helps reduce the high administrative overhead of managing SANs by providing a more easily managed environment, which can be used to back up, archive, and recover data in a shorter period of time and makes the complexity of a SAN appear less formidable. The idea behind storage virtualization is to pool and share storage resources. This type of virtualization offers the capability for storage services such as thin provisioning, replication, and data migration. It also allows virtualization with hardware and software hybrid appliances, as shown in Figure 1.9.

Service Virtualization

Service virtualization is associated with service-oriented architecture (SOA). An SOA is fundamentally a collection of services that connect through some means and then communicate with one another. This means of connecting the services to one another is usually a service intermediary sitting between the service client and the service implementation. This service intermediary is the central premise behind all service virtualization architectures, as shown in Figure 1.10.

In this type of virtualization, all communication through the service intermediary, the clients, and the service implementations never directly interact.

In service virtualization, all the service components used in delivering an application function independently and can work together regardless of where those pieces physically reside. It

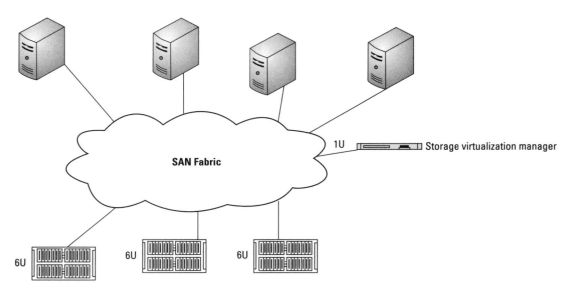

Figure 1.9 Storage Virtualization Concepts

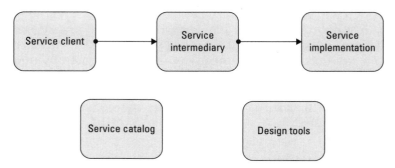

Figure 1.10 Service Virtualization Concepts

allows independent ownership of each layer within a typical SOA. It allows for a wide range of flexibility from beginning to end. Developers can develop service interfaces, and operations can dictate endpoint policies and messaging standards. The architecture allows all stakeholders involved in a project to work together through the central repository. Service virtualization can also help put organizations in a position to leverage new cloud computing opportunities without requiring any changes to existing service code. An example of this is Microsoft Services SOA Infrastructure, which provides a service virtualization called the *Managed Services Engine* with the intention of using it for cloud computing on the Azure Services Platform.

Benefits of Virtualization

There are many benefits to virtualization. As mentioned earlier, with power becoming more expensive and a trend towards going green, virtualization offers cost benefits by decreasing the number of physical machines required within an environment. There are additional benefits that virtualization offers such as more effective disaster recovery and better resource management. In the "Rise of the Virtual Machine," Orakwue (2009) describes additional benefits of virtualization, including testing, business continuity, and server consolidation. Several of those benefits will be discussed as well.

The cost and complexity of disaster recovery and business continuity management are greatly reduced by using virtualization technology. Because OSes can be encapsulated with applications and data, it is much easier to move and implement for immediate access. VMs consist entirely of software, so transportation to an offsite location can be done just as with transmitting a data file. This capability alone can reduce downtime in the event of system failure. With virtualization, organizations can do full mirroring and backups of primary systems without duplicating the hardware for those systems. Conversely, hosts running the same platform can access saved files of configured OSes from a repository.

Virtualization management tools help to effectively manage server resources. In virtualization, since the machine hardware and OS are independent, an OS can readily be moved to run on another server. This comes in handy when server space gets low, or memory capacity is reduced. Additionally servers can be readily put up and taken down in seasonal businesses such as tax return preparation. The need for more physical resources during times of high usage can be easily compensated for with virtualization.

Virtualization is an ideal environment for testing applications. Multiple OS configurations can be easily stored, then downloaded to build, verify, and validate software applications, and just as easily deleted when testing is completed. This type of environment can also be used to test malware actions. Additional benefits of virtualization include server consolidation. For example, organizations can run as many as 15 applications in a VE on a single server. Virtualization technology can be used in technical support services to help walk customers and clients through support issues in the environment they are experiencing. It can also be used to isolate business applications from portable devices that workers bring into the workplace. Most importantly, it can be used by forensic investigators to view the environment as the suspect used it.

Cost of Virtualization

Although virtualization has many benefits, it may not be appropriate for every situation or environment, and there are also costs associated with virtualization such as tracking not only authorized VMs but also unauthorized VMs, configuration management, and virtual sprawl. There are also hidden costs such as security and management.

A virtualized infrastructure is often more complex to manage than the conventional physical server environments. In reality, many organizations have a combination of virtual and physical servers. This mixed mode environment increases operational complexity. With this increased complexity, configuration management can become unmanageable. VMs need to have correct permissions and configuration settings and be patched and updated. They are susceptible to the same issues as a host OS. The security concerns of VEs begin with the guest OS. If a VM is compromised, an intruder can gain control of all the guest OSes.

In addition, because hardware is shared, most VMs run with very high privileges. This can allow an intruder who compromises a VM to compromise the host machine too. With VMs, security zone enforcement control can be easily overlooked because data can be inadvertently commingled, resulting in possible data corruption, leak, or loss. For example, if VMs that contain sensitive information are hosted on the physical machines that contain VMs for testing, the risk to the sensitive information is greatly increased. A virtualized environment needs special consideration when deploying financial applications on virtualized shared hosting and secure storage on SAN technologies.

VEs are susceptible to vulnerabilities, just as much as physical environments are. For example, a few years ago, VMware's network address translation (NAT) service had a buffer-overflow vulnerability that allowed remote attackers to execute malicious code by exploiting the VM itself. Because of the ease with which virtualization can be implemented and deployed, organizations can easily end up with lost assets, lack of standardization, and noncompliance with established internal security policies.

Although virtualization is touted to be green, physical server running many VMs may run at a constant or higher utilization rate than if there was single use. This means that the hardware is pulling quite a bit more power than a nonvirtualized server running on much lower utilization. The number of VMs allocated per physical host quickly translates to a rapid increase of resources that require network configuration and IP addresses. The capability to quickly mass produce VMs can present not only licensing compliance issues but also storage issues. Local and network storage capacities are quickly reduced since the VMs take up more space than a regular office document but are just as easy to copy.

Unauthorized VMs are quite possible and can become a problem on the network. VM software is freely available and downloadable. Employees can independently install these applications onto their laptops, workstations, or removable media. It is not uncommon to find unauthorized or rogue VMs. This issue is discussed in Chapter 7, "Finding and Imaging Virtual Environments."

Due to the dynamic nature of VMs, when they go down, it will be hard to identify the physical server on which they were residing, what systems they were hosting, and what their custom configuration settings are unless there is detailed, updated documentation in place. On the flip side, network and storage components are not exempt from failure. When using this type of environment, any outage or failure of the network or storage device will affect a large number of VMs relying on that device for services.

Summary

In this chapter, we have discussed how virtualization happens along with the various methods of virtualization, hypervisors, and the main categories of virtualization. We also covered the benefits and costs associated with using VEs.

An investigator must understand these concepts in order to properly assess the environment. You will need to ask questions about the use of these environments not only to get a good picture of the examination environment but also to determine what exactly will need to be examined and where evidence might be found.

References

Adams, K., & Agesen, O. (2006). A comparison of software and hardware techniques for x86 virtualization. Retrieved from http://www.vmware.com/pdf/asplos235_adams.pdf.

Dubie, D. (2010, January 20). Gartner: CIOs look to lighter-weight, social technologies to transform IT. *Network World*. Retrieved from http://www.cio.com.au/article/333035/gartner_cios_look_lighter-weight_social_technologies_transform_it?eid=-1533.

Ferrie, P. (2007). Attacks on more virtual machine emulators. Retrieved from www.symantec.com/avcenter/reference/Virtual_Machine_Threats.pdf

Gammage, B., & Jump, A. (2009, February 17). Emerging technology analysis: hosted virtual desktops. *Gartner group*. Retrieved from http://www.gartner.com/DisplayDocument?ref=g_search&id=887912&subref=simplesearch.

Garfinkel, T., & Rosenblum, M. (2005). When virtual is harder than real: security challenges in virtual machine based computing environments. *Proceedings of the 10th Workshop on Hot Topics in Operating Systems*, June 12–15. Santa Fe, NM.

Messmer, E. (2009, October 20). Gartner predicts nearly half of server workloads will be virtualized. *Network World*. Retrieved from http://www.networkworld.com/news/2009/102009-gartner-server-virtualization.html

Murphy, A. (n.d.) Virtualization defined – eight different ways. *F5*. Retrieved from http://www.f5.com/pdf/white-papers/virtualization-defined-wp.pdf

Orakwue, E. (2009, February). Rise of the virtual machine. *ISSA* Journal. Retrieved from http://www.issa.org/Library/Journals/2009/February/Orakwue-Rise%20of%20the%20Virtual%20Machine.pdf

Paravirtualization API version 2.5. Copyright 2005, 2006. VMware, Inc. Retrieved from www.vmware.com/pdf/vmi_specs.pdf

Popek, G. J., & Goldberg, R. P. (n.d.) *Formal requirements for virtualizable third generation architectures*. Los Angeles: University of California, Honeywell Information Systems and Harvard University.

VMWare, Inc. (n.d.). Understanding full virtualization, paravirtualization, and hardware assist. Retrieved from www.vmware.com/files/pdf/VMware_paravirtualization.pdf

Virtual Data Center E-Zine, (2010, January), Volume 18. Retrieved from http://searchdatacenter.techtarget.com/generic/0,295582,sid80_gci1313630,00.html

Bibliography

Embedded Hypervisor

www.scribd.com/doc/17770659/VirtualizationReport-for-Seminar

http://www.cio.com.au/article/333035/gartner_cios_look_lighter-weight_social_
technologies_transform_it?eid=-1533.

http://www.gartner.com/DisplayDocument? id=5651

VMware Understanding Full Virtualization, Paravirtualization, and Hardware Assist.

Vmware

www.wmware.com

Parallels

www.parallels.com

Windows Virtual PC

http://www.microsoft.com/windows/virtual-pc/

Sun VirtualBox

http://www.virtualbox.org/manual/UserManual.html

Virtual Infrastructure products: features comparison

Xen

http://www.xen.org/support/documentation.html

SERVER VIRTUALIZATION

INFORMATION IN THIS CHAPTER

- What Is Server Virtualization?
- Differences between Desktop and Server Virtualization
- Common Virtual Servers

Server virtualization is the forerunner in the adoption of virtualization, primarily because of the visible benefits of consolidation, reduced operating expenditure, and limited impact on user operations. In 2008, about 25 percent of servers sold were virtualization enabled, and that percentage is increasing rapidly as computing power increases, and budgets are reduced. With hypervisors available for low cost, as well as improved management tools for managing both physical and virtual servers, this figure is expected to grow to about 60 percent in a few years (Frost & Sullivan, 2009). The entry of market participants such as Microsoft has changed the dynamics of the market, making server virtualization solutions more affordable for a variety of end users. There are nearly 100 providers of products adapted for the server virtualization management marketplace. This section discusses some of the major players and more popular products used for server virtualization.

What Is Server Virtualization?

Server virtualization, like the other virtualization definitions we've discussed so far, is simply the separation of computing functions such as the processors, memory, and operating system from the actual physical server with the intent of allowing system administrators to run multiple virtualized servers on a single, physical server.

To achieve this, an administrator uses special software to carve the physical server's resources into a number of isolated virtual machines (VMs), which are appropriately referred to as virtual private servers. Some other terms for these virtual environments are guests, instances, and containers.

As mentioned in Chapter 1, "How Virtualization Happens," there are a number of virtualization approaches. The three most popular approaches for server virtualization are as follows:

- The VM approach
- The paravirtual machine approach
- The operating system virtualization approach

Each approach has strengths and weaknesses and is often chosen based on the needs of the organization.

The Purpose of Server Virtualization

There are a number of reasons why an organization would want to utilize server virtualization. The most common answer is to save money. According to research done by Brown Associates, Inc. in Port Chester, NY, a typical server runs at only 15 to 20 percent of its capacity.

Naturally, with a figure like this, it's easy to see why an organization would rather operate in a virtualized environment and reclaim the 80 to 85 percent of the lost clock cycles that aren't being used.

However, the money savings don't stop with simply getting the most out of a physical server. Some of the other benefits of server virtualization are space savings in an organization's data center and fewer physical machines. It's rather simple. Fewer machines also mean fewer servers to maintain. The opposite of this is called *server sprawl*, in which several underutilized servers take up more space and consume more electricity than can be justified. In short, they become part of the problem. Server sprawl is primarily caused by the availability of inexpensive servers and the administrative practice of dedicating one server to one application.

In addition to reducing server sprawl, server virtualization helps reduce wasteful energy consumption, which eases the strain on the overburdened power grid and has positive benefits for the environment. Virtual servers also give an organization a much more flexible operating environment in which code and machine crashes can now be reset with the click of a mouse, not with the rebuilding or reimaging of an entire server.

Server Virtualization: The Bigger Picture

In the upcoming chapters, we'll dive into some of the bigger virtualization trends with respect to large enterprise and global area network environments, but for now, we'll focus on the ones that relate directly to server virtualization.

In this section, we'll look closely at three virtualization trends:
- Storage virtualization
- Network virtualization
- Workload management

Storage Virtualization

Storage virtualization is similar to other virtualization in that the physical hard drive is separated from the function of storing data. There are a number of ways to package storage virtualization, but the most common way is when several physical disks appear as a single unit of storage space. Aside from the convenience of behaving as a single unit of hard drive space, storage virtualization also allows for easier data migration between drives without any downtime, which is a huge advantage in almost any environment.

Storage virtualization has the following characteristics:
1. The availability of logical volumes separate from physical hard disk constraints
2. The capability of abstracting multivendor storage devices into one group and reallocating storage space independently of size or physical location
3. The capability of having automated storage optimization and management

With this kind of flexibility, there are three issues that are immediately resolved. The first is manageability; storage virtualization increases the effectiveness of administrators by streamlining the management process. The second is scalability, which by design is able to add new capacity rapidly as demand changes. The third is availability, which reduces downtime due to drive failures or configuration changes. Having this level of inherent convenience allows for significantly improved data management and storage efficiency.

Storage virtualization has the following five valuable properties:
1. A single point of administration: all the storage administration occurs at the virtualization layer.
2. Information life cycle management: it is possible to transparently relocate frequently accessed data to more expensive, high-performance storage and move less frequently accessed data to less expensive storage.

3. Improved efficiencies: preallocation of storage and shared free space across applications optimizing unused disk are the most expensive storage assets.
4. Seamless data migrations: migrations often require application outages. With Storage Area Network (SAN) virtualization, the storage team can execute disk array swap-outs without impacting anyone else.
5. Seamless replication: SAN virtualization can aid in disaster recovery replication by providing a single method of replication for multiple types of storage arrays and a limited number of management points.

Storage Virtualization Methods

Currently there are three methods of storage virtualization:
1. Server-based virtualization: this method places a management program on the host system and has the benefit of leveraging the SAN asset as it is.
2. Fabric-based virtualization: this can be done via network switches or appliance servers. In both instances, independent appliances, such as switches, routers, and dedicated servers, are placed between servers and storage and have a storage virtualization function. The purpose behind this is to reduce the impact on the existing SAN and servers.
3. Storage array-based virtualization: this is a virtualization implemented at the storage-system level.

As the need for storage virtualization increases, vendors will bring new virtualized storage products to market. It is likely that whatever form these new storage virtualization products take they will fall into one of these categories.

Network Virtualization

Network virtualization is the method of splitting up network resources into separate bandwidth channels that are each independent from one another, and that can be assigned and reassigned to servers or other network devices. Its purpose is to optimize the speed, reliability, and flexibility of the network. It is particularly useful when a network experiences a large, and usually unforeseen, spike in usage.

Network virtualization can be categorized as either external or internal. External network virtualization is the combining of one or more local networks or parts of networks into a whole "virtual" network with the intended goal of improving the efficiency of a large network or data center. Its two key components are the virtual local area network (VLAN) and the network switch. Using these two together, system administrators can configure systems that are physically attached at the same local network into many different virtual networks.

Internal network virtualization is a network confined to a single machine and provides network functionality to the different VMs using a single system. Sometimes, it is also referred to as *network in a box*, and it improves the overall efficiency of a single system by isolating the separate virtual environments and allowing them to communicate over a virtual network interface. This type is most commonly seen on the workstation versions of VMware and Parallels.

Virtual networks have the following basic components:

1. Network hardware (including network interface cards, virtual switches, and VLANs)
2. Network storage devices
3. Network media (usually Ethernet or Fiber Channel)

Workload Management

Workload management is used to handle some of the more difficult server consolidation problems. Workload management tools allow for the management of virtual server instances and the optimization of server applications. It also allows a system administrator to control the access users have to system resources to provide optimal performance for users and applications.

Workload management consists of the following elements:

- Services
- Connected load balancing
- A framework to ensure high availability
- Load balancing advisory
- Failover capabilities

Workload management is very different than server virtualization; it comes from very different places on the information technology (IT) landscape, but it can be used together to solve difficult server consolidation problems.

Server virtualization is definitely a technology that is here to stay and will continue to evolve as the demands for more computing power grow. It will continue to be used to eliminate server sprawl, centralize server administration, increase performance and efficiency, and assist in disaster recovery and development capacities.

Differences between Desktop and Server Virtualization

As we have seen so far, server virtualization has a number of uses, specifically to consolidate server resources for more efficient computing and storage solutions. Both server and desktop virtualization tools (which will be discussed in Chapter 3, "Desktop Virtualization") are efficient from a cost and management standpoint; however, in spite of their similarities, there are actually a number of significant differences between them that should be explored.

The first significant difference between server and desktop virtualization is the predictable versus unpredictable workload requirements that are placed on the different virtual environments. Servers are by their very design meant to be running all the time, whereas a desktop environment isn't nearly so crucial and can be powered down and moved or modified when a user is not working on it. The second big difference is in the networking requirements: a virtualized server is centrally located and thus does not contribute greatly to the network load, whereas a virtualized desktop often operates entirely over the network. The third big difference is how storage is handled. Virtualized servers require high-performance SAN infrastructure in order to access data across multiple data stores, whereas a virtualized desktop does not require even a fraction of the performance and can operate just fine in a direct access or Redundant Array of Independent Disks (RAID) configuration.

Other differences include the different requirements for the graphical user interface (GUI). In a server environment, the GUI is not of paramount importance, beyond being able to manage the server effectively. In a desktop environment, the GUI is far more important, contributing greatly to the user's overall experience. Additionally, organizational changes and differences in integration procedures further differentiate virtual servers and desktops.

Common Virtual Servers

In this section, we'll explore some of the most common virtual server products you are likely to encounter during your investigations. We'll cover the basics, giving you some background on each product, as well as the feature sets.

VMware Server

Arguably, the best known virtualization vendor is VMware. VMware invented its virtualization tool for the x86 platform in the 1990s to address underutilization in computer hardware. VMware Server can be installed and run as an application, Type 2 hypervisor, on top of a Windows or Linux host operating system. As with all software hypervisors, a thin virtualization layer divides up the physical server's resources, so multiple virtual servers can be run on one physical machine. The physical server's resources are divided up equally and can be assigned to the various VMs at the discretion of the administrator.

VMware Server is also responsible for isolating each VM from both the host operating system and all the other VMs that may be running at the time. This segmentation ensures that any instability in one VM does not affect another or the host operating system. The only way VMs and the applications they are running can communicate is over a configured network connection just as though they were isolated physical machines on a network. VMware Server encapsulates each virtual environment into a set of files, which like a text or picture file can be easily moved, copied, and backed up.

VMware Server now supports Windows Server 2008, Windows Vista, Red Hat Enterprise, and Ubuntu 8.04. VMware also has a new Remote Console application that allows for access of VM consoles through a Web-based management interface, as well as its standard Server Console, as shown in Figure 2.1. It also has Volume Shadow Copy Service (VSS) support, which leverages the Windows Shadow Copy function to properly back up the state of a Windows VM when using the snapshot feature. The VSS

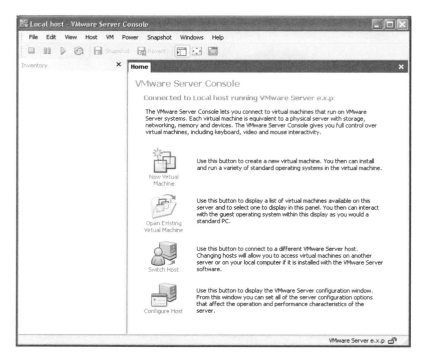

Figure 2.1 VMware Server Console

support feature allows the snapshot to maintain the integrity of the applications running inside the VM, which can be potentially very useful during a forensic investigation.

Microsoft Virtual Server

Microsoft Virtual Server is presented as a full suite of technologies for enabling comprehensive virtualized infrastructure. Microsoft Virtual Server's emphasis on virtualization technologies is rooted in creating what is called a *dynamic IT environment*. Microsoft's solution includes servers, desktops, and applications VM management and virtualization acceleration.

Hyper-V and Application Virtualization

Hyper-V provides software infrastructure and basic management tools in Windows Server 2008 that can be used to create and manage a virtualized server computing environment, as shown in Figure 2.2. It requires an x64-based processor, hardware-assisted virtualization, and hardware data execution protection. Microsoft offers preconfigured Virtual Hard Disks that can be downloaded and evaluated similar to the virtual appliance market.

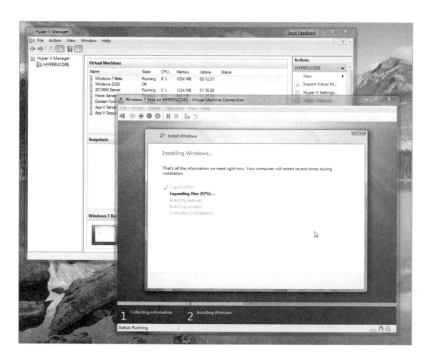

Figure 2.2 Microsoft Virtual Server Hyper-V Manager

Microsoft Hyper-V Server 2008 R2

Since Hyper-V Server is a dedicated stand-alone product, which contains only the Windows hypervisor, Windows Server driver model, and virtualization components, it provides a small footprint and minimal overhead. It easily plugs into customers' existing IT environments, leveraging their existing patching, provisioning, management, support tools, processes, and skills. Some of the key new features that are available in Microsoft Hyper-V Server 2008 R2 are live migration, cluster shared volume support, and expanded processor and memory support for host systems.

Server 2008 R2 also includes the following features:
- Failover clustering: host clustering functionality is included in R2 to enable support for unplanned downtime.
- Live migration: enables customers to move running applications between servers without service interruptions.
- Processor and memory support: R2 beta now supports up to 8-socket physical systems and provides support for up to 32 cores. Additionally, R2 supports up to 1 TB of random access memory on a physical system.

Citrix XenServer

Another major virtualization competitor is XenSource. XenSource is a free, open-source software hypervisor but sells related products. Essentially, XenSource is the core engine for a variety of other virtualization products. Xen is a Type 1, or bare-metal, hypervisor, installing directly to the hardware. Xen uses paravirtualization technology in its virtualization platform making it very fast and secure.

Citrix XenServer, which is managed by the XenCenter Console, as shown in Figure 2.3, is an enterprise-class, cloud-proven server virtualization platform that delivers the critical features of live migration and centralized multiserver management at no cost. XenServer is an open (and powerful) server virtualization solution designed to radically reduce data center costs.

Oracle VM

Oracle VM is server virtualization software that fully supports both Oracle and non-Oracle applications and delivers more efficient performance. It provides a single point of enterprise-class support for entire virtualization environments, including Oracle Database, Fusion Middleware, Applications, and Linux, which can be managed by the Oracle VM Manager, as shown in Figure 2.4.

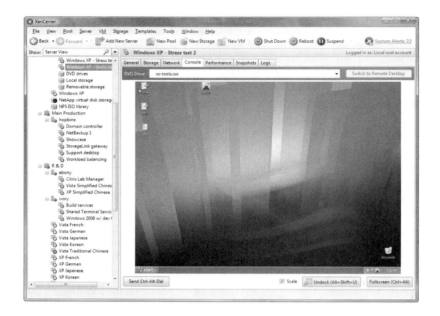

Figure 2.3 Citrix XenCenter
Management Console

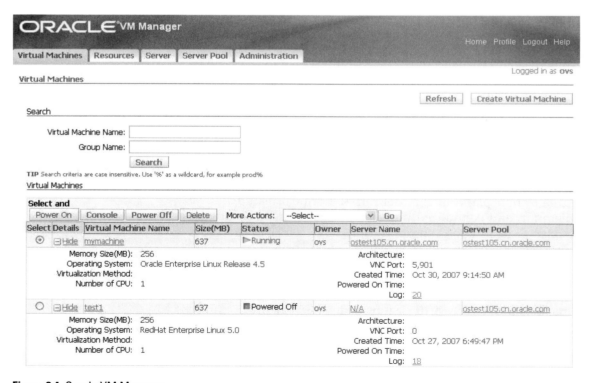

Figure 2.4 Oracle VM Manager

The Oracle VM architecture is made up of two primary components: the Oracle VM Manager and the Oracle VM Server. The VM Manager provides a Web-based user interface for managing virtual servers, machines, and other resources. It is also capable of performing load balancing functions across a wide array of resource pools. The VM Server component is the self-contained virtualization environment. It is based on open-source technology and is tailored by Oracle to allow for more refined management of VMs.

Summary

In this chapter, we have discussed how server virtualization happens along with exploring many of the most common server virtualization products and hypervisors. We learned that server virtualization is the separation of server computing functions from the physical resources they reside on and that the purpose of server virtualization is ultimately to save money by more efficiently utilizing server capacity, saving room and power in data centers by having fewer machines, and creating a much more flexible operating environment for the organization. We looked at the growing trends in server virutalization, including storage virtualization, network virtualization, and workload management.

We also took a closer look at the differences between server virtualization and desktop virtualization, showing that while the virtualization concepts are the same, servers and desktops have radically different requirements in both functionality and their overall place in a larger enterprise environment. Finally, we concluded this chapter with summary descriptions of some of the more common virtual servers you are likely to encounter during your investigations.

References

Frost & Sullivan. (2009, November 30). Although in its nascent stage, the future of virtualization market in India looks promising, notes Frost & Sullivan. *Frost & Sullivan*. Retrieved from http://www.frost.com/prod/servlet/press-release. pag?docid=185829213

Bibliography

What Is Server Virtualization?

Kusnetzky, D. (2007, June). Virtualization and virtual machine software. We help you to choose the best VM. *Hacking IT Security Magazine*.

Sturdevant, C. (2009, November 17). Is virtualization becoming the turducken of the IT World? *eWeek.com*. Retrieved from http://www.eweek.com/c/a/Virtualization/Is-Virtualization-Becoming-the-Turducken-of-the-IT-World-231429/

Suzuki, Y., & Moriyama, M. (2006, March). What issues does storage virtualization solve? The benefits of Hitachi's virtualization solutions. *Techrepublic.com*. Retrieved from http://whitepapers.techrepublic.com.com/abstract.aspx?docid=344989

Peterson, B. (2007, October 10). SAN-based storage virtualization: five benefits for your customers. *Search Storage Channel.com*. Retrieved from http://searchstoragechannel.techtarget.com/tip/0,289483,sid98_gci1274842,00.html

Differences between Desktop and Server Virtualization

Preimesberger, C. (2009, November 23). 10 key differences between desktop and server virtualization deployments. *eWeek.com*. Retrieved from http://www.eweek.com/c/a/Data-Storage/10-Key-Differences-Between-Desktop-and-Server-Virtualization-Deployments-152781/

Oracle. (2009, August). *Introduction to workload manager. Chapter 6 in*: Database Oracle Clusterware and Oracle Real Application Clusters Administration and Deployment Guide. Retrieved from http://download.oracle.com/docs/cd/B19306_01/rac.102/b14197/hafeats.htm#RACAD7120

DESKTOP VIRTUALIZATION

Desktop virtualization is similar in form to server virtualization but with some differences, specifically in usage and performance demands that are made on them. Today there are several commercially available virtual machine (VM) platforms on the market that you will likely encounter during an incident response or an investigation, which we will cover in this chapter. Additionally, virtual appliances, preconfigured VMs that are designed for specific functions, are available and growing in popularity. We will explore some of the more common virtual appliances that are available for forensic investigations.

As virtual environments have steadily grown more and more popular, using these environments as repositories for forensic evidence has also become somewhat common. This chapter explores this in detail and outlines the strengths and limitations of using virtual environments as forensic platforms.

What Is Desktop Virtualization?

As we've discussed in previous chapters, virtualization is the emulation of hardware. The same is true for desktop virtualization. Desktop virtualization is often the most dynamic of all the virtualized environments with far more changes made inside the environment both locally and over the network than a virtualized server. A virtual desktop is based on a computing architectural model in which a VM detects and responds to changing business requirements on demand. This allows for all types of configurations that can be created, deleted, copied, archived, and downloaded over a network or remotely hosted with administration times dropping from hours to minutes.

As we discussed in Chapter 2, "Server Virtualization," when highlighting the differences between desktop and server virtualization, the desktop requires the most flexibility and resources and is often used for more customized work. Desktop virtualization is also an excellent digital testing ground and "clean room." Viruses, malware, Web site redirects, Trojan horses, and all the other potentially dangerous software are unable to reach out to other parts of the network. This type of infection would only be possible if these malicious programs are able to push through the virtual machine monitor (VMM) layer and access the underlying operating system (OS) before the session is terminated, or the VM is reset to a previous configuration.

Virtualization also has benefits when working on development (including the development of OSes); running the new system as a guest avoids the need to reboot the physical computer whenever a bug occurs. A "sandboxed" guest system can also help in computer-security research, which enables the study of the effects of some viruses or worms without the possibility of compromising the host system.

Why Is It Useful?

The uses of desktop virtualization are as follows:

- Run multiple OSes on a single computer including Windows, Linux, and more. With computers permeating every facet of modern life, the flexibility of this use reduces frustration and increases productivity to a whole new level. Finally, it gives access to the Linux environment without having to dual boot.
- Let your Macintosh (Mac) run Windows, creating a virtual PC environment for all your Windows applications. With the runaway successes of the iPod and all the iterations that followed, the OS X platform has steadily increased its market share over the past 10 years and is showing up in a lot more homes and businesses that used to run Windows exclusively.
- Reduce capital costs by increasing energy efficiency, requiring less hardware, and increasing the number of servers without the need for additional administrators. This trend, which directly affects the bottom line, is here to stay and will only expand, becoming more refined as time passes.

- Improve enterprise desktop management and control with faster deployment of desktops and fewer support calls due to application conflicts. Virtualization reduces an entire functioning computer down to just a couple of files, which is obviously far easier to manage than the thousands and thousands of files found in the Windows directory alone. With virtualization, it is not only practical but also logical to simply discard an old or infected VM in favor of a fresh copy.

Common Virtual Desktops

In this section, we'll explore some of the most common virtual desktop products you are likely to encounter during your investigations. We'll cover the basics, giving you some background on each product, as well as the feature sets.

VMware

VMware software provides a completely virtualized set of hardware to the guest OS. Now, VMware is still the leading provider of virtualization software. VMware's desktop software runs on Microsoft Windows, Linux, and Mac OS X and is designed to use the CPU to run code directly whenever possible to provide the best possible performance in the virtualized environment. Figure 3.1 shows the VMware Workstation Management Console. VMware Workstation takes a more optimized path to running target OSes by emulating instruction sets for the hardware that is physically present. Sometimes, this can cause problems when moving VMs between hardware hosts using different instruction sets (such as between different processors) or between hardware hosts with different numbers of CPUs.

VMware software virtualizes the hardware for a video adapter, a network adapter, and hard disk adapters. The host provides pass-through drivers for guest Universal Serial Bus (USB), serial, and parallel devices.

When direct execution cannot operate normally, VMware products use a process called *binary translation* to rewrite the code dynamically. The translated code gets stored in spare memory, which allows VMware to operate dramatically faster than other emulators, running at more than 80 percent of the speed that the virtual guest operating system would run directly on the same hardware. VMware claims an overhead as small as 3 to 6 percent for computationally intensive applications.

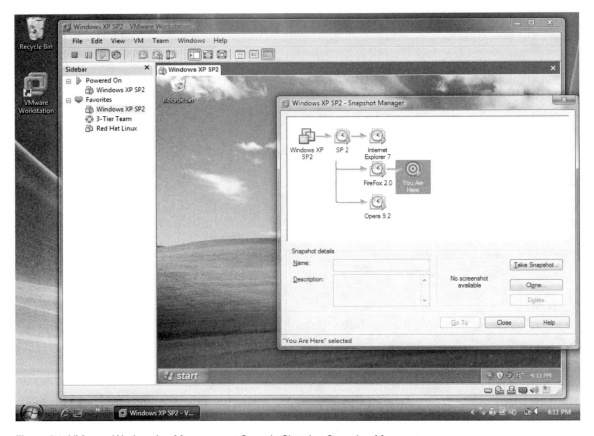

Figure 3.1 VMware Workstation Management Console Showing Snapshot Manager

VMware Fusion

A variant of VMware is the version for the OS X operating system called *VMware Fusion*. Fusion is a Cocoa-based Mac application that is essentially the same core virtualization engine that is used for VMware Server. Cocoa is Apple's name for the frameworks, application program interfaces (APIs), and runtimes that make up the development layer of Mac OS X. Figure 3.2 shows the VMware Fusion Machine Library and Settings functions. VMware Fusion integrates nicely with the OS X operating system (Figure 3.3) and is capable of providing many of the same, if not more, features that the Windows version of VMware has.

Some of these features include the following:

* Support for 64-bit guest OSes for Linux, Solaris, and Windows as long as the host hardware is 64 bits
* Provides one or two processors to a VM

Figure 3.2 VMware Fusion Machine Library and System Settings Options

Figure 3.3 VMware Fusion Running a Windows XP Guest inside OS X

- Supports up to 8 GB of random access memory (RAM) per VM
- Supports Windows DirectX 8.1 graphics acceleration

Microsoft Virtual PC

Microsoft Virtual PC is an emulation program for Mac OS X on PowerPC-based systems and emulates a standard PC with its associated hardware, and the program is free, as shown in Figure 3.4. The only disadvantage is that it is dedicated to run only on Microsoft OSes; however, it can run on some versions of Linux, but it is not officially supported by Microsoft.

The newest release "Windows" Virtual PC, as opposed to "Microsoft" Virtual PC, is available only for Windows 7 hosts, and discussed later in this section. Microsoft Virtual PC and Windows Virtual PC are designed to support the following versions of Windows (the versions are listed from newest to oldest) to varying degrees:

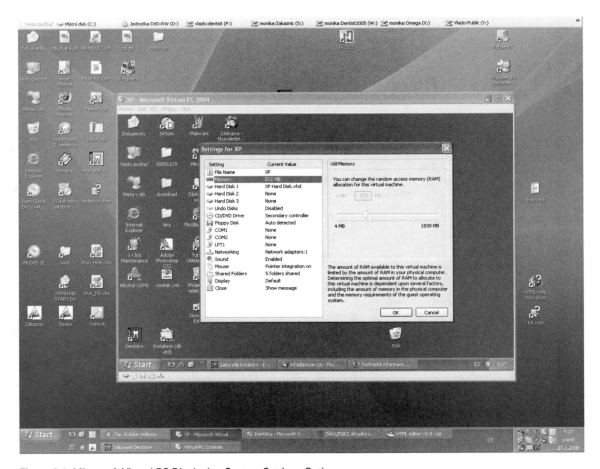

Figure 3.4 Microsoft Virtual PC Displaying System Settings Options

- Windows 7 Ultimate
- Windows 7 Enterprise
- Windows 7 Professional
- Windows 7 Home Premium
- Windows 7 Home Basic
- Windows 7 Starter
- Windows Server 2008 Standard
- Windows Vista Ultimate
- Windows Vista Enterprise
- Windows Vista Home Premium
- Windows Vista Home Basic
- Windows Vista Starter
- Windows Server 2003 Standard
- Windows XP Professional
- Windows XP Tablet PC Edition
- Windows XP Media Center Edition
- Windows XP Home Edition
- Windows XP Starter Edition
- Windows 2000 Server
- Windows 2000 Professional
- Windows Me
- Windows 98 Second Edition
- Windows 98 (original release)
- Windows 95
- Windows NT 4.0 Workstation
- Windows NT 3.51 Workstation
- Windows NT 3.1 | NT 3.5
- IBM OS/2 (select editions)
- Windows 3.1
- MS-DOS 6.22

Virtual PC emulates the following:
- Intel Pentium processor (32 bits)
- Standard Super Video Graphics Array (SVGA) graphics cards
- Basic input/output system (BIOS)
- Sound card
- Ethernet card

Windows Virtual PC

Unlike Microsoft Virtual PC, Windows Virtual PC, as shown in Figure 3.5, supports only Windows 7 host OSes and requires hardware virtualization support.

Windows Virtual PC includes the following features:
- USB support and redirection
- Application launching: run Windows XP Mode applications directly from the Windows 7 desktop

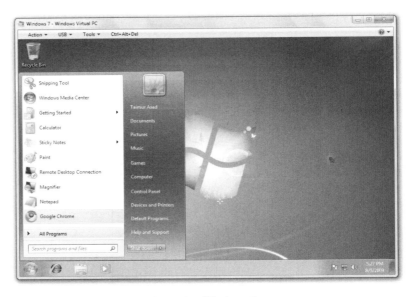

Figure 3.5 Windows Virtual PC Running Windows 7

- Multithreading: run multiple VMs concurrently, each in its own thread for improved stability and performance
- Smart card redirection: use smart cards connected to the host
- Integration with Windows Explorer: manage all VMs from a single Explorer folder (%USER%\Virtual Machines)

Parallels

Parallels Workstation is a VM suite for Intel x86-compatible computers that operate on Microsoft Windows, Linux, and Mac OS X platforms. Like many of the other virtualization software programs we've looked at so far, Parallels Workstation uses Type 2 hypervisor technology allowing for the simultaneous creation and execution of multiple x86 virtual computers, as shown in Figure 3.6.

Note

Awareness of the differences between Microsoft Virtual PC and Windows Virtual PC is important for your forensic investigations. Specifically, if you encounter Windows Virtual PC, you know you will very likely be dealing with a limited set of OSes, specifically Windows XP and later.

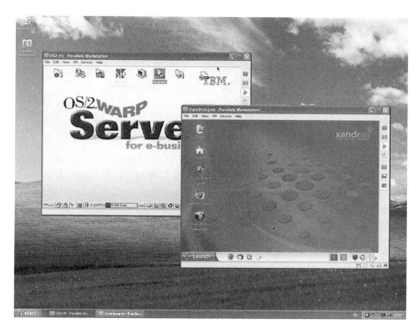

Figure 3.6 Parallels Running OS/2Warp and Xandros Linux inside Virtual Environments

Parallels Workstation uses hardware emulation allowing each VM engine to work with its own processor, RAM, floppy drive, CD/DVD drive, input and output devices, and hard disk – everything a physical computer contains. It virtualizes all devices within the virtual environment, including the video adapter, network adapter, and hard disk adapters. It also provides pass-through drivers for parallel port and USB devices.

Parallels Workstation is capable of virtualizing standard PC hardware, such as
- Pentium or AMD Duron processors
- Generic motherboards compatible with Intel i815 chipset
- Up to 1.5 GB of RAM
- VGA and SVGA video cards
- A 1.44 MB floppy drive
- Serial ports
- Parallel ports
- Ethernet network cards
- USB 1.1
- Sound cards
- Standard keyboard and wheel mouse

Known limitations of Parallels Workstation include the following:

- It can only run 32-bit OSes.
- It has an inability to assign multiple CPUs to your VM.
- The supported memory limit for all VMs is 4 GB, and the memory limit for a single VM is 1500 MB.
- Network emulation does not support Network Address Translation (NAT).

Parallels Desktop for Mac

In 2006, Parallels was the first software product to bring virtualization mainstream for the Mac OS X platform, as shown in Figure 3.7. It is similar in form and function to the Windows and Linux versions.

Parallels Desktop for Mac is capable of virtualizing a full set of standard PC hardware, such as

- A virtualized CPU of the same type as the host's physical processor
- Advanced Configuration and Power Interface (ACPI) compliance system
- A generic motherboard compatible with the Intel chipset
- Up to 8 GB of RAM for guest VMs

Figure 3.7 Parallels for Mac Running a Windows Vista Virtual Environment

- Up to 256 MB of video RAM
- VGA and SVGA video adapter
- A 1.44 MB floppy drive
- Virtual CD/DVD-read-only memory ROM drives can be mapped to either physical drives or ISO image files
- DVD/CD-ROM "pass-through" access
- Serial ports
- Parallel ports
- Ethernet network cards
- USB 2.0 devices and USB 1.1 devices
- Sound card
- Standard keyboard and wheel mouse

Another feature of Parallels for Mac is called *Coherence*, which removes the Windows desktop and virtualization frames to create a more seamless desktop environment between Windows and OS X applications. Additionally, Parallels for Mac can boot existing "Boot Camp" Windows XP partitions, which is a utility within OS X that allows users to install Windows XP or Vista on Intel-based Mac computers.

As new versions of Parallels have been released (version 5 is currently the most recent edition), and there have been additional features added that allow for greater use of the Mac platform. Some of those features are as follows:

- The capability to start and stop a VM via the iPhone
- *MacLook*, which themes Windows applications and makes them look like a Mac
- The capability to use Multi-Touch gestures with the recently released Magic Mouse in Windows applications, as well as using the standard Apple Remote to control Windows applications

Sun VirtualBox

Sun VirtualBox supports host OSes including Linux, Mac OS X, OS/2 Warp, Windows XP, Windows Vista, Windows 7, and Solaris. However, for OS X, aside from Apple's licensing restriction, it also requires a Streaming SIMD Extensions 3 (SSE3) – capable CPU for both native and virtualized Mac OS X. VirtualBox supports both Intel's hardware virtualization VT-x and AMD's AMD-V.

The VirtualBox feature set includes the following:

- 64-bit guests
- Snapshots
- Seamless mode
- Clipboard
- Shared folders
- Special drivers and utilities to facilitate switching between systems

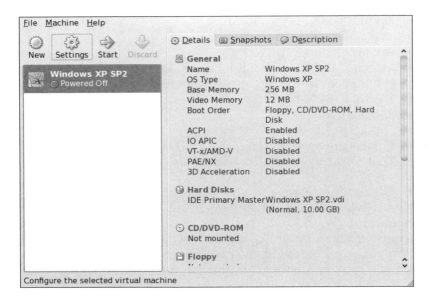

Figure 3.8 Sun VirtualBox Settings Menu

- Public API (Java, Python, Simple Object Access Protocol [SOAP], Cross Platform Component Object Model [XPCOM]) to control VM configuration and execution
- Remote display
- Raw hard disk access – allowing physical hard disk partitions on the host system to appear in the guest system
- VMware VM disk format support – allowing VirtualBox to exchange disk images with VMware
- Microsoft Virtual Hard Disk (VHD) support
- 3D virtualization
- Symmetric multiprocessing (SMP) support – up to 32 virtual CPUs

Figures 3.8 and 3.9 show the Sun VirtualBox settings option and VMs running inside Ubuntu.

Xen

Xen (pronounced Zen) is a powerful VMM for x86, x86-64, Itanium, and PowerPC 970 architectures and allows multiple OSes to run concurrently on the same physical server hardware. Figure 3.10 shows Xen running a Windows XP virtual environment inside Linux. Xen's hypervisor uses paravirtualization, a technique that presents a software interface that is similar, though not identical, to the underlying hardware. Xen systems are structured in which the Xen hypervisor is the lowest and most privileged layer. Above this layer comes one or more guest OSes, which the hypervisor schedules across the physical CPUs. Xen includes features such as 32- and 64-bit guest support, live

Figure 3.9 Sun VirtualBox Running Multiple Virtualized Environments within Ubuntu

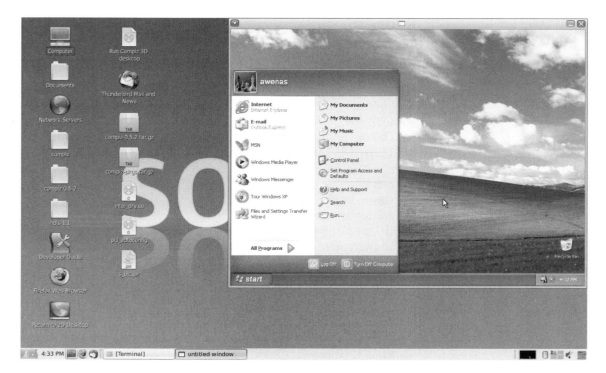

Figure 3.10 Xen VMM Running a Windows XP Virtual Environment inside Linux

migration, and support for the latest processors from Intel and AMD, along with other experimental non-x86 platforms.

Additionally, Xen's hypervisor is available as an open-source release, as well as a commercially supported release. XenSource has been acquired by Citrix. It offers a comprehensive end-to-end virtualization solution with the main purpose to enable information technology to deliver applications to users anywhere.

Virtual Appliances and Forensics

Virtual appliances are VM images, usually with a specific configuration, designed to run on a virtual platform such as VMware, Parallels, and VirtualBox. They are designed to reduce or eliminate the installation, configuration, and maintenance costs associated with running large or complicated suites of software. There are a number of virtual appliances available for download from vendor Web sites, such as VMware, that are specifically built for conducting forensic investigations.

Penguin Sleuth Kit

The goal of the Penguin Sleuth project was to bring the Linux Forensics platform to the common investigator without the intimidation of Linux, while maintaining the power and functionality of the Linux OS. The Penguin Sleuth Kit has been around for many years and is still widely used in bootable CD format. It has also evolved into a virtual appliance with some of the uses being that an investigator can run a Linux platform within Windows (Figure 3.11) and can image in Linux and conduct an exam at the same time in Windows.

The advantage of the Penguin Sleuth Kit as a virtual appliance is that there is an immediate reduction in installation and development time – it is essentially a forensics computer ready to go right away.

Some of the forensic tools already included in the virtual appliance are as follows:
- Sleuth Kit–Forensics Kit: a collection of file system tools that allows you to examine file systems of a suspect computer
- Forensics Browser Autopsy: a browser interface that allows you to investigate the file system and volumes of a computer
- dcfldd – DD Imaging Tool: an enhanced version of GNU dd optimized for forensics
- Data Carver command-line tool: a console program to recover files based on their headers, footers, and internal data structures
- MD5 Hashing Program

More information about the Penguin Sleuth Kit can be found at www.linux-forensics.com.

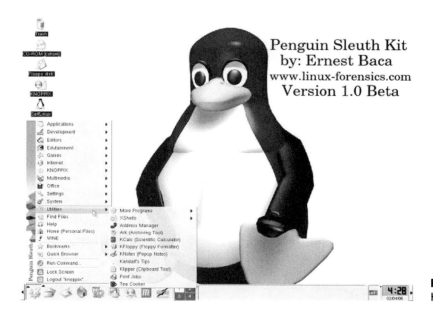

Figure 3.11 The Penguin Sleuth Kit Desktop

The Revealer Toolkit

The Revealer Toolkit is a framework of tools running on Debian Linux and is used for conducting computer forensics. The foundation program is The Sleuth Kit created by Brian Carrier, but Revealer Toolkit has a number of other free tools included. The goal of Revealer Toolkit is to automate tasks and to manage sources.

Intelica IP Inspect Virtual Appliance

This virtual appliance is more of a security tool than a forensics tool; however, there is some strong overlap. Intelica IP Inspect monitors, detects, and reports unusual network traffic and activities in real time. It's designed to passively monitor Ethernet traffic and provides full visibility into an enterprise network. The value to forensic investigators is the long-term full packet recording feature, which allows a user to peer back in time to perform detailed network analysis for intrusions or other unauthorized activities. Intelica IP Inspect also has session monitoring and supports most common network applications, such as the Web and File Transfer Protocol, and has the capability to export the collected data as evidence.

Helix 2008R1

Helix, by e-fense, is probably one of the most common tool packages out in the forensics community today. It has existed as a bootable CD for a number of years, so it is no real surprise that it has evolved into a virtual appliance. Helix 2008 uses the

Ubuntu Linux OS and comes with a number of installed forensic applications and utilities, such as
• Adepto – a drive imaging utility
• Autopsy – a forensic browser
• GtkHash
• Bless
• Hierarchical File System (HFS) volume browser – allowing you to browse Mac volumes
• Linen
• Meld
• Ophcrack
• Regviewer
• Wireshark
• Xfprot

For more information about this virtual appliance, visit the Helix Web site at www.e-fense.com/helix.

CAINE 0.3

CAINE, which stands for computer-aided investigative environment, is a GNU/Linux live CD and virtual appliance. It offers a complete forensic environment that is organized to integrate existing software tools as software modules and primarily uses a graphical interface, as shown in Figures 3.12 and 3.13. The CAINE virtual appliance was designed to support an investigator during

Figure 3.12 The CAINE Desktop Environment

Figure 3.13 The Analysis Functions Available through the CAINE Interface

all phases of a digital investigation and includes a semiautomated reporting function.

Virtual Desktops as a Forensic Platform

There is a lot of potential for virtual environments to be used in the forensic analysis process; however, there are limits that must be understood. Although a VM is nearly identical to an actual computer system, there are differences that the hypervisor abstracts, which can cause problems in some situations. However, this does not discount the advantages of using virtual desktops as an analysis platform.

The first big advantage is the capability to boot a forensic image into a virtual environment. This process saves a tremendous amount of time, as opposed to the alternative, which is restoring an image to the actual hardware the OS was running on when it was imaged. By leveraging the virtual environment, the process can be done quickly and be repeated as often as necessary.

This also has the added benefit that it makes a visual inspection of the OS much easier and easier to present to just about anyone who may have a need to see and understand the evidence since most users are familiar with a modern computer interface. Booting a forensic image into a VM can also distribute workload during a large case where a junior investigator can conduct a preliminary examination on a number of evidence drives, setting aside the high-value images for more senior investigators to more closely examine.

In extreme cases, where obtaining an image is not possible, virtual environments can be used to examine original media without writing changes back to the drive. Using a write blocker to protect the original media, the drive can be booted into a VM without changing the contents of the evidence. This process varies from vendor to vendor and requires adjustment to the VM configuration files, so be sure you have a thorough understanding of the tool before attempting this. With that being said, and again restating that this is not considered the best practice, this is a possible option when time is of importance.

Summary

In this chapter, we have discussed the fundamentals of desktop virtualization and explored a number of virtual desktop platforms that are available today, looking closely at their similarities, differences, and feature sets. We also discussed virtual appliances and some of the preconfigured packages available for conducting digital forensics. We concluded by outlining the benefits and limitations of using a virtual desktop environment to restore and examine forensic images.

Bibliography

What Is Desktop Virtualization?

VMware Understanding Full Virtualization, Paravirtualization, and Hardware Assist Vmware

www.wmware.com

Common Virtual Desktops

Vmware

www.wmware.com

Parallels

www.parallels.com

Windows Virtual PC

http://www.microsoft.com/windows/virtual-pc/

Sun VirtualBox

http://www.virtualbox.org/manual/UserManual.html

Xen

http://www.xen.org/support/documentation.html

Virtual Appliances and Forensics

Penguin Sleuth Kit

http://www.linux-forensics.com/

Revealer Toolkit, Virtual Appliances

http://www.vmware.com/appliances/directory/213673

Intelica IP Inspect Virtual Appliance

http://www.vmware.com/appliances/directory/813

e-fense

http://www.e-fense.com/helix3pro

Caine

http://www.vmware.com/appliances/directory/57815
http://www.caine-live.net/
Bem, D., & Huebner, E. (2007, Fall). Computer forensic analysis in a virtual
environment. *International Journal of Digital Evidence 6(2)*.

PORTABLE VIRTUALIZATION, EMULATORS, AND APPLIANCES

INFORMATION IN THIS CHAPTER

- MojoPac
- MokaFive
- Preconfigured Virtual Environments
- Virtual Appliance Providers
- JumpBox Virtual Appliances
- VirtualBox
- Virtualization Hardware Devices
- Virtual Privacy Machine
- Virtual Emulators
- Future Development

Virtualized environments, especially those run from a removable drive, can make forensics investigation more difficult. Technological advances in virtualization tools can transform removable media into a portable personal computer (PC) that can be carried around in a shirt pocket or on a lanyard around a neck. Running operating systems (OSes) and applications in this fashion leaves very little evidence on the host system. This chapter discusses some of the various virtual environments that can be run on portable devices such as thumb drives, iPods, and cell phones. The use of virtualization is growing in the individual use market, as many corporate organizations use devices such as the IronKey. IronKey partnered with MokaFive and RingCube to provide portable virtual machines, which can allow applications and secure OSes to be carried on an

IronKey-encrypted drive. This section explores the technology being used with PCs that do not necessarily alter the current environment, but instead it can use a Universal Serial Bus (USB) device to run a virtual environment, thereby leaving the original system intact.

MojoPac

MojoPac was developed by RingCube Technologies. RingCube was founded in 2004 to 2005 and launched its first virtual portable environment, MojoPac Freedom 1.0 in 2006. The version used in all the examples in this book is 2.1.1, which was released on October 14, 2008. In essence, MojoPac is a Windows environment run on a USB drive. MojoPac's virtualization technology encapsulates a complete Windows desktop environment, including applications, files, and settings, isolating it from the underlying host PC. This virtualized environment can be loaded onto a host computer, a portable USB storage device, or a network-attached storage and can run on any Windows host computer. As MojoPac starts up, it loads a user profile and configuration file. Figure 4.1 shows the user profile. Previous versions allowed the user to copy all documents and personal items to the USB drive before launching.

The first time MojoPac is run, it configures personal settings just as the first time Windows XP is run, as shown in Figure 4.2.

Figure 4.3 shows the MojoPac environment when it first loads on the USB drive. As one can see, it looks exactly like Windows XP.

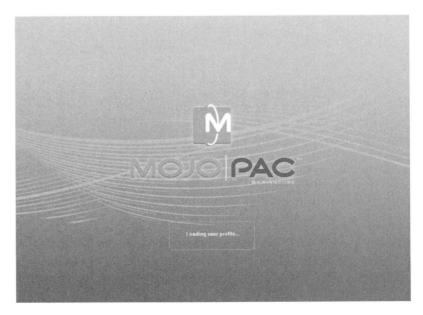

Figure 4.1 MojoPac Environment Loading User Profile

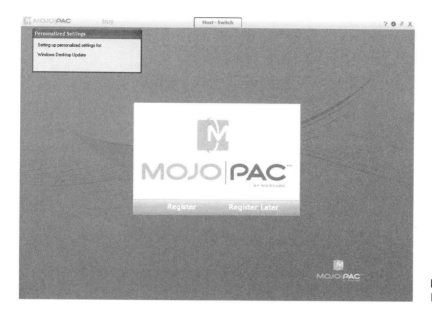

Figure 4.2 MojoPac Configuring Personal Settings

Figure 4.3 MojoPac Environment Loaded on a USB Drive

The professional version has policy isolation settings such as preventing the MojoPac user from switching to the host PC and accessing printers, network drives, and optical drives. However, by default, once started, access to the local hard drive is eliminated, as shown in Figure 4.4. We will go into further detail on the specifics of

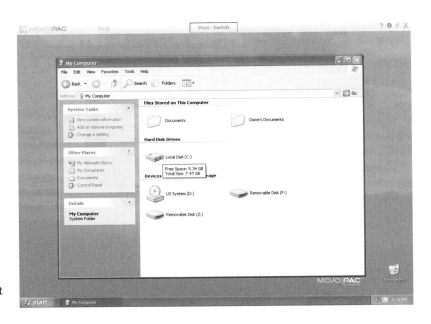

Figure 4.4 MojoPac Environment as the User Sees It

MojoPac in Chapter 5, "Investigating Dead Virtual Environments," as we discuss artifacts, the registry, and install files.

Early versions of MojoPac were quite slow and also required administrative privileges on the host computer to execute. Because the USB environment used the host's resources, loading the user settings and profiles was time consuming. A plug-in called *MojoPac Usher* was introduced so that MojoPac could run on the host with limited mode access. Once MojoPac was installed on the host computer, it could execute on that computer even when used with limited access user login. MojoPac 2.0 was launched in 2008. Here are the host machine requirements for installation:

- A Windows PC running Windows XP (SP2 or SP3)
- Minimum 256 MB of memory
- Administrator login capability
- If installing on a portable drive, USB 2.0 media
- 100 MB of free space for MojoPac installation
- Sufficient free space for data and application installations within MojoPac

In addition to USB installations, MojoPac can be installed on some cell phones. Phones that have USB connections for direct PC connections and storage space can store files like any external USB storage device. MojoPac is installed on cell phones in the same way you install it on any external USB device. According to MojoPac's support site, when using MojoPac with an iPod, the iPod must be set to be "manually managed by iTunes," or the user will not be able to access the iPod as a USB storage device. It also states that installing MojoPac on an iPod will not alter its behavior as a music player or change its performance when iTunes software installed on the host PC detects the iPod.

MojoPac supports only Windows XP. There was a Vista upgrade, but it appears that there were some issues with getting everything worked out, and it never fully worked correctly. It's possible that it could have been because of Microsoft user account control. However, in experimenting with running FileMon to track changes to files made by MojoPac, the system blue screened every time it started to load the configuration file. This happened not on one but on two machines, yet it loaded fine without FileMon running, so there is some type of host to USB interaction at a rudimentary level.

As per an e-mail with support at RingCube, MojoPac will not be upgraded to run on Vista. Macintosh (Mac) users can run MojoPac within Parallels Desktop software or VMware Fusion, and there's no immediate plan to support any Linux OSes.

MojoPac enterprise solution was also launched, which included mojostation, mojodrive, and mojonet. These products provided secure workspace, portable desktops, and network desktop solutions. RingCube is no longer developing products under the MojoPac name, and based on its current product offering, it has switched its focus to a technology called *vDesk*. RingCube's Web site describes vDesk as a technology that allows a virtualized desktop to be synchronized to any number of devices. It can be stored and run locally on the user's PC; stored on portable drives such as USB, flash, or smartphone; stored on a network file share and run locally; and stored in the data center and accessed remotely using Virtual Desktop Infrastructure (VDI). In December 2009, RingCube became a member of the Microsoft System Center Alliance. The vDesk product is being integrated into Microsoft's System Center Configuration Manager 2007 server management product. This environment offers a virtualized workspace that can be stored on a portable USB drive, on the unmanaged PC itself, or on a network file. More importantly, it encrypts the virtual workspace using a Microsoft Virtual Hard Disk (VHD) format. For an investigator, this can be looked at as either an advantage or a disadvantage. The advantage being that the format is now standard. On the downside, if the environment is encrypted, it may be mountable but not readable.

This environment has been implemented by companies such as Fenwick & West LLP, Prometric, and Cloud 10 Corporation. It was also included in Gartner, Inc.'s report titled "Cool Vendors in PC Technologies, 2007."

MokaFive

Like MojoPac, MokaFive began as a virtual environment that could be run from a portable device. It is a spin-off from Stanford University's Computer Science Department and was founded in 2005. Stanford's portable virtual machine research started in 2001 and was based on the thin-client computing model. The original group that was led by Dr. Monica Lam consisted of four PhDs from Stanford University and industry professionals. MokaFive's product called *LivePC* was introduced in September 2006. It came in two versions: for Windows and for bare-metal installations. LivePC depends on VMware Player. It imported existing LivePCs or created new ones using a very basic .vmx generator. MokaFive technology advances used the MokaFive Engine technology to permit LivePCs to launch without needing to start MokaFive Engine. By simply dragging and dropping LivePC shortcuts to the desktop or start menu, Live PCs were able to launch, making it possible to have the LivePC links automatically download MokaFive Engine. Around the same time, password protection was added for the MokaFive Engine.

In September 2007, IronKey and MokaFive partnered to deploy virtual desktop solutions on an encrypted USB flash drive. In April 2008, MokaFive Engine became MokaFive Player. The virtual environment is still called a LivePC. LivePCs contain everything needed to run a virtual computer: an OS and a set of applications. LivePCs can be run from a USB flash drive, USB hard disk, iPod, or desktop computer. At that time, MokaFive introduced a solution, which basically is a console to centralize the management of multiple LivePCs.

The idea behind MokaFive is to allow consumers to carry virtual PCs on a portable storage device so that a user can walk up to any Windows PC and plug-in a device such as an iPod, launch MokaFive, and run Damn Small Linux (DSL) in a window. MokaFive Player, which actually is a VMware Player, runs the LivePCs and can be downloaded or distributed and preloaded on a USB device, phone, or laptop. The LivePC can automatically be backed up while the USB drive is plugged into a computer. Premade LivePCs are downloadable from MokaFive's Web site. This is similar to the VMware and Parallels virtual appliance concept that will be discussed in the next section.

A LivePC can be downloaded from a public repository of LivePC images created by both MokaFive and outside entities. Figure 4.5 shows MokaFive's LivePC Library.

The technology can stream and prefetch LivePCs, so they can be shared. LivePCs are always live. This means that users automatically receive updates to the LivePCs as the maintainers make changes. With MokaFive Player, users can run multiple LivePC images irrespective of the underlying OS. It also provides complete

Figure 4.5 MokaFive's LivePC Library

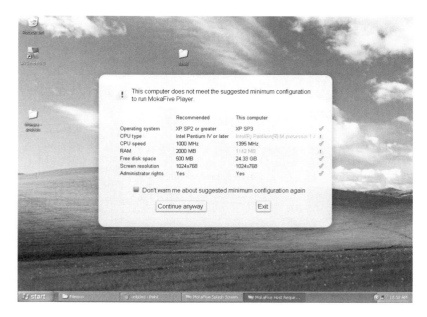

Figure 4.6 MokaFive's System Configuration Check

isolation from the underlying OS, so users can run corporate LivePC images securely on any personal or unmanaged device.

As the MokaFive Player starts on a computer, a configuration check is done to determine if the OS and hardware meet the requirements to run the player, as shown in Figure 4.6.

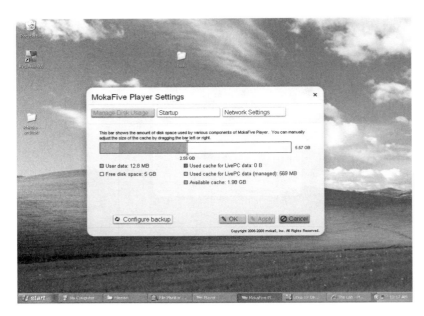

Figure 4.7 MokaFive's Settings

Figure 4.8 MokaFive's Startup Settings

After MokaFive Player is finished loading, the user screen loads. At this point, the user can load an already downloaded LivePC, add a new LivePC, or change the settings, as shown in Figure 4.7.

It is in this area where the LivePC startup and network and backup settings can be set. For example, the user can configure the LivePC that starts automatically or only starts upon entering a password, as shown in Figure 4.8.

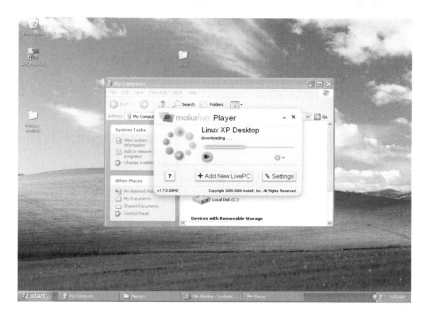

Figure 4.9 LivePC Updating

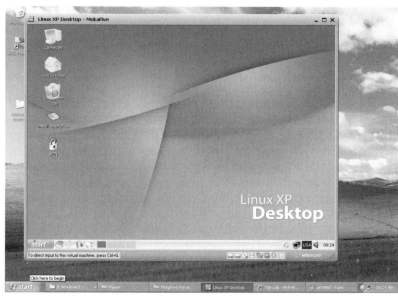

Figure 4.10 Linux XP Desktop Running as the User Sees It

At this point, the LivePC will check for updates or download the default LivePC, which is Linux XP Desktop, for the version used in this book (1.7.0.20942). This is shown in Figure 4.9.

Once the LivePC is updated, it is ready to run. Figure 4.10 shows the Linux XP Desktop running.

MokaFive has entered the enterprise virtual desktop arena, just as MojoPac has.

MokaFive Suite is a Desktop-as-a-Service (DaaS). Chapter 10, "Cloud Computing and the Forensic Challenges," discusses DaaS in further detail. It is basically a platform with desktop management capabilities, so Information Technology (IT) administrators can centrally create, deliver, secure, and update a fully contained virtual environment and then make it available to a large number of users. Users download their secure virtual desktop via a Web link and run it locally on any Mac or Windows computer. MokaFive Creator is the authoring tool that enables IT administrators to create the LivePC image; MokaFive Enterprise Server integrates with standard corporate infrastructure, and the Web-based MokaFive Console allows administrators to centrally manage, distribute, and control LivePC images.

According to MokaFive's Web site, MokaFive Service is a hosted desktop service designed for small- to medium-sized organizations with up to 500 users. This solution is a hosted service, where the organization receives a dedicated secure account within the MokaFive infrastructure. Then, IT administrators create and upload user information along with customized corporate LivePC images to MokaFive's server. The images are managed via MokaFive's Web-based console.

This environment has been implemented by companies such as Sheridan Institute of Technology and Advanced Learning, Panasonic, and healthcare facilities.

Preconfigured Virtual Environments

Preconfigured virtual appliances are available from a variety of vendors including VMware, Microsoft, and Parallels. Virtual appliances come ready to start up. They have a preinstalled, preconfigured OS inside a virtual machine environment. The user merely donwloads the appliance and loads it. According to a white paper titled "Virtualization from the Datacenter to the Desktop," virtual appliances are fundamentally changing how software is developed, distributed, deployed, and managed. In addition to commercial virtual appliance marketplaces, open-source vendors are also supporting the virtual appliance model. Examples are Ubuntu Server Edition JeOS, Lime JeOS, and Red Hat's Appliance Operating System.

VMware

VMware offers a wide variety of services and products. Of particular interest are the preconfigured appliances that can be readily downloaded and implemented using VMware Player. In the last section, we covered VMware Player's use in MokaFive's technology, but VMware also offers its VMware Player for use

Figure 4.11 VMware Virtual Appliance Marketplace

with preconfigured appliances downloadable through its appliance marketplace. VMware Player makes it simple to quickly evaluate one of the many virtual appliances available through the VMware Virtual Appliance Marketplace. The VMware Appliance Marketplace is shown in Figure 4.11.

Virtual appliances are created using virtual appliance authoring tools, and then, the appliance is posted for use. Due to the nature of virtualization, most virtual appliances have a stripped down version of an OS. VMware's Marketplace contains downloadable appliances in VMware's format and can be loaded into any application that will understand the format. Currently there are over 1000 virtual appliances available for use with the VMware format. These include not only OSes but also applications such as e-mail servers and firewalls.

Microsoft

Microsoft provides a full suite of technologies to enable an integrated, end-to-end virtualized infrastructure. Microsoft's solution includes servers, desktops, and applications virtual machine management and virtualization acceleration as described in Chapter 2, "Server Virtualization," and Chapter 3, "Desktop Virtualization." According to Microsoft's Web site, its emphasis on virtualization technologies is rooted in creating what is called a *Dynamic IT environment*. Microsoft uses the VHD file format for its virtual appliances. We will be discussing dynamic VHD in Chapter 5, "Investigating Dead Virtual Environments." The Microsoft VHD file format specifies a virtual machine hard disk that can reside on a native host file system encapsulated within a single file. This is now a standard format used by Virtual PC 2007, Virtual Server 2005 R2, and Hyper-V. Microsoft plans to use this format for future versions of Microsoft Windows Server with hypervisor-based virtualization technology.

Microsoft's Web site offers a VHD Test Drive Program, which provides software vendors with a place to distribute preconfigured applications within Windows Server-based virtual machines to their customers. This gives Microsoft partners a way to offer their prospective and current customers more choices and flexibility for evaluating application software and makes it easier to assess complex solutions through the distribution of preconfigured virtual machines. These preconfigured virtual machines currently run on Virtual Server 2005 R2 or Hyper-V System Center Virtual Machine, as shown in Figure 4.12. If the program is successful, the offerings are sure to expand.

Manager can also be used to manage all the virtual machines in an environment. Beyond that, the VHD format is broadly applicable. Since June 2005, Microsoft has made the VHD Image Format Specification available to third parties under a royalty-free license, and as noted earlier, MojoPac has partnered with Microsoft to leverage their technology. Microsoft offers preconfigured VHDs

Figure 4.12 Microsoft's Test Drive Program

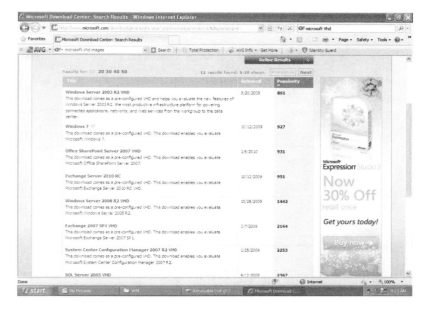

Figure 4.13 Microsoft VHD Images

that can be downloaded and evaluated similar to the virtual appliance market of VMware. Figure 4.13 shows the readily available VHD images.

However, the images that are offered are a bit different than those offered by VMware's Appliance Marketplace. Microsoft currently only offers VHDs that are evaluation copies due to licensing.

Parallels

Parallels is similar to VMware in that it provides virtualization solutions along with preconfigured appliances, except it is used on the Mac platform. Parallels provides server, desktop, automation, and management solutions. Based on the Web site offerings, Parallels offers a library of more than 350 software downloads that can be used to easily create and manage OSes and applications running in virtual environments. A Parallels Virtual Appliance is a target service or application installed and configured inside a prebuilt virtual machine for Parallels Desktop, Parallels Workstation, or Parallels Server. Because Parallels Virtual Appliance can be built on any supported guest OS (Windows, Linux, Solaris, BSD, OS/2, eComStation, and DOS), appliances can be created for almost any application.

The Parallels Virtual Appliance is a self-contained archive that includes an archive of all virtual appliance files in a single file using the zip format whenever possible. The archive

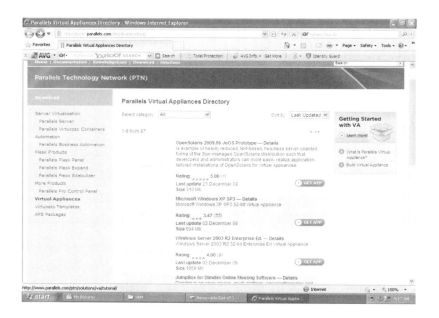

Figure 4.14 Parallels Virtual Appliances Directory

must contain the .pvs configuration file, virtual disk(s) files, the Parallels Virtual Appliance's description document, and all documentation that the end-user will need. All this information can be entered into the Parallels template supplied on the Parallels Web site.

The Parallels also supplies Virtuozzo Templates. A template in Parallels Virtuozzo Containers is a set of application files and registry settings installed on the Host OS in such a way as to be usable by any Container by mounting over Virtuozzo File System. Parallels also offers service providers access to applications for software-as-a-service that conform to the Application Packaging Standard for. Figure 4.14 shows the readily available appliances.

Xen

Another major virtualization competitor in the virtual appliance marketplace is XenSource. XenSource distributes its hypervisor as free, open-source software, but it sells related products. It was acquired by Citrix in 2007. According to Citrix's Web site, Citrix Delivery Center is the only end-to-end solution for virtualizing both the desktop and the data center.

Citrix Project Kensho is a tool developed for assisting in the creation and use of virtual appliances that is available to Citrix

Partners and administrators. Kensho facilitates the export and import of virtual machines and virtual appliances through the use of the Open Virtual Machine Format (OVF) and Common Information Model industry standards developed by the Distributed Management Task Force (DMTF). OVF and the DMTF will be discussed in Chapter 7, "Finding and Imaging Virtual Environments." This allows the virtual appliances to be used by multiple hypervisor platforms including Citrix XenServer and Microsoft Hyper-V. You can also build virtual appliances using the XenServer and the tools provided by Citrix. Once a virtual machine is created, it is saved as a .xva file, and any other steps recommended to finish the creation of the virtual appliance image should be completed. You may compress your .xva file to reduce the size of the virtual appliance. The file formats of the commercial and open-source Zen are totally different. The open source is a standard image file, and you can mount it, fdisk it, or do whatever else you like with it. The Citrix Xen Virtual Appliance file is quite different.

Virtual Appliance Providers

In addition to virtual appliance marketplaces, there are virtual appliance providers. For example, at http://virtualappliances .net lightweight, virtual machines based on Ubuntu Linux are built with portability and optimization in mind. Once the appliances are built, they are posted for download. The appliances use Ubuntu's own repositories for update management, so updates and patches are very easy to manage. There are also hundreds of applications that can be installed on the appliances from the Ubuntu repositories.

JumpBox Virtual Appliances

JumpBox is an open-source solution for virtual appliances. It provides ready-to-go virtual computers containing a preconfigured application. This takes the learning curve out configuring, optimizing, and securing open-source software. The premise behind JumpBox is simplified server software deployment with software applications that are prebuilt, preconfigured, and packaged for deployment on virtualization platforms including VMware, Parallels, VirtualBox, Microsoft Hyper-V, Virtual Iron, Xen and Amazon EC2 Server, and Virtual Iron, as shown in Figure 4.15.

Figure 4.15 JumpBox Virtual Appliances

VirtualBox

VirtualBox was originally the product of InnoTek, a German company. In early 2007, the product went open source. There were two versions offered: an open-source version and a full version with additional features aimed at enterprise customers. Sun Microsystems, Inc. announced that it entered into a stock purchase agreement to acquire InnoTek in February 2008. Sun continues development of VirtualBox. VirtualBox 3.1.0 was released on November 30, 2009, with the most recent maintenance release being on February 12, 2010. VirtualBox has the capability of virtualizing a wide variety of OSes including Windows, from 3.1 through 7, Linux, Solaris, and OpenBSD for use as guest OSes. The configuration settings of virtual machines are stored entirely in XML and are independent of the local machine allowing for easier portability. The closed-source edition supports the standard Remote Desktop Protocol (RDP), USB, and RDP over USB. The RDP support allows a virtual machine to act as an RDP server so that the virtual machine can be run remotely on some thin client that merely displays the RDP data. The emulator is based on QEMU. The virtual drive format used by VirtualBox is .vdi. Figure 4.16 shows an image of VirtualBox.

Virtualization Hardware Devices

Besides the above-named companies, there is a wide variety of other companies that offer virtual solutions. Since the market is growing at a very fast pace, included in this section are only a

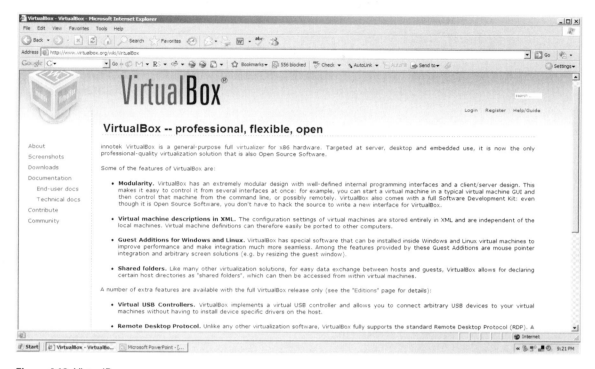

Figure 4.16 VirtualBox

few of the solutions the authors thought might be relevant to the computer forensic examiner.

According to Pano Logic's Web site, the company offers a complete desktop virtualization solution. Pano Logic has moved the PC and all its software off the desktop and into the data center. Pano's solution is contained in a small device that connects a keyboard, mouse, display, audio, and USB peripherals over an existing Internet Protocol network to an instance of Windows XP or Vista running on a virtualized server. The Pano device is a zero client. It has no CPU, no memory, no OS, no drivers, no software, and no moving parts. A management device sits between the Pano device and the virtualization server; see Figure 4.17.

InBoxer was founded in 2003. The InBoxer Anti-Risk Appliance combines e-mail archiving, electronic discovery, and real-time content monitoring in a single appliance. The technology behind the InBoxer is based on advanced mathematical techniques and language research capabilities to filter messages and documents. The InBoxer virtual appliance runs on and can adopt storage virtualization.

Figure 4.17 Pano Device (© Photo copyright Pano Logic. Used with permission.)

Figure 4.18 NComputing Device (© Photo copyright NComputing. Used with permission.)

In November 2009, NComputing launched the industry's first USB-connected virtual desktop (model U170) at the Consumer Electronics Show (CES) in Las Vegas (Figure 4.18).

Virtual Privacy Machine

The Portable Virtual Privacy Machine by MetroPipe contains a complete virtual Linux machine with privacy-enabled open-source Internet applications. Carry your Internet applications, e-mail, bookmarks, history, Web cookies, and download files in your pocket. The Portable Virtual Privacy Machine is based on DSL and

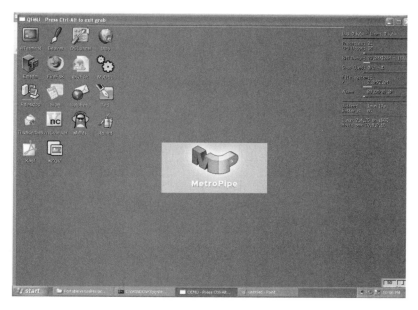

Figure 4.19 Virtual Privacy Machine Running

QEMU releases. QEMU is a generic, open-source processor emulator. The Virtual Privacy Machine running is shown in Figure 4.19

Virtual Emulators

Virtual emulators are a bit different than virtual machines. Virtual emulators allow OSes to be run that have different processor requirements. In other words, emulators simulate an entire environment, not just the OS. An example of this is running Windows Vista on a Mac-based PowerPC. Due to fact that the entire environment must be simulated, emulators tend to be slower than VMs.

Bochs

Bochs is open-source x86 PC emulator written by Kevin Lawton. It includes emulation of the entire x86 PC platform, including the x86 processor, hardware devices, and memory. Bochs is written in C++ and can be complied to emulate many x86 Intel platforms including the 386, 486, and the Pentium family of processors. The most current version, Bochs 2.4.2, was released on November 12, 2009. Bochs is capable of running many OSes inside the emulation including Linux, DOS, and most Microsoft OSes. Figure 4.20 shows the Bochs console and start menu. The creation of an image is show in Figure 4.21.

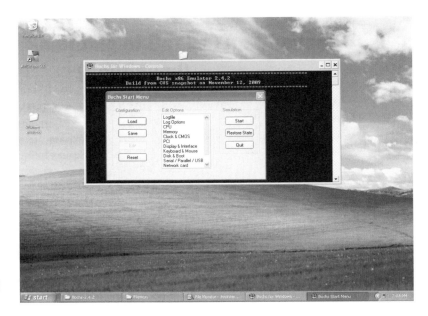

Figure 4.20 Bochs Console and Start Menu

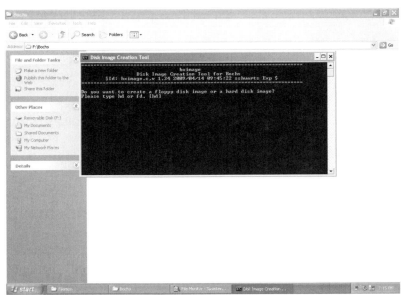

Figure 4.21 Creation of a Bochs Image

DOSBox

DOSBox is another emulated x86 machine. It is integrated with DOS for the main purpose of running old DOS games and applications. The emulation offers support of old sound and video cards and speed control for old games. The integrated DOS eliminates the need for DOS to be set up as a virtual machine before

Figure 4.22 DOSBox Console

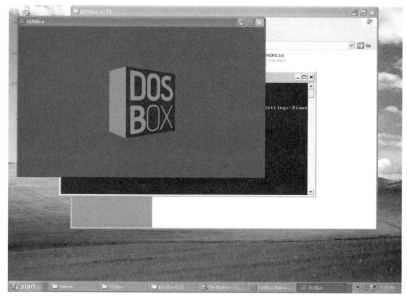

Figure 4.23 DOSBox Completed
Installation

a game can be started. It also has the ability to simulate peer-to-peer networking.

DOSBox was created shortly after the release of Windows 2000 because many games became unplayable under the platform. The intended audience is people who want to play DOS games and preferably already have a familiarity with DOS. Figures 4.22 and 4.23 show the DOSBox environment.

Future Development

Currently most portable environments save at least some part of the information in the system registry or configuration files. In "Portable Desktop Applications Based on P2P Transportation and Virtualization," Zhang, Wang, and Hong (2000) propose an application that can work without installation by making a two-part application. One part is portable and enables the application to run in a sandbox where it can access and store the data associated with it, and the second part can run in an isolation mode. Other similar environments include Feather-weight Virtual Machine and Progressive Deployment System.

Summary

In this chapter, we have discussed the various portable virtualization programs, emulators, and appliances that an examiner may run into during the course of an investigation. It is important to know about these environments because as the investigator, you will need to ask questions about the use of these environments not only to get a good picture of the examination environment but also to determine what exactly will need to be examined and where evidence might be found. This information can also tip you off to potential problem areas.

References

Marshall, D. (2008). Parallels virtuozzo containers offers 350 templates. *InfoWorld virtualization report.* Retrieved from http://weblog.infoworld.com/virtualization/archives/2008/02/parallels_virtu.html

Zhang, Y., Wang, X., & Hong, L. (2000). Portable desktop applications based on P2P transportation and virtualization. *Proceedings from LISA '08: The 22nd Large Installation System Administration Conference.*

Bibliography

MojoPac

RingCube. *MojoPac* http://www.mojopac.com/enterprise/products/index.html

MokaFive

LivePCs. *Moka5.* http://www.moka5.com/products/index.html

Fiering, L., Silver, M. A., Gammage, B., Unsworth, J., & Smith, D. M. (2007). Cool vendors in PC technologies, 2007. *Gartner, Inc.* Retrieved from www.gartner.com/DisplayDocument?id=502005

Preconfigured Virtual Environments

Microsoft

Run IT on a virtual hard disk – test drive program. *Microsoft TechNet*. Retrieved
from. http://technet.microsoft.com/en-us/bb738372.aspx

Virtualization from the datacenter to the desktop. *Microsoft TechNet*. Retrieved
from http://technet.microsoft.com/en-us/virtualserver/bb676673.aspx

VMware

www.wmware.com

Parallels

www.parallels.com

Xen

http://www.xen.org/support/documentation.html

Deliver IT as an on-demand service: Transform datacenters into delivery centers.
Citrix. Retrieved from http://www.citrix.com/English/ps2/products/product
.asp?contentID=683711.

Project kensho v1.3 technology preview. *Citrix Community*. http://community.citrix
.com/display/xs/Kensho

Virtual Appliances

http://www.vmware.com/appliances/getting-started/learn/faq.html

Virtual Privacy Machine

The free portable privacy machine. *MetroPipe*. http://www.metropipe.net/
ppm.php?SID=4e38766ea6a3fab4792ced91b2bdbe48

FORENSICS

INVESTIGATING DEAD VIRTUAL ENVIRONMENTS

INFORMATION IN THIS CHAPTER

- Install Files
- Remnants
- Registry
- Microsoft Disk Image Formats
- Data to Look for
- Investigator Tips

Traditionally, investigators have used virtual machines to create contained environments for malware isolation or to view the environment as a suspect used it. Suspect machines. For example, VMware can be used to mount a dd image, and applications such as LiveView and Virtual Forensic Computing (VFC) can be used to create a VMware virtual machine from a raw disk image or physical disk. VFC uses a combination of VMware's VMPlayer and forensic disk mount tool Mount Image Pro to create and mount the disk. This allows the forensic examiner to boot the image or the disk in a virtual environment and to view the system in a user-level perspective of the system. This method is a controlled setting that doesn't modify the host operating system, and after the investigator examines the subject system, the changes can be discarded. The original machine is preserved and can be used without any adverse effects.

However, now instead of using virtual environments to examine the suspect's machine, virtual environments themselves need to be examined. As described previously, virtualization technology is used in all facets of corporate environments from data centers to virtual desktops. In addition, the applications discussed in the Chapter 4, "Portable Virtualization, Emulators, and Appliances," allow mobile employees to leave hardware behind and take only software with them. Entire environments can now be carried on micro devices such as a USB drive or iPod. An operating system on removable media and external devices can function on its own as described in the Chapter 4, "Portable Virtualization, Emulators, and Appliances." It is possible with removable media that the only place that evidence is located is in the random access memory, which is cleared when the computer is powered off. These environments combined with the concept of downloading a virtual machine through a browser on a borrowed machine and cloud computing have changed the evidence landscape. All these technological changes present new challenges to the traditional methods of performing forensic analysis.

Many forensic examinations are still carried out using the traditional method of creating a forensic copy of the suspect's drive using a write blocker and then using that image to create a case in the forensic examination software. This method does not allow the investigator to view inside the virtual machine. Instead the investigator must look for telltale signs that a virtual environment has been used and then mount that environment to examine the files inside.

As discussed previously, virtual machines are merely files on a hard drive, and these files can be easily copied, deleted, or stored in remote locations. Many virtual environment products are capable of taking a snapshot of a virtual machine, so the virtual machine can later be reverted back to the state in which the snapshot was taken. The concept behind snapshots is similar to Windows restore points. Snapshots will be discussed in further detail in Chapter 7, "Finding and Imaging Virtual Environments." It is possible that if snapshots exist, there may be evidence in these files as well.

This chapter covers the notable installation files, registry entries, artifacts, and other remnants an investigator may find when dealing with individual virtual environments. VMware and Virtual PC will be the first applications discussed in each category because they are the most common virtual environments an investigator will encounter. In fact, at the recent Paraben's Forensic Innovations Conference (PFIC), several attendees asked questions about how to examine VMware environments as they are running into them more often. Other virtual environments will be discussed so that investigators can be aware of their existence in the event that they are not finding evidence that should be there. Often in cases of theft of proprietary information, file activity between the network and the suspects' external devices is usually the first item of evidence to be requested. Furthermore, tying that evidence to the external device is also requested. In the next few sections, we will cover some of the notable findings from the various applications we have discussed previously.

Install Files

Most Windows applications need to be installed before they can run normally. Even most applications that can work without installation save their customizations into the system registry and/or into configuration files located in some system folders. Then an application can be regarded as including two parts: Part 1 is all of the files and folders and registry keys and environment variables created by its installation process, and Part 2 is the customization produced during the runtime. As each application installs, there will be notable information that may help the investigator in recognizing that a particular environment was used.

VMware Server

Table 5.1 shows a portion of the files that File Monitor reports as changed when VMware server is installed.

Table 5.1 Sampling of VMware Server File Changes

C:\WINDOWS\Prefetch\VMWARE-SERVER-2.0.2-203138.EX-38A11171.pf

C:\Documents and Settings\My Documents\VmWare\VMware-server-2.0.2-203138.exe.Local\

C:\WINDOWS\WinSxS\X86_Microsoft.Windows.Common-Controls_6595b64144ccf1df_6.0.2600.5512_x-ww_35d4ce83

C:\WINDOWS\WindowsShell.Config

C:\DOCUME~1\ LOCALS~1\Temp\vminst.log

C:\DOCUME~1\ LOCALS~1\Temp\vmmsi.log

C:\Documents and Settings\ My Documents\VmWare\1033.bmp

C:\WINDOWS\system32\config\software.LOG

C:\DOCUME~1\ LOCALS~1\Temp\{AF08C71F-F822-4416-87A9-2BBF5A8A5F12}~setup\

C:\DOCUME~1\ LOCALS~1\Temp\{AF08C71F-F822-4416-87A9-2BBF5A8A5F12}~setup

C:\DOCUME~1\ LOCALS~1\Temp\{AF08C71F-F822-4416-87A9-2BBF5A8A5F12}~setup\instmsiw.exe

C:\WINDOWS\system32\MSI.DLL

C:\Documents and Settings\ My Documents\VmWare\WINTRUST.dll

C:\Documents and Settings\ My Documents\VmWare\CRYPT32.dll

C:\Documents and Settings\ My Documents\VmWare\MSASN1.dll

C:\Documents and Settings\ My Documents\VmWare\rsaenh.dll

C:\Documents and Settings\ My Documents\VmWare\xpsp2res.dll

C:\Documents and Settings\My Documents\VmWare\netapi32.dll

Continued

Table 5.1 Sampling of VMware Server File Changes (Continued)

```
C:\Documents and Settings\ Application Data\Microsoft\SystemCertificates\My\Certificates\
C:\Documents and Settings\ Application Data\Microsoft\SystemCertificates\My\CRLs\
C:\Documents and Settings\ Application Data\Microsoft\SystemCertificates\My\CTLs\
C:\Documents and Settings\ Application Data\Microsoft\SystemCertificates\My
C:\Documents and Settings\ My Documents\VmWare\cryptnet.dll
C:\Documents and Settings\ My Documents\VmWare\PSAPI.DLL
C:\Documents and Settings\ My Documents\VmWare\SensApi.dll
C:\Documents and Settings\ My Documents\VmWare\WINHTTP.dll
C:\Documents and Settings\ My Documents\VmWare\setupapi.dll
C:\Documents and Settings\ My Documents\VmWare\Cabinet.dll
C:\Documents and Settings\ My Documents\VmWare\Cab8.tmp
C:\Documents and Settings\ My Documents\VmWare\MSISIP.DLL
C:\Documents and Settings\ My Documents\VmWare\msi.dll
C:\Documents and Settings\ My Documents\VmWare\sfc_os.dll
C:\DOCUME~1\ \LOCALS~1\Temp\3f78a20.msi
```

VMware Workstation

Table 5.2 shows a portion of the files that File Monitor reports as changed when VMware Workstation is installed.

As one can see, VMware products install quite a few .dll files, load in the Prefetch, and put files in the Temp directory. We will discuss Prefetch later in this chapter. VMware is not intended to be a stealth application and therefore it will leave a lot of telltale signs.

Microsoft Virtual PC – Microsoft Virtual PC 2007

Table 5.3 shows a portion of the files that File Monitor reports as changed when Microsoft Virtual PC is installed.

Microsoft products install quite a few .dll files, load in the Prefetch, and put files in the temp directory just as VMware products do. Virtual PC is not intended to be a stealth application and therefore it will leave a lot of telltale signs.

MojoPac

Table 5.4 shows a portion of the files that File Monitor reports as changed when MojoPac is installed.

Table 5.2 Sampling of VMware Workstation File Changes

C:\Documents and Settings\VMware Workstation\dbghelp.dll
C:\Documents and Settings\VMware Workstation\deploypkg.dll
C:\Documents and Settings\VMware Workstation\farexec-service.exe
C:\Documents and Settings\VMware Workstation\hqtray.exe
C:\Documents and Settings\VMware Workstation\iconv.dll
C:\Documents and Settings\VMware Workstation\icustbundlegen.dll
C:\Documents and Settings\VMware Workstation\libcurl.dll
C:\Documents and Settings\VMware Workstation\libeay32.dll
C:\Documents and Settings\VMware Workstation\libeaynf32.dll
C:\Documents and Settings\VMware Workstation\libxml2.dll
C:\Documents and Settings\VMware Workstation\messages\ja\vmappsdk-ja.dll
C:\Documents and Settings\VMware Workstation\messages\ja\vmnetui-ja.dll
C:\Documents and Settings\VMware Workstation\messages\ja\vmplayer-ja.dll
C:\Documents and Settings\VMware Workstation\messages\ja\vmui-ja.dll
C:\Documents and Settings\VMware Workstation\mspack.dll
C:\Documents and Settings\VMware Workstation\ntwrap.dll
C:\Documents and Settings\VMware Workstation\p2vhlpr.dll
C:\Documents and Settings\VMware Workstation\p2vjobmanager.dll
C:\Documents and Settings\VMware Workstation\p2vsupport.dll
C:\Documents and Settings\VMware Workstation\p2vwizard.dll
C:\Documents and Settings\VMware Workstation\p2vxml.dll
C:\Documents and Settings\VMware Workstation\pixops.dll
C:\windows\system32\atl71.dll
C:\windows\system32\comdlg32.ocx
C:\windows\system32\mfc71.dll
C:\windows\system32\mfc71u.dll
C:\windows\system32\mscomct2.ocx
C:\windows\system32\msflxgrd.ocx
C:\windows\system32\msvcp71.dll
C:\windows\system32\msvcr71.dll
C:\windows\system32\richtx32.ocx
C:\windows\system32\v2idisklib.dll
C:\windows\system32\vmnat.exe
C:\windows\system32\vmnc.dll
C:\windows\system32\vmnetbridge.dll
C:\windows\system32\vmnetdhcp.exe
C:\windows\system32\vnetinst.dll
C:\windows\system32\vnetlib.dll

Table 5.3 Sampling of Microsoft Virtual PC File Changes

```
C:\$ConvertToNonresident
C:\DOCUME~1\
C:\DOCUME~1\\LOCALS~1\
C:\DOCUME~1\\LOCALS~1\Temp\
C:\DOCUME~1\\LOCALS~1\Temp\msxml6-KB927977-enu-x86.exe
C:\DOCUME~1\\LOCALS~1\Temp\msxml6-KB927977-enu-x86.exe.Manifest
C:\DOCUME~1\\LOCALS~1\Temp\Virtual_PC_2007_Install.msi
C:\Documents and Settings\\Local Settings\Temp\Virtual_PC_2007_Install.msi
C:\Documents and Settings\\My Documents\MSFT Virtual PC\Microsoft Virtual PC 2007 (English)\en_virtual_pc_2007_x32.exe
C:\Documents and Settings\\My Documents\MSFT Virtual PC\Microsoft Virtual PC 2007 (English)\en_virtual_pc_2007_
x32.exe.Local\
C:\Documents and Settings\\My Documents\MSFT Virtual PC\Microsoft Virtual PC 2007 (English)\msi.dll
C:\Documents and Settings\\My Documents\MSFT Virtual PC\Microsoft Virtual PC 2007 (English)\msiexec.exe
C:\Documents and Settings\\My Documents\MSFT Virtual PC\Microsoft Virtual PC 2007 (English)\msiexec.exe
C:\WINDOWS\AppPatch\sysmain.sdb
C:\WINDOWS\AppPatch\sysmain.sdb
C:\WINDOWS\AppPatch\systest.sdb
C:\WINDOWS\AppPatch\systest.sdb
C:\WINDOWS\Prefetch\EN_VIRTUAL_PC_2007_X32.EXE-3218130F.pf
C:\WINDOWS\system32\
C:\WINDOWS\system32\Apphelp.dll
C:\WINDOWS\system32\comctl32.dll
C:\WINDOWS\system32\comctl32.dll.124.Config
C:\WINDOWS\system32\comctl32.dll.124.Manifest
C:\WINDOWS\system32\IMM32.DLL
C:\WINDOWS\system32\msiexec.exe.Config
C:\WINDOWS\system32\msiexec.exe.Manifest
C:\WINDOWS\system32\SHELL32.dll
C:\WINDOWS\system32\SHELL32.dll.124.Config
```

MojoPac files are most often installed directly on the thumb drive, so these files will not be found on the hard drive. In the "Remnants" section, the Prefetch folder as well as the MojoPac environment will be addressed.

MokaFive

Table 5.5 shows a portion of the files that File Monitor reports as changed when MokaFive is installed.

Table 5.4 Sampling of MojoPac File Changes

C:\WINDOWS\Prefetch\MOJOPACINSTALLER2.EXE-3720EC86.pf
C:\$Directory
C:\WINDOWS\Registration
C:\WINDOWS\system32\CRYPTUI.dll.2.Manifest
C:\WINDOWS\system32\CRYPTUI.dll.2.Config
C:\DOCUME~1\Diane\LOCALS~1\Temp\RingThreeInstallerHelper.Dll.1000.Manifest
C:\DOCUME~1\Diane\LOCALS~1\Temp\RingThreeInstallerHelperENU.dll
C:\DOCUME~1\Diane\LOCALS~1\Temp\RingThreeInstallerHelperLOC.dll
C:\Program Files\ringthree\config\Mojo1Cx.dat
C:\Program Files\ringthree\config\LastKnownGood\Mojo1Cx.dat
C:\Program Files\ringthree\config\Mojo1Cx.dat
C:\WINDOWS\system32\digest.dll
C:\WINDOWS\system32\msnsspc.dll
C:\WINDOWS\system32\msv1_0.dll
C:\WINDOWS\system32\cryptdll.dll
C:\WINDOWS\system32\mswsock.dll
C:\WINDOWS\system32\hnetcfg.dll
C:\WINDOWS\System32\wshtcpip.dll
C:\WINDOWS\system32\MLANG.dll.123.Manifest
C:\WINDOWS\system32\MLANG.dll.123.Config
C:\WINDOWS\system32\rasadhlp.dll
C:\Documents and Settings\Diane\Start Menu\Programs\RingCube
C:\Documents and Settings\Diane\Start Menu\Programs\RingCube\MojoPac (RingCube).lnk
C:\WINDOWS\Prefetch\MOJOPACINSTALLER2.EXE-3720EC86.pf
C:\Documents and Settings\Diane\Start Menu\Programs\RingCube\
C:\Documents and Settings\Diane\Start Menu\Programs\RingCube\MojoPac Website.lnk
C:\WINDOWS\Prefetch\RINGTHREEMAINWIN32.EXE-30ECE670.pf

Table 5.5 Sampling of MokaFive File Changes

C:\WINDOWS\Prefetch\M5LAUNCH.EXE-11B7C3B6.pf
C:\WINDOWS\system32\SHELL32.dll.124.Manifest
C:\WINDOWS\system32\SHELL32.dll.124.Config
C:\Documents and Settings\ Application Data
C:\Documents and Settings\ Application Data\moka5\Engine\.config
C:\Documents and Settings\ Application Data\moka5\Engine\.config\m5engine.log

Continued

Table 5.5 Sampling of MokaFive File Changes (Continued)

C:\DOCUME~1\ LOCALS~1\Temp\m5usb-6302
C:\DOCUME~1\ LOCALS~1\Temp\m5usb-6302\m5usb.exe
C:\DOCUME~1\ LOCALS~1\Temp\m5usb-6302\sleep.exe
C:\DOCUME~1\LOCALS~1\Temp\m5usb-6302\m5util.dll
C:\DOCUME~1\ LOCALS~1\Temp\m5usb-6302\util_all.dll
C:\DOCUME~1\ LOCALS~1\Temp\m5usb-6302\gui-unicode.dll
C:\DOCUME~1\ LOCALS~1\Temp\m5usb-6302\m5tk-unicode.dll
C:\DOCUME~1\ \LOCALS~1\Temp\m5usb-6302\wxbase28u_vc_custom.dll
C:\DOCUME~1\ LOCALS~1\Temp\m5usb-6302\wxbase28u_xml_vc_custom.dll
C:\DOCUME~1\ LOCALS~1\Temp\m5usb-6302\wxmsw28u_adv_vc_custom.dll
C:\DOCUME~1\ \LOCALS~1\Temp\m5usb-6302\wxmsw28u_core_vc_custom.dll
C:\DOCUME~1\ \LOCALS~1\Temp\m5usb-6302\wxmsw28u_html_vc_custom.dll
C:\DOCUME~1\ LOCALS~1\Temp\m5usb-6302\wxmsw28u_xrc_vc_custom.dll
C:\DOCUME~1\ LOCALS~1\Temp\m5usb-6302\boost_date_time-vc71-mt-1_35.dll
C:\DOCUME~1\ \LOCALS~1\Temp\m5usb-6302\boost_system-vc71-mt-1_35.dll
C:\DOCUME~1\ LOCALS~1\Temp\m5usb-6302\boost_thread-vc71-mt-1_35.dll
C:\Documents and Settings\ Local Settings\Temp\m5usb-6302\m5usb.exe
C:\Documents and Settings\ Local Settings\Temp\m5usb-6302
C:\Documents and Settings\ Start Menu\Programs\Startup\moka5 USB Clean-6302.lnk
C:\Documents and Settings\ Start Menu\Programs\Startup\

In the "Remnants" section, the Prefetch folder will be addressed as will the MokaFive environment itself.

Virtual Privacy Machine

Table 5.6 shows a portion of the files that File Monitor reports as changed when Virtual Privacy Machine is installed.

This environment is little different than MojoPac and MokaFive because it is based on QEMU. This environment and its files will be discussed later in this chapter.

Bochs

Table 5.7 shows a portion of the files that File Monitor reports as changed when Bochs is installed.

Table 5.6 Sampling of Virtual Privacy Machine File Changes

C:\WINDOWS\Prefetch\QEMU.EXE-32A2B1AB.pf
C:\WINDOWS\system32\IPHLPAPI.DLL
C:\WINDOWS\system32\WS2_32.dll
C:\WINDOWS\system32\WS2HELP.dll
C:\WINDOWS\system32\WINMM.DLL
C:\WINDOWS\system32\wshbth.dll
C:\WINDOWS\system32\SETUPAPI.dll
C:\WINDOWS\System32\mswsock.dll
C:\WINDOWS\system32\DNSAPI.dll
C:\WINDOWS\System32\winrnr.dll
C:\WINDOWS\system32\rasadhlp.dll
C:\WINDOWS\system32\uxtheme.dll
C:\WINDOWS\system32\MSCTF.dll
C:\WINDOWS\system32\msctfime.ime
C:\WINDOWS\system32\hnetcfg.dll
C:\WINDOWS\System32\wshtcpip.dll
C:\WINDOWS\web\wallpaper\Bliss.bmp

Table 5.7 Sampling of Bochs File Changes

C:\WINDOWS\Prefetch\BOCHS-2.4.2.EXE-1CC2A7E0.pf
C:\WINDOWS\SYSTEM32\SHFOLDER.DLL
C:\WINDOWS\WIN.INI
C:\WINDOWS\system32\config\software.LOG
C:\DOCUME~1 \LOCALS~1\Temp
C:\DOCUME~1 \LOCALS~1\Temp\nsb3.tmp
C:\Program Files\Bochs-2.4.2\bochs.exe
C:\Program Files\Bochs-2.4.2\
C:\Program Files\Bochs-2.4.2\bochsdbg.exe
C:\Program Files\Bochs-2.4.2\bxcommit.exe
C:\Program Files\Bochs-2.4.2\bximage.exe
C:\Program Files\Bochs-2.4.2\niclist.exe
C:\Program Files\Bochs-2.4.2\sb16ctrl.exe

Continued

Table 5.7 Sampling of Bochs File Changes (Continued)

C:\Program Files\Bochs-2.4.2\CHANGES.txt
C:\Program Files\Bochs-2.4.2\TODO.txt
C:\Program Files\Bochs-2.4.2\bochsrc-sample.txt
C:\Program Files\Bochs-2.4.2\sb16ctrl-example.txt
C:\Program Files\Bochs-2.4.2\bochs.ico
C:\Program Files\Bochs-2.4.2\penguin.ico
C:\Program Files\Bochs-2.4.2\unbochs.ico
C:\Program Files\Bochs-2.4.2\keymaps\sdl-pc-de.map
C:\Documents and Settings \Start Menu\Programs\Bochs 2.4.2\Readme.lnk
C:\Documents and Settings \Start Menu\Programs\Bochs 2.4.2\Bochs Sample Setup.lnk
C:\Documents and Settings \Start Menu\Programs\Bochs 2.4.2\Disk Image Creation Tool.lnk
C:\Documents and Settings \Start Menu\Programs\Bochs 2.4.2\NIC Lister.lnk
C:\Documents and Settings \Start Menu\Programs\Bochs 2.4.2\Help.url

DOSBox

Table 5.8 shows a portion of the files that File Monitor reports as changed when DOSBox is installed.

This sampling of files will be discussed in the next few sections. In addition, the notable files along with all pertinent information will be described for future reference. When dealing with the possibility of virtual environments, it is a good idea to have a keyword list that can be run against the suspect's drive.

Remnants

In order to explore what remnants are left by virtual environments that were run from a USB drive, the environments MojoPac, MokaFive, Virtual Privacy Machine, and a VMware appliance were examined.

The methodology used was kept as simple as possible in order to gain an accurate picture of the environments. Forensic Toolkit (FTK) Imager was used to make a dd image from a clean Windows XP installed on a 20 GB drive. The USB device was plugged in, the virtual environment was started, several actions

Table 5.8 Sampling of DOSBox File Changes

C:\WINDOWS\Prefetch\DOSBOX0.73-WIN32-INSTALLER.EX-07AD09EB.pf
C:\WINDOWS\system32\SHFOLDER.dll
C:\DOCUME~1\LOCALS~1\Temp\nsf4.tmp
C:\DOCUME~1\LOCALS~1\Temp\nsq5.tmp
C:\Documents and Settings\All Users\Start Menu\Programs\DOSBox-0.73
C:\Documents and Settings\All Users\Start Menu\Programs\DOSBox-0.73\Video
C:\Documents and Settings\All Users\Start Menu\Programs\DOSBox-0.73\Configuration
C:\Documents and Settings\All Users\Start Menu\Programs\DOSBox-0.73\Uninstall.lnk
C:\Documents and Settings\All Users\Start Menu\Programs\DOSBox-0.73\
C:\Documents and Settings\All Users\Start Menu\Programs\DOSBox-0.73
C:\Documents and Settings\All Users\Start Menu\Programs\DOSBox-0.73\Video
C:\Documents and Settings\All Users\Start Menu\Programs\DOSBox-0.73\Configuration
C:\Documents and Settings\All Users\Start Menu\Programs\DOSBox-0.73\Uninstall.lnk
C:\Documents and Settings\All Users\Start Menu\Programs\DOSBox-0.73\
C:\Documents and Settings\All Users\Start Menu\Programs\DOSBox-0.73\DOSBox.lnk
C:\Documents and Settings\All Users\Start Menu\Programs\DOSBox-0.73\DOSBox (noconsole).lnk
C:\Documents and Settings\All Users\Start Menu\Programs\DOSBox-0.73\README.lnk
C:\Documents and Settings\All Users\Start Menu\Programs\DOSBox-0.73\Configuration\Edit
Configuration.lnk
C:\WINDOWS\system32\OPENGL32.DLL
C:\WINDOWS\system32\GLU32.dll
C:\WINDOWS\system32\DDRAW.dll
C:\WINDOWS\system32\DCIMAN32.dll
C:\WINDOWS\system32\DINPUT.DLL
C:\WINDOWS\system32\KBDUS.DLL
C:\WINDOWS\system32\DSOUND.DLL
C:\WINDOWS\system32\HID.DLL

were performed such as Internet surfing, and then the device was ejected. FTK was used to take another dd image of the machine. The dd image chunks were reconstructed into one file using A.F.7 Merge. Beyond Compare software was used initially to look for differences in the dd images. FTK was also used to search for signs of the virtual environment. The observations made during examination of these environments are described in the following sections.

MojoPac

MojoPac technology was described in Chapter 4, "Portable Virtualization, Emulators, and Appliances." Specific points related to this technology are listed below:

- In some versions, all documents and personal items can be copied to the drive, before launching.
- Once started, access to the local hard drive is eliminated.
- Access to CD and removable drives is still possible.
- May need administrative rights on the host machine in order to run.
- Currently, it will run only on Windows XP.
- MojoPac has its own separate registry and shell.
- Programs of the same name may be running on both the USB drive and the host machine at the same time.
- MojoPac implements paging between memory and the hard drive to take place on the host PC instead of on the portable drive.
- Browsing and multimedia history stays inside MojoPac.

Notable findings:

- The NTUSER.DAT file contained the line: Autorun Action Run MojoPac.
- The Windows SysEvent.evt log file contained the phrase: To see your password hint, please move the mouse over the question mark in the MojoPac Login Dialog.
- All three Prefetch files listed: \DEVICE\HARDDISK1\DP(1) 0-0+9\PROGRAM FILES\RINGTHREE\BIN\MOJOPAC.DLL.
- Pvm.sys and ringthree.ico were found stored on the host machine.
- Phones home for updates.

MojoPac allows all documents and personal settings to be copied to the drive, before launching. If this happens, there will be .lnk files. Although the application does not allow access to the local hard drive once the application is started, access to the CD/DVD drive and removable drives is still possible. MojoPac implements paging between memory and the hard drive to take place on the host PC instead of on the portable drive, so remnants of activity from the drive would be in the page file. Browsing and multimedia history stays inside MojoPac. It has a separate registry and shell stored on the USB device. Currently, it will run only on Windows XP and needs administrative rights on the host machine in order to run, unless an application such as MojoUsher is installed on the host PC for limited mode authority. MojoPac runs under the RingThreeMainWin32 process. Since there are essentially two XP environments running, programs of the same name may be running on both the host and the virtual environments.

"Automatic Updates" is enabled by default in MojoPac to download the latest updates and install them when they becomes available. MojoPac Deluxe customers can disable "Automatic Updates," but MojoPac Freedom users will *not* be able to disable it.

MokaFive

MokaFive technology was described previously. Specific observations related to this technology are listed below:

- Installs VMware Player
- Asks whether you want to leave it installed for easier load next time
- Streams and prefetches LivePCs
- Captures any changes made during a session in separate file systems on a RAM disk
- Creates folders in the My Documents folder for LivePC

Notable findings:

- Folders are created in the My Documents folder for LivePC and LivePC documents. These folders are not removed when the drive is ejected.
- Entry in the user's Startup folder for MokaFive USB Clean 2238, which points to an executable file in the host machine's C: drive: C:\Documents and Settings\Local Settings\Temp\m5usb-2238\m5usb.exe.
- Folder labeled m5usb-2238 inside the Temp folder contained a total of 23 MokaFive-related files.
- Evidence of registry keys created or modified.
- Log file containing information on a MokaFive automatically updates client on the host machine and the path of the MokaFive engine on the thumb drive from which it was run.
- Phones home for updates upon launch.
- LivePCs are stored with .lpc extension that is a small pointer file.
- Data stored in flat.0.
- .lpc extension is just an ID file.

MokaFive technology is based on VMware Player. The application asks whether you want to leave it installed for easier load next time, so there will be evidence in both the Temp folder and the Application Data folder with VMware references. MokaFive used the same technology as VMware for its LivePC except that instead of using a .vmdk extension, it stores the data in a flat.0 file in the cache folder with the .lpc used as a pointer file (Figure 5.1). The .0 extension is a compressed hard disk data format.

The MokaFive engine will stream and prefetch LivePCs. Any changes made during a session are captured in separate file systems on a RAM disk. Browsing and multimedia history stays inside the virtual machine.

Figure 5.1 MokaFive Flat File

Virtual Privacy Machine

Portable Virtual Privacy Machine technology was described previously. Issues related to this technology are listed below:

- Very small Linux distro was designed to boot from a USB drive.
- No installation was needed.
- Just plug the drive into any Windows or Linux computer and click on the Virtual Privacy Machine icon.

Notable findings:

- NTUSER.DAT and NTUSER.LOG files changed.
- Prefetch data files are present.
- Phones home.

Portable Virtual Privacy Machine technology is designed to just plug the drive into any Windows or Linux computer, and the Virtual Privacy Machine will run a contained environment including portable applications. All browsing and multimedia history stays inside the virtual machine. According to a notice posted on MetroPipe's Web site, as of July 2008, the version of the Portable Virtual Privacy Machine that was tested is no longer maintained nor supported. A new version is in development using updated software and operating system. This environment will be reexamined, once the new version is released.

VMware

In many of the aforementioned technologies, virtual devices are exclusive to the virtual machine and are files on the host. For example, VMware creates virtual adapters as well as files with the following extensions: .vmx, .vmdk, .vmsn, and .vmss. "What Files Make Up a Virtual Machine?" posted on VMware's Web site is an explanation of all the file extensions that are associated with VMware along with the purpose of the file. A brief explanation of the file extensions is provided below.

.vmdk – virtual hard drive for the guest operation system
.vmem – backup of the virtual machine's paging file
.vmsn – snapshot file
.vmsd – snapshot metadata
.nvram – virtual machine bios information
.vmx – virtual machine configuration file
.vmss – virtual machine suspended state file
.vmtm – team data configuration
.vmxf – supplemental team configuration file

Additionally, there is .log file created for each virtual machine, which is stored in the directory that holds the configuration (.vmx) file. Since some forensic software lists these extensions as unknown file types, a forensic examiner should become familiar with these files because the presence of only one of these files may be an indication that a virtual machine existed on the media and further investigation may be warranted.

Bares (2009) from the University of Central Florida researched memory allocation in virtual machines in a paper titled "Hiding in a Virtual World: Using Unconventionally Installed Operating Systems." The paper was published on June 11, 2009 by IEEE and appears in *IEEE International Conference on Intelligence and Security Informatics, 2009* (ISI '09). Bares tested the ability to recover data on a 10GB New Technology File System (NTFS) partition with VMware Server installed that was hosting three virtual machines. His research showed that the biggest factor in determining how many and what files are recoverable is whether the virtual machine was shut down correctly or not. When virtual machines are improperly shutdown, less information is recoverable.

Microsoft

Microsoft's virtual products, just like VMware's products, have other files associated with the virtual machine where the VHD format is used. The files and their descriptions are as follows: the virtual machine configuration (.vmc) file, the virtual hard disk (.vhd) file, any virtual machine saved-state (.vsv) files, and virtual machine undo disk (.vud) files associated with the virtual machine. The saved-state and undo disk files are stored in the same folder as the .vmc file. If you save the state of a virtual machine instead of shutting it down, all data from the virtual machine's memory is stored in a saved-state file (.vsv file) instead of in a .vhd file. Microsoft recommends that you either restore the virtual machine or discard the changes and then shut down the virtual machine before moving or copying a .vhd file.

Versions prior to Microsoft Virtual Server 2005 supported splitting of disk images, if the disk image grew larger than the maximum supported file size on the host file system.

Some file systems, such as the FAT32 file system, have a 4 GB limit on file size. If the hard disk image expands to more than 4 GB, Microsoft Virtual PC 2004 and previous versions will split the hard disk image into another file. The split files are stored in the same directory as the main hard disk image. They only have raw data, no headers or footers except for the last one, which has a footer stored at the end of the file. The first file in the split disk image has an extension of .vhd. The subsequent split files use a number convention similar to an EnCase image, so they would show as .v01, .v02, and so on. The maximum number of split files that can be present is 64, and the size of the split file cannot be altered.

Citrix Xen

Citrix Xen offers several different formats, including Open Virtualization Format (OVF), VHD file format, and an Open Virtual Appliance (OVA) package. OVF is an XML file format defined by the Distributed Management Task Force (DMTF) that contains the guest virtual machine metadata. A single OVF can contain information on several guest virtual machines. A VHD file is the disk image of the virtual machine as described in Chapter 4, "Portable Virtualization, Emulators, and Appliances." This is the same format that Microsoft has adopted, but it works a little differently in Xen. Each VHD represents a virtual disk that when joined with an OVF can characterize multiple virtual machines. The last type of format supported by Xen is called an *OVA Package*, which contains the OVF and VHD in an individual uncompressed tape archive file. An OVA Package is created after exporting an OVF and is the format used for Xen's virtual appliances. Project Kensho, which was described in Chapter 4, "Portable Virtualization, Emulators, and Appliances," supports the OVF standard but does not support compression of the OVA file.

Bochs

Bochs only provides the user with virtual hardware. It is a command line emulator. Therefore, the user must know something about hardware, the environments they are working on, and the environment they wish to create and must also have ability to navigate without a graphical user interface. Bochs will run on as variety of operating systems including Windows, Linux, and OpenSolaris. Bochs is attractive because it is one of the only choices available for running x86 software on a non-x86 machine. Bochs has been known to work on a wide variety of hardware platforms, including Sparc, PowerPC, and MIPS.

Bochs uses a lot of macros to compensate for the slow speed at which it runs. It is not meant to be run as a stealth application, so there will be a directory created when it is installed.

DOSBox

The DOSBox emulator is a program that acts as a computer running the DOS operating system. Once the game or program is downloaded and installed, the DOSBox program is run. There will be a DOSBox Status Window that is similar to the window that opens when QEMU is used. Since this environment is used to run DOS-based games, it's working are very similar to running an .exe file at a command prompt. As of 2008, the gp2x file archive now hosts a section on working configs for various games. The files associated with games made to run in this environment include: dosbox.conf, xxx.gpe (xxx being the game name), and mapper.txt files, along with a text file explaining how the keys are mapped as well as any other notes about the configuration.

Virtual Appliances

Preconfigured virtual appliances were described previously. Issues that this technology presents are listed below:
• No installation is needed, runs via VMware Player.
• Virtual applications can be combined. For example, BackTrack2 with Metasploit 3.

Notable findings:
• Runs via VMware Player
• Creates two VMware network adapters

When VMware Player is used, there will be traces associated with VMware, such as C:\program files\common files\vmware. This type of environment is perhaps the most obvious to spot.

There will be virtual adapters created and a host of VMware-referenced files. The user activity is contained in the virtual appliance. File associations maintained in the registry will indicate which program will be started based upon a specific file being selected. This information is found in the Windows registry, under HKEY_CLASSES_ROOT, file associations.

Registry

Just about every application that runs on a Microsoft operating systems touched the registry in some way. This section discusses the registry files associated with the various programs discussed in this chapter. In order to determine what files were placed in the registry, after each application was installed, the machine was booted with Knoppix and the registry hive files were copied to a thumb drive. Then RegRipper was used to examine the registry hives.

MojoPac

MojoPac has its own registry. Depending on the version of the software being used, the location is different. In older versions, it was located in a root directory. With the later release, it is located in the Mojo\Program Files\RingThree\Settings\LastKnownGood folder on the removable device.

In addition, there may be the following files located in the NTUSER.DAT file:

```
MRUList = a
a -> C:\Documents and Settings\Diane\My Documents\tools\
    ProcessMonitor\mojoshutdown.CSV
MRUList = dcba
d -> E:\Installers\MojoPacInstaller2.exe
UEME_RUNPATH:F:\MojoPac\Start.exe
```

MokaFive

MokaFive creates folders for LivePCs as shown in Figure 5.2.

There will also be files with .lpc extensions for any LivePCs created on the host drive. This environment will be discussed in further detail in Chapter 7, "Finding and Imaging Virtual Environments." Notable NTUSER.DAT files are as follows:

```
UEME_RUNPATH:F:\Installers\MokaFive-Win-Player-Installer
    .exe
UEME_RUNPATH:G:\Moka\m5launch.exe
```

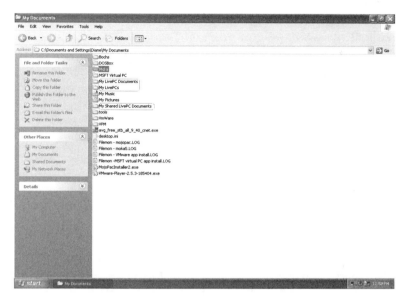

Figure 5.2 LivePC Folders Created on Host Machine

Bochs

Notable NTUSER.DAT files are as follows:

```
UEME_RUNPATH:C:\Program Files\Bochs-2.4.2\bochs.exe
UEME_RUNPIDL:%csidl2%\Bochs 2.4.2\Bochs 2.4.2.lnk
UEME_RUNPIDL:%csidl2%\Bochs 2.4.2
UEME_RUNPIDL:%csidl2%\Bochs 2.4.2\Disk Image Creation
    Tool.lnk
UEME_RUNPATH:C:\Program Files\Bochs-2.4.2\bximage.exe
UEME_RUNPATH:F:\Bochs\Bochs-2.4.2.exe
```

DOSBox

Notable NTUSER.DAT files are as follows:

```
UEME_RUNPATH:F:\DOSBox\DOSBox-0.73\dosbox.exe
UEME_RUNPATH:F:\DOSBox\DOSBox-0.73\dosbox.exe
```

VMware and Microsoft

File associations maintained in the registry will indicate which program will be started based upon a specific file being selected. In the Windows registry, under HKEY_CLASSES_ROOT, file associations. In addition, there is a wealth of information in many of the registry keys. A couple of registry entries that indicate the use of VMware are listed below.

```
MUICache
Software\Microsoft\Windows\ShellNoRoam\MUICache
LastWrite Time Mon Jan 4 22:42:25 2010 (UTC)
C:\Program Files\VMware\VMware Server\tomcat\bin\tomcat6w
    .exe (Procrun Service Manager)
Mon Jan 4 22:03:42 2010 (UTC)
UEME_RUNPIDL:%csidl2%\VMware (3)
UEME_RUNPIDL:%csidl2%\VMware\VMware Web Access (2)
UEME_RUNPIDL:%csidl2%\VMware\VMware Web Access\Tomcat 6.0
    Program Directory.lnk (1)
Mon Jan 4 22:02:36 2010 (UTC)
UEME_RUNPIDL:%csidl2%\VMware\VMware Web Access\Configure
    Tomcat.lnk (1)
UEME_RUNPATH:C:\Program Files\VMware\VMware Server\tomcat\
    bin\tomcat6w.exe (1)
Mon Jan 4 21:51:19 2010 (UTC)
```

Detailed information on registry artifacts can fill an entire book. For additional information on what the registry keys are and what artifacts they hold, please see Harlan Carvey's *Windows Forensic Analysis* (2009).

Microsoft Disk Image Formats

When you are examining virtual environments, virtual formats may have different file locations and headers than an actual physical environment. One of the best documented examples of this is Microsoft's document titled "Virtual Hard Dive Specifications," (2009) which explains the VHD format. This documentation outline VHD formats supported by Virtual PC and Virtual Server and provides information about how to store the data. The following types of VHD formats are supported by Microsoft Virtual PC and Virtual Server:

- Fixed hard disk image – It is an image file allocated to the same size as the fixed disk size.
- Dynamic hard disk image – It is an image file that is as large as the current data written to it and includes the size of the header and footer.
- Differencing hard disk image – It is a block representation of the current state of the VHD in comparison to a parent image.

A dynamic hard disk image is a constantly adjusting image file that can grow up to the allocated size with an upper limit of 2040 GB. Microsoft provides the following information about the basic format and how it works. The basic format of a dynamic hard disk is shown in Table 5.9

Table 5.9 Basic Format of a Dynamic Hard Disk

Dynamic disk header fields
Copy of hard disk footer (512 bytes)
Dynamic disk header (1024 bytes)
BAT (block allocation table)
Data block 1
Data block 2
...
Data block n
Hard disk footer (512 bytes)

The hard disk footer is a crucial part of the hard disk image. The footer is mirrored as a header at the front of the file for purposes of redundancy, so whenever a data block is added, the hard disk footer is moved to the end of the file.

A differencing hard disk is a block representation of the current state of the VHD in comparison to a parent image. A differencing disk is dependent on the parent hard disk to be fully functional. The parent hard disk image can be a fixed, dynamic, or differencing disk image. Because the differencing hard disks store the file locator of the parent hard disk inside the differencing hard disk itself, when this type of disk is opened by a VM, the parent disk is opened as well. Since the parent hard disk can also be a differencing hard disk, it is possible to encounter a chain of differencing hard disks until a fixed or dynamic disk is found.

The hard disk format is designed to store parent hard disk file locators for different platforms at the same time in order to support the movement of hard disks across platforms.

In dynamic and differencing disk images, the data offset field within the image footer points to a secondary structure that provides additional information about the disk image. The dynamic disk header should appear on a sector (512 byte) boundary. The VHD specifications document the following dynamic disk header fields and their sizes in bytes as shown in Table 5.10.

The first sector of the virtual disk is actually the Master Boot Record (MBR). From here, the partitions in the virtual disk can be determined. Usually, the first entry is the boot (primary) partition. Using the structures for the MBR, the starting sector can be determined. The starting sector is the boot sector from the partition. The chain from the first sector (footer) to the boot sector is consistent and can be determined by code based on the spec.

Table 5.10 Dynamic Disk Header Fields

Dynamic Disk Header Fields	Size (bytes)
Cookie	8
Data offset	8
Table offset	8
Header version	4
Max table entries	4
Block size	4
Checksum	4
Parent unique ID	16
Parent time stamp	4
Reserved	4
Parent unicode name	512
Parent locator entry 1	24
Parent locator entry 2	24
Parent locator entry 3	24
Parent locator entry 4	24
Parent locator entry 5	24
Parent locator entry 6	24
Parent locator entry 7	24
Parent locator entry 8	24
Reserved	256

Most people probably wouldn't bother with this. However, there is value because there is a gap between the sectors in the VHD file versus the files that are contained in the VHD itself. This gap has caused a few different problems. One issue is that it is impossible to know which files live in what parts of the VHD.

Data to Look for

The host's critical resources such as memory, processor time, video, and sound are shared with the virtual machines. In applications such as MojoPac, the host resources must be used for better performance. Log files are created by most software; virtual machines are no exception, look for these. Since many of these technologies use a USB drive for access, there will be remnants in the registry. The March 2007 edition of *Digital Investigation* includes an article titled "Tackling the U3 Trend with Computer Forensics" by

Spruill and Pavan (2007) explored the artifacts left behind by U3 devices. The information provided is a good base for some general items to be on the lookout for:

- MRU cache
- Link files
- Prefetch files
- Page file
- Unique identifiers associated with the program
- Artifacts in processes, file system, and/or registry
- Artifacts in memory
- VME-specific virtual hardware, processor instructions, and capabilities

The Prefetch folder and the "layout.ini" file will defragment itself every 72 h and will self-clean older Prefetch files from your system. You will hardly ever see more than 130 Prefetch files in your Prefetch folder. A sample of the Prefetch folder is shown in Figure 5.3.

Research conducted found that this list can be used as a starting point. Since individual environments vary, not all these will exist, especially with applications such as MojoPac and Virtual Privacy Machine.

In the corporate environment, application-layer security such as application proxies can capture some evidence that can help track actions. Application-layer firewall logging can capture more

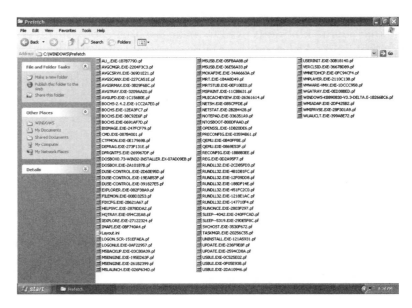

Figure 5.3 Prefetch Folder

than the IP address and port number. Many firewalls are capable of intercepting packets traveling to or from an application such as a browser. This provides a more thorough examination of network traffic and can capture evidence from applications such as MokaFive and portable Virtual Privacy Machine. Corporations also have the option of not allowing removable media. This can eliminate the issues that arise from using many of the technologies mentioned in this chapter.

Investigator Tips

When you are looking for these types of environments, having a keyword list similar to one used for spoliation tools may come in handy. Just as the returned hits on any keyword search can turn up information that requires additional analysis or can be misinterpreted, the same applies here. For example, there are very few applications that use the .lpc extension so a hit on this extension may not be all that common. However, .lpc's primary association is to linear predictive coding, which is used in audio signal and speech processing.

Since devices are becoming smaller, with larger capacity, they can easily be hidden in ordinary everyday things such as a gum wrapper. The physical environments need to be examined very closely for all CDs and removable devices. Search warrants may need to include examining wall jacks for hidden devices.

When examining a removable device, sound procedures dictate that a write blocker is used to make the image, but the investigator should take caution and consider previewing the drive for utilities such as USB Hacksaw, which may compromise the examination machine. In addition, using tools such as Switchblade to acquire information can subject the investigator's machine to compromise.

Summary

In this chapter, we discussed many methods that can be used to determine what files can be associated with what programs for the examination of dead drive environments. Specifically, we also discussed the artifacts that are created and left behind from the virtualization process as well as the registry, prefetch data, and cache files. We also glanced at the file images that Microsoft's VHD format uses.

References

Bares, R. (2009). Hiding in a virtual world using unconventionally installed operating systems. *IEEE International Conference on Intelligence and Security Informatics*. Dallas, TX. Retrieved from http://ieeexplore.ieee.org/Xplore/login.jsp?url=http%3A%2F%2Fieeexplore.ieee.org%. 2Fiel5%2F5089313%2F5137253%2F05137326.pdf%3Farnumber%3D5137326&authDecision=-203

Microsoft Corporation. (2009). Virtual hard disk image format specification. Retrieved from download.microsoft.com/.../Virtual%20Hard%20Disk%20Format%20Spec_10_18_06.doc

Spruill, A., & Pavan C. (2007). Tackling the U3 trend with computer forensics. *Journal of Digital Investigation, 4*(1). Retrieved from http://www.sciencedirect.com/science?_ob=ArticleURL&_udi=B7CW4-4N440CB-1&_user=8303832&_coverDate=03%2F31%2F2007&_rdoc=1&_fmt=high&_orig=search&_sort=d&_docanchor=&view=c&_searchStrId=1285052568&_rerunOrigin=google&_acct=C000000593&_version=1&_urlVersion=0&_userid=8303832&md5=a1cb63ae1f78f6b950cc2a28c540f4ed.

What Files Make Up a Virtual Machine? *VMWare*. http://www.vmware.com/support/ws55/doc/ws_learning_files_in_a_vm.html

Bibliography

VMware and Microsoft

Carvey, H. (2009). *Windows forensic analysis DVD toolkit* (2nd ed.). Burlington, MA: Syngress.

INVESTIGATING LIVE VIRTUAL ENVIRONMENTS

INFORMATION IN THIS CHAPTER

- The Fundamentals of Investigating Live Virtual Environments
- Artifacts
- Processes and Ports
- Log Files
- VM Memory Usage
- Memory Analysis
- ESXi Analysis
- Microsoft Analysis Tools
- Moving Forward

For a long time, digital forensics used only static or "dead" drive analysis. In fact, in many cases, it is still the main method of finding evidence. In this type of acquisition, often the evidence found is sparse or partially missing. As technology advances, dead drive forensics will be faced with challenges such as complex networking, larger drive capacity, and encryption.

With the increase in the amount of recoverable evidence, live investigations and acquisitions are becoming more common. In fact, many large organizations have moved to mostly live investigation, especially those bound by legislation and government-contracting agreements. For example, in a large organization, data preservation can be quite burdensome with 500,000 employees. Evidence acquired when imaging entire drives of multiple employees can require several terabytes of storage. In certain situations, there may be no choice but to do a live investigation such as with a distributed file system or large storage area networks.

As organizations move to a virtual environment for servers and desktops, there is a good chance of running into a virtual environment when conducting a live investigation. There are some specific issues related to this type of environment that an investigator should be aware of when conducting a live investigation.

The Fundamentals of Investigating Live Virtual Environments

All forensic acquisitions require that methodologies used to collect evidence are sound and that they ensure that the evidence will be admissible in a court of law. Forensic methodologies are also based on being verifiable and repeatable. Although live forensics is becoming more acceptable, there are still some issues associated with this type of acquisitions. The main issue being that live investigation changes the state of the investigated system, and the examination results may not be repeatable. Any change of the system state and inconsistencies in verification and repeatability are against accepted principles in forensics. By now, great strides have been made with limitations imposed on the acceptability of live investigation evidence collected, but virtual environments may complicate the matter a bit further.

Live forensics investigations help protect sensitive and easily altered digital evidence and can be conducted in a number of ways. Many commercial forensic packages offer the ability to push out a small program to user workstations in order to constantly monitor the work environment. The machine can be acquired, and data can be downloaded from the machine over the network in real-time, including screenshots, applications running, and other data. Other packages allow live acquisitions via a Web browser. These applications provide the same capabilities as an installed applet but are used upon request or incident as opposed to constant monitoring. Finally, there is the first-responder acquisition, where live acquisitions are done upon notification of an incident.

Regardless of the acquisition method used, the principle of live forensics is based on the premise of collecting data from a running system in order to gather pertinent information that is not available in a dead drive analysis. The information gathered in this process usually consists of the system volatile data such as memory, current applications and processes running, as well as open ports, raw sockets, and active connections. Live acquisitions also limit the data gathered to relevant data.

Best Practices

RFC 3227: Guidelines for Evidence Collection and Archiving defines best practices for responding to a security incident. It outlines the order of volatility collection procedures from the most volatile to the least volatile and provides the following example collection order for a typical system:

- registers, cache
- routing table, arp cache, process table, kernel statistics, memory
- temporary file systems
- disk
- remote logging and monitoring data that is relevant to the system in question
- physical configuration, network topology
- archival media

In a live response collection, some of most practical ways to save the volatile information besides using commercial tools are to use a remote forensic system, a bootable CD/DVD, or a removable USB drive. There are many tools available for this purpose. In addition to commercial tools, there are also many open-source tools. Netcat, and its encryption version, cryptcat have been around for quite some time. Both are free tools used to create a reliable, and in cryptcat's instance, encrypted connection between the target system and the forensic workstation. The Forensic Server Project is another open-source tool that can be used for remote forensic acquisitions. Bootable CD/DVD environments include DFLCD, Helix, CAINE, the Farmers boot CD, and Knoppix STD. There are many more available tools that provide this environment. Advances in the amount of data that a removable drive can hold and basic input/output system (BIOS) support for boot capability make this type of media attractive for live forensic acquisition tools. Many of the CD/DVD utilities have been ported over for use on removable media. In addition, tools have been specifically designed for this purpose. Perhaps the most high-profile tool is Microsoft's Computer Online Forensic Evidence Extractor (COFEE).

Virtual Environments

Virtualized environments are becoming more and more common from the server to the desktop. In a live acquisition, depending on the tools used, the virtual environment may or may not be captured. Let's look at a scenario where an organization uses an enterprise solution that includes a tool that monitors the user's workstation through an installed program such as an applet. The intent of this environment is to offer system administrators the ability to monitor target machines in the network. This can be accomplished by pushing small surveillance programs from a central server onto a target machine without alerting the user to the process. A silent mode allows the program to run without detection. The applet is part of a larger suit of forensic tools. Although the applet can be pushed to the user's workstation, if the user uses a virtual environment that uses the host network adapter, traffic can be monitored, but the applet may not be able to be pushed into that environment and may only show the host activity. In late 2007, this theory was tested with several of the commercial tools available. Most of the tools were unsuccessful in being pushed to the virtual environment when given their own IP address. The negative results ranged from not being able to install at all to the famous Microsoft blue screen of death, which came to be a regular occurrence in the experiment. In one instance, the applet recognized the virtual environment running, but it did not have the capability to install in that environment. This was the most promising result because the tool actually was intuitive enough to realize the environment was virtual and popped-up a nice box saying that the environment was virtual and it could not install. We suspect these issues are most likely the result of the stealthy way applets are designed to work and how the hypervisor interacts with the host computer.

Physical installation of the applet in the virtual environment was also tested. The results were a bit more successful, some of the applets installed, some didn't install, and one told us it couldn't install because the environment was virtual.

As our tools advance to account for virtual environments, the likelihood of capturing the required evidence from these environments will increase significantly. With all the recent developments for managing, provisioning, and monitoring virtual machines (VMs), it gives investigators more concrete places to find evidence. In the meantime, any organization that is combining forensic monitoring and virtualized environments should be sure to check with the software vendor about the capability of the tool to monitor this environment. If building VMs for desktop distribution, installing the applet inside the environment will probably prove to be successful so that the machine can be monitored in the same way as a physical machine, provided the tool has the capability to run on this platform.

Another area of interest is tracking the applet inside the VM from machine to machine and how to be sure it can be monitored when employees drop the VM to a thumb drive or take it home. When a VM is added to or removed from a work environment, it doesn't set off the metal detector. Now, methods are being developed to detect rogue VM environments. Once the VM is detected, the pushing of an applet into the environment can happen.

Artifacts

In a live virtual environment investigation, there are many similarities in the types of evidence collected as compared to a standard live environment investigation because in some respects, the evidence will be the same whether the environment is physical or virtual. The following are still acquired:

- Currently logged user
- Open ports
- Running processes
- System and registry information
- Attached devices

When you are conducting live investigations on virtual environments, some additional considerations are as follows:

- Is the environment physical or virtual?
- Is there hardware virtualization, software virtualization, or both?
- Are there identifiable specific Mac addresses?
- Are there identifiable vendor strings?
- Are there identifiable hardware drives?

The answers to these questions may seem unimportant, but they can affect the outcome of a case. For example, a live investigation was conducted in a civil case where the defendant was accused of the theft of proprietary information in the amount of $300,000.00. In an attempt to absolve the accused of the crime, the expert witness testimony went something like this:

Mr. Defense: Ms. Barrett is there a difference between physical and virtual environments?

Ms. Barrrett: Yes

Mr. Defense: Was the environment you examined physical or virtual?

Ms. Barrett: Physical

Mr. Defense: How do you know?

Ms. Barrett: Because I had access to the physical machine

Mr. Defense: Did you run any tools on the machine that specifically checked if the environment you were examining was physical or virtual?

Ms. Barrett: No

Mr. Defense: If you did not use a tool to validate the environment, how can you say for sure that the environment was physical?

Courtroom testimony and depositions include questions about virtualization, and the expert witness and examiner must be ready to answer these questions. In the above-mentioned case, there may be number of ways of explaining that the environment was not virtual such as the absence of virtual adapters, running processes, or open ports. However, the point is that when conducting live investigations, spending a few extra minutes or asking a few extra questions may not only save an embarrassing moment but also affect the outcome of a case.

Processes and Ports

In any live investigation, open ports and services are important to capture. But things aren't always as they appear, so it is important for an investigator to examine the processes and ports carefully. The following section will discuss the running processes and ports associated with some of the environments examined in Chapter 5, "Investigating Dead Virtual Environments."

Virtual Environment File Ports and Processes

When MojoPac is running, the following unique events will occur:
- MojoPac runs RingThreeMainWin32.
- MojoPac performs a netstat that will show an open connection to ringcube.com as shown in Figure 6.1.
- MojoPac prefers port 3819.
- MojoPac also establishes a connection on port 3823.

When MokaFive is running, the following unique events will occur:
- MokaFive runs m5backup.exe, m5usb.exe, and m5engine.exe.
- MokaFive prefers ports 29524 and 26662 as shown in Figure 6.2.

Figure 6.1 MojoPac Netstat

- MokaFive uses duse-control.exe when restoring the system state and stays running during the duration of the session.

When a browser is open in the virtual machine, the connection will look like the image in Figure 6.3.

Figure 6.2 MokaFive Netstat

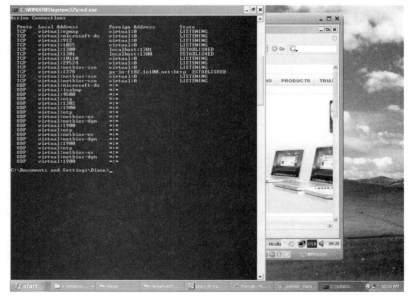

Figure 6.3 MokaFive Netstat with Browser Open

Portable Virtual Privacy Machine uses QEMU. There will be an open-command prompt running when QEMU is started that stays open during the time the application is running as shown in Figure 6.4 (process qemu.exe will be running).

VMware player will show the following:

- VMware player runs vmount2.exe, vmnat.exe, vmnetdhcp.exe, and vmware-authd.exe.
- VMware player prefers ports 8222 and 8307.

Figure 6.5 shows the netstat from VMware Player.

VMware and Tomcat

VMware Server 2.0 uses a Web interface that is presented over a local tomcat instance. Although VMware changed the default http and https ports, the start-up http and https, Tomcat's default support ports 8005 and 8009 are used. This might be misleading to an investigator. Figure 6.6 shows the default tomcat install directory.

IronKey and Tor

Virtual environments can be run from a thumb drive such as an Ironkey. IronKey uses AES 256-bit encryption, and it works by tunneling your entire Web browsing communications through a Tor-based proxy on the device. Tor stands for the onion router.

Figure 6.4 QEMU Running

The premise behind Tor is to route communications through a distributed network of relays worldwide to hide traffic paths and maintain privacy. IronKey has its own Tor, so the session tunnel connects over an encrypted connection to IronKey's servers, routes the traffic between a network of servers, and then

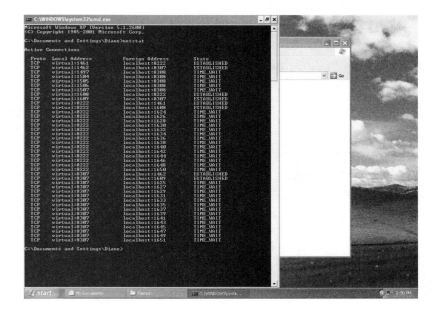

Figure 6.5 VMware Player Netstat

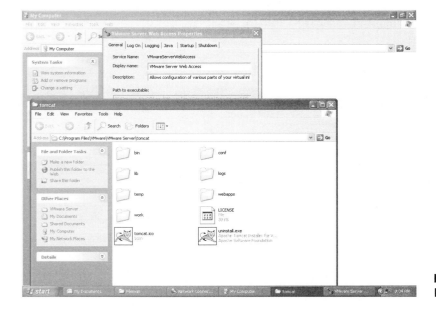

Figure 6.6 Default Tomcat Install Directory

Figure 6.7 IronKey Traffic

eventually out to the destination Web site. Since IronKey uses Tor, when the drive is running with an open Internet connection, it looks very similar to Tor traffic as shown in Figure 6.7.

In addition, under the Task Manager, Processes tab processes SecureSessions.exe, Privoxy.exe, vidalia.exe, IronKey.exe, IkPwdMgr. exe, and LKINJ.exe will be running. Note that Privoxy and Vidalia are used in regular Tor traffic, so the investigator must look closely at the processes before making assumptions.

SPICE

SPICE stands for Simple Protocol for Independent Computing Environment. It is a Red Hat open-source Virtual Desktop Protocol that is one of the components of the Red Hat Enterprise Virtualization for Desktops application. There are SPICE guest drivers for Windows operating systems (OSes) that will render virtual instances of Microsoft Windows XP and Windows 7, as well as Red Hat Enterprise Linux. At the server level, it runs on 64-bit Linux platforms. The SPICE server listens on port 5930.

Log Files

Most virtualization vendors are now providing centralized management capabilities for VMs and support for Simple Network Management Protocol (SNMP) and Windows Management Instrumentation (WMI), but standardization of remote logging is not quite perfected yet. In addition to Windows logging events

Table 6.1 VMware Log Files and Locations

Log	Location
Virtual machines	vmware.log
Web access	/var/log/vmware/webAccess
Authentication log	/var/log/secure
VMkernel	/var/log/vmkernel
ESX server host agent log	/var/log/vmware/hostd.log
VirtualCenter agent	/var/log/vmware/vpx
System events	/var/log/messages

such as those found in Event Viewer, VMware-specific logs for virtual environments are listed in Table 6.1.

VM Memory Usage

Memory analysis is one of the main components of a live investigation. When a virtual machine is created, memory is allocated to that virtual machine. Limits on the amount of host computer memory available for use can also be set for each virtual machine and the amount of the host computer's memory that can be used for virtual machines. In addition, the extent to which the host OSes allows the memory manager to swap virtual machines out of physical random access memory (RAM) can be set. Changes to memory settings affect the virtual machines and system performance. Using VMware Server as an example, it limits the total amount of RAM that can used by virtual machines so that virtual machines do not use too much memory and cause the host to thrash. As a general rule, the total memory of all the running virtual machines added to the overhead for the VMware Server processes cannot be greater than the amount of physical memory on the host excluding additional memory reserved for the host to operate properly while virtual machines are running. The reserved amount depends on the host OS and the amount of memory in the host computer. Although the amount of host RAM that VMware Server uses can be reserved, the memory is not allocated in advance and any unused RAM is available for use by other applications if the VMs are not using it. However, if the entire RAM is in use by the VMs, the host OS itself or any other application can use it. The VM overhead varies based on disk size and memory allocated. For example, VMware has listed the numbers in Table 6.2 as the typical amount of overhead needed for various virtual machine memory allocations for the GSX server.

The following memory options can be used in VMware Server:

- Putting all virtual machine memory into reserved host RAM restricts the number and the memory size of virtual machines that may run at a given time.
- Allowing some virtual machine memory to be swapped allows a moderate amount of virtual machine memory to be swapped to disk if necessary.
- Allowing most virtual machine memory to be swapped allows as much virtual machine memory to be swapped to disk as the system wants.

Memory Management

Memory management processes in virtual machines can affect the amount of recoverable information from the virtual machine. For example, VMware makes use of shadow page tables while the XenSource approach does not, except on a temporary basis. XenSource, through kernel modifications provides limited access for the guest OS directly to physical memory page tables.

In shadow paging, a table is maintained to efficiently virtualize memory access between the virtual memory pages of the guest OS and the underlying physical machine pages. Shadow page tables shield guest OSes from their dependence on specific machine memory. This allows the hypervisor to optimize that memory.

Virtual machine memory virtualization is based on the same principle as the virtual machine monitor (VMM) used for regular OS page files, where the OS keeps an address table of virtual page numbers for each process that corresponds to physical page numbers. In VMware's ESX server, one of two techniques is used

Table 6.2 VMware GSX Server Memory Overhead Requirements

Memory Allocated to the Virtual Machine	Amount of Overhead Needed
Up to 512 MB	Up to 40 MB
Up to 1 GB	Up to 50 MB
Up to 2 GB	Up to 70 MB

for dynamically increasing or reducing the amount of memory allocated to virtual machines. Either a memory balloon driver is loaded into the guest OS or paging is implemented from the VM to a server swap file. When a VMware virtual machine is powered up, a swap file is created in the same directory as the virtual machine configuration file. The memory balloon driver is part of the VMware Tools package and if it is not installed, ESX server hosts use swapping to forcibly recover memory.

Memory Analysis

The memory analysis of some virtual environments is more simplistic than other analysis. Investigation of a VM's memory contents in VMware Server or Workstation is most easily conducted by acquiring the .vmem file. This is the virtual machine's paging file and is a backup of the guest OS main memory. It is located on the host file system and is created at startup of the virtual machine. To acquire the file, you can use the Pause VM action and then use your tool of choice to analyze the file. VMware Server can function without the .vmem file. So if the file is not found, check the .vmx file for the line mainmem.useNamedFile = "FALSE." If it's there, the .vmem file should be turned off.

There are many tools available to do such acquisitions from commercial tools to open-source tools such as dd, the Volatility Framework, Mandiant's Memoryze, and HBGary Responder. Simple memory analysis on a machine running a single virtual environment is usually pretty straightforward. In this next analysis example, a Windows XP machine with 1 GB of RAM was used. MojoPac was run from a thumb drive and a browser was opened. Mandiant Memoryze was used to image the memory and then Mandiant Audit View was used to view the contents. Figure 6.8 clearly shows RingThreeMainWin32.exe and MojoPac.

Figure 6.9 clearly shows Internet Explorer (IE) running.

Keep in mind that in this example, there was very little running on the host machine, and the image was taken while browsing was going on in MojoPac. The imaging was done while the browsing was happening. Catching a suspect in the act and being able to immediately image the memory requires a whole lot of luck in an actual investigation. In addition, the environment was running from an application that swaps information between the thumb drive and the host resources.

Bares (2009) from the University of Central Florida researched memory allocation in virtual machines in a paper titled "Hiding in a Virtual World: Using Unconventionally Installed Operating Systems." The paper was published on June 11, 2009 by IEEE and appears in *IEEE International Conference on Intelligence and Security Informatics, 2009* (ISI '09). His research confirms the way the host OS and virtual environment memory allocations interact in a VMware environment. The host computer virtualizes the memory management to support the guest OS. As a result, direct access

Figure 6.8 MojoPac Memory Analysis

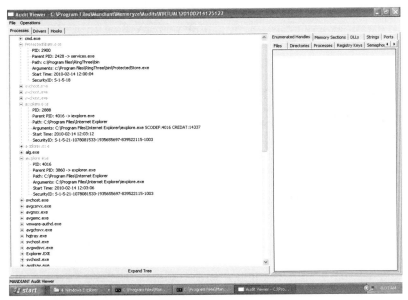

Figure 6.9 Web Surfing Memory Analysis

to actual physical memory is not allowed by the guest OS. The VMM uses shadow page tables to map the guest OS memory allocation and coordinates that mapping with the physical machine memory. As part of his research, Bares used a New Technology File System (NTFS) partition as the testing environment to determine the recoverability of files based upon how much memory was allocated to VMware Server VMs. The test VMs were respectively allocated 256, 512, and 1024 MB of RAM. Activity that was attempted to be recovered consisted of e-mail communications, instant messenger traffic, creation of a Word document, and Web traffic. One of the interesting points of his research shows that the amount of RAM allocated to the individual VMs has a minimal effect on the number of recoverable files and hits. Most of the tests conducted on the VM with the largest amount of allocated RAM resulted in fewer recoverable files and hits than the tests conducted on the VMs with less RAM. This result is mostly likely due to the way that VMware Server reserves RAM for virtual machines. Bares's research shows that although more physical RAM allocated to a virtual machine should allow it to operate without accessing the virtual memory as often, none of the tests in the VM with the smallest amount of RAM consistently proved that there was a decline in the amount of data recoverable from the swap file as the amount of RAM increased.

ESXi Analysis

Fiterman and Durick (2010) published an article in the second edition of *Digital Forensics Magazine* (February, 2010) titled "Ghost in the Machine: Forensic Evidence Collection in the Virtual Environment." Their research supports the theory expressed previously that tools and options for conducting examinations on virtual data are currently limited. Interestingly, their research covers an area that should be of specific interest to all forensic examiners, the examination of VMware's ESXi 4 server product. Although the technologies that compose the ESXi server environment such as VMware's proprietary Virtual Machine File System (VMFS) are discussed in Chapter 9, "Virtualization Challenges," there are some interesting points that investigators should be aware of when examining this type of environment. Their best practices and response methodology framework consists of the same principles that apply in a nonvirtualized environment:

1. Generating an image without invoking any code within the guest VM
2. Establishing the integrity and the fidelity of the acquired evidence files
3. Supporting proper chain of custody

These are accomplished by first collecting a snapshot of the VM and the .vmsn file. A live system acquisition will not capture the .vswp file. It is possible that the partition on which the file resides will have to be acquired. Next, connect to the ESXi service console over Secure Shell (SSH), and using the command-line interface (CLI), determine where the VM files are saved. The esxcfg-info command is used for this purpose. Table 6.3 provides some useful CLI commands.

Next, capture and hash the pertinent files such as the. vmx, .vmsn, and .vmdk files. This can be done through the console since ESXi 4 Update 1 comes with an implementation of OpenSSL. Finally, verify the acquisition.

Microsoft Analysis Tools

Quite a few sections of this chapter have been devoted to VMware functions and processes. It's time to look at tools that can be used in the live investigation of Microsoft virtualized environments. Harley Stagner published an article titled "How to Examine the Compromised Microsoft Virtual Server 2005 Host Server after a Security Breach" on February 20, 2007. This article is posted in on http://searchservervirtualization.com. It outlines suggested procedures that should be considered before a compromised Microsoft Virtual Server 2005 is taken offline. The first step listed is to export or backup the event logs along with the export of the events. Next, if possible, obtain a screenshot of the Virtual Server 2005 Administration page. Then, it recommends running Sysinternal tools such as accessenum.exe, autoruns.exe, pendmoves.exe, and logonsessions.exe before shutting down any virtual machines running on the server. The premise is to capture services, open ports, and abnormal files from the server or the virtual machines. The description of each of these tools and their purpose are as follows:

- AccessEnum provides user access permission information on the file system and registry security settings through the use of standard Windows security application program interfaces (APIs).

Table 6.3 CLI Commands

vim-cmd vmsvc/getallvms	Lists all VMs running on the hypervisor
vim-cmd vmsvc/destroy vmid	Deletes the .vmdk and .vmx files from disk
chkconfig -l	Shows daemons running on hypervisor and can also be used for configuration
esxcfg-info	Lists a wealth of information about the ESX host
esxcfg-nics-l	Lists information about network interface cards (NICs)

- Autoruns provides information on what programs are configured to run during system bootup or login, and it shows the entries for items such as toolbars and browser helper objects in the order they are processed.
- Pendmoves provides information on scheduled file renames and deletions for the next system boot. Essentially, it reports any actions queued to happen after a reboot using the MoveFileEx API.
- Logonsessions provides information on active logon sessions. The –p switch will list the active processes under each session.

These tools are mentioned to inform the investigator of their capabilities and are merely suggestions. They were written specifically for Microsoft environments, so they can easily gather information that may be of value. Since most of these tools are run from a command line, they can be incorporated in a script or batch file quite easily. There are many excellent tools available for gathering pertinent information from a Microsoft environment. No matter what tools are used, the processes and documentation are what's most important. The processes outlined in the previous section on the ESXi server should be considered especially if the server or virtual machine cannot be shutdown. As we move to a more virtualized and cloud environment, the prospect of shutting down a server is rapidly decreasing. The files associated with a Microsoft VM are as follows: the virtual machine configuration (.vmc) file, the virtual hard disk (.vhd) file, any virtual machine saved-state (.vsv) files, and virtual machine undo disk (.vud) files associated with the virtual machine.

Moving Forward

In order to see the issues arising from trying to properly collect information from virtual machines, one only needs to look at the patent applications in relation to VMs. In late 2009, VMware patent applications were published for the following:

- Trace Collection for a Virtual Machine
- Separate Swap Files Corresponding to Different Virtual Machines in a Host Computer System
- Profile Based Creation of Virtual Machines in a Virtualization Environment
- System and Methods for Enforcing Software License Compliance with Virtual Machines
- System and Method for Improving Memory Locality of Virtual Machines
- Mechanism for Providing Virtual Machines for Use by Multiple Users

Many more patent applications are listed in www.patentstorm
.us/attorney-applications/VMware_Inc_/241723/1.html.

These patent applications will be discussed briefly in the following sections. This is to provide the investigator with an idea of
how the evidence landscape will change and the ability to collect
information may improve. However, the self-service VM store and
allowing a user to share a VM seem a bit scary from the investigative side.

Trace Collection for a Virtual Machine

The invention components consist of computer-implemented
methods of trace collection for a virtual machine. In particular, one such embodiment is a computer-implemented method
comprising: executing a sequence of instructions from an initial
state of the virtual machine; accessing an event log of data relating to nondeterministic events, which data includes an execution
point; making at least a portion of the data available to the virtual
machine when the sequence reaches the execution point; collecting trace information in response to expansion parameters; and
storing the trace information in a trace file.

Separate Swap Files Corresponding to Different Virtual Machines in a Host Computer System

This invention relates to a virtualized computer system; in particular, to a method and system for using swap space for host physical memory with separate swap files corresponding to different
virtual machines.

Profile Based Creation of Virtual Machines in a Virtualization Environment

Self-service VM store – In big data centers, this will reduce the
task of creating hundreds of VMs, which is enormously time consuming. It will also eliminate optimization issues due to the inex-
perience of the person creating VMs.

System and Methods for Enforcing Software License Compliance with Virtual Machines

The license-control algorithms implemented by application programs cannot discern changes in the underlying hardware platform, allowing the application program, including the virtual
computer environment, to be copied and executed without regard

to licensing. The current process defeats the ability of the application program to discern whether a hardware dongle is available to just one application instance or shared by many.

System and Method for Improving Memory Locality of Virtual Machines

A method for migrating a virtual machine and memory pages from a first node to a second node is provided. The method includes migrating the virtual machine from the first node to the second node, monitoring memory access requests of the virtual machine and identifying priority pages for migration from the first node to the second node, and initiating a page migration process and migrating at least a subset of the priority pages from the first node to the second node.

Mechanism for Providing Virtual Machines for Use by Multiple Users

This is a method for allowing multiple users to share a common computer system image, the method comprising: generating a state vector representing the total machine state for a virtual machine configured with one or more commonly used applications; establishing the state vector for the virtual machine as a read-only common computer system image for use by multiple users; loading the state vector into a first virtual machine for use by a first user and into a second virtual machine for use by a second user; and allowing the first user to use the first virtual machine and allowing the second user to use the second virtual machine and allowing the first and second users to enter different data in the first and second virtual machines, respectively, so that the processing paths of the first and second virtual machines diverge.

Summary

In this chapter, we have discussed the challenges that come with the live investigation of virtual environments, including running processes and ports used by many virtual environments. We also discussed memory allocation and analysis along with the research findings into how adjusting the memory allocated to a VM affects the ability to recover data. Furthermore, the procedures that should be followed when examining an ESXi server were also covered. Based on the recommendations of Fiterman and Durick, when working with live virtual environments, the investigator should have the following characteristics:

- Be familiar with the virtualization technologies that are likely to be encountered.
- Have a strategy for extracting evidence.
- Do some testing to find out how things work.

Finally, some recommendations on tools that can used to examine a Microsoft Virtual Server 2005 host server after a compromise from Harley Stagner were examined.

References

Bares, R. (2009). Hiding in a virtual world using unconventionally installed operating systems. *IEEE International Conference on Intelligence and Security Informatics.* Dallas, TX. Retrieved from http://ieeexplore.ieee.org/Xplore/login.jsp?url=http%3A%2F%2Fieeexplore.ieee.org%. 2Fiel5%2F5089313%2F5137253%2F05137326.pdf%3Farnumber%3D5137326&authDecision=-203

Fiterman, E. M., & Durick, J. D. (2010). Ghost in the machine: Forensic evidence collection in the virtual environment. *Digital Forensics Magazine, 2,* 73–77.

Stagner, H. (2007, February 20). How to examine the compromised Microsoft Virtual Server 2005 host server after a security breach. *SearchServerVirtualization.com.* Retrieved from http://searchservervirtualization.techtarget.com/tip/0,289483,sid94_gci1244430,00.html.

Bibliography

Memory Management

VMware GSX server documentation. http://www.vmware.com/support/gsx25/doc/performance_memory_reserved_gsx.html

Moving Forward

VMware patents applied for: http://www.patentstorm.us/attorney-applications/VMware__Inc_/241723/1.html

http://searchservervirtualization.techtarget.com/tip/0,289483,sid94_gci1244430,00.html

FINDING AND IMAGING VIRTUAL ENVIRONMENTS

INFORMATION IN THIS CHAPTER

- Detecting Rogue Virtual Machines
- Is It Real or Is It Memorex?
- Imaging Virtual Machines
- Snapshots
- VMotion
- Identification and Conversion Tools
- Environment to Environment Conversion

As an investigator, especially in a live environment, it may be necessary to find and image rogue virtual machines (VMs). Additionally, there may be the need to acquire virtual machine snapshots and use conversion tools. The investigator may have to determine if the environment is indeed physical or virtual. More importantly, the investigator may have to testify to the type of environment examined in court.

Detecting Rogue Virtual Machines

In principle, rogue VMs are no different than rogue physical servers. A rogue server is one that was not put into place through the means of normal business requirements and is not controlled by the IT department. The most common example of this is a rogue Dynamic Host Configuration Protocol (DHCP) server because it provides IP addresses and will allow network access. In many organizations, policies are in place to prevent rogue physical servers, and vendors like Microsoft have incorporated measures to prevent this from happening in the application software. But most organizations do not have a policy in place addressing rogue VMs.

Due to the nature of VMs, creating a rogue VMs is relatively easy, especially in the user environment. The user can bridge the network connection between the VM and the desktop using the IP address of the desktop. VMs can be installed inside the application software such as Virtual PC or VMware Workstation. However, if the user is typical, easy is best. This means downloading preconfigured appliances and using an application to play them such as VMware Player. Another option available is to run the VM from a USB thumb drive or iPod using an environment such as MokaFive. Since these appliances are "ready to go," the user typically doesn't think about installing virus software or patches. After all, it's "ready to go."

One of the main features of VMs that allows rogues to happen is the ability to use the host resources for connectivity. The network configuration settings for a VM can be either bridged networking or network address translation (NAT). Bridging in its simplest terms is a forwarding technique allowing unlike platforms to communicate. The physical network interface card (NIC) forwards traffic from the VMs to the network. NAT works by modifying individual packets. It modifies the header to have a new address for the source address, destination address, or both. Figure 7.1 shows these settings in Virtual PC.

Figure 7.1 Networking Options in Virtual PC

A VM that uses bridged networking will appear on the network as a normal machine showing its own Mac and IP addresses. NAT allows a VM to connect to the network through the physical network card. This type of traffic appears on the network as originating from the physical system and shows the Mac and IP addresses of the physical machine. The VM's NAT driver translates the addresses and provides the typical domain name system (DNS) and DHCP network services. Figure 7.2 shows the VMware virtual adapters.

If using NAT, unmanaged VMs can easily access the network. Allowing unmanaged access to the network presents the following issues:

- Malicious software installation
- Network vulnerability due to unpatched and outdated VMs
- Misdirected clients and client networking issues

Having policies in place to deal with such situations would go a long way to securing the network, but many organizations have not addressed these issues. Auditing should be in place and if it is, it may detect the presence of rogue VMs. As you will see in Chapter 8, "Virtual Environments and Compliance," compliance auditing and tracking licensing compliance may prove to be difficult in a virtual environment, especially if users are allowed to install them at will.

In Chapter 5, "Investigating Dead Virtual Environments," it was discussed that by default VMware products automatically

Figure 7.2 VMware Virtual Adapters

install two network adapters. A telltale sign that a user-installed a VM would be the presence of these adapters. If an organization is aware that users might be installing VMs, the VMware Bridge Protocol and the Virtual Machine Network Services driver might be disabled. This disables the bridged networking support and disables the device emulator's operating system (OS) from emulating its own network connection, thus preventing VMs from using networking functions that allow the VM access to outside resources. The two virtual network interfaces installed by VMware on physical host machines are as follows:

- VMware Network Adapter VMnet1
- VMware Network Adapter VMnet8

VMnet1 allows VMs to communicate with the physical host system. VMnet8 allows VMs to use NAT for communication with the network.

In the event an investigator or first responder has to look for rogue VMs, here are two scripts you will want to have in your toolbox: domainvhdaudit.vbs and vhdaudit.vbs. Wolf (2007) explains how to use both of these scripts in "Inventorying Virtual Hard Disk Files on a Server or Domain." Domainvhdaudit.vbs is used in Active Directory domains and generates a list of virtual hard disk files; both .vhd and .vmdk files are found on each computer in the domain. The vhdaudit.vbs script provides the same output information as domainvhdaudit.vbs, expect it is meant to be used locally on a single computer. The scripts also find files larger than 800 MB. The minimum file size that the script will list is configurable. These scripts provide a method to locate .vhd and .vmdk files as well as alert the investigator of large files that might possibly be VMs. This is good for applications like MojoPac and MokaFive, or for identifying the user that thinks changing a file extension makes it undetectable. Besides these scripts, VMware and some third-party vendors have begun to offer auditing tools capable of auditing and tracking VMs across both client and server systems.

Alternate Data Streams and Rogue Virtual Machines

Running a script like the ones listed in the section "Detecting Rogue Virtual Machines" (Wolf, 2008) may not find the entire rogue VMs. The fact that scripts look for large files is good because it helps identify hidden data, but what about alternate data streams (ADS)? ADSes are possible due to the structural make up of New Technology File System (NTFS) and the Master File Table (MFT). An optional element is file data streams. NTFS supports multiple data streams. A handle can be opened to each data stream. This feature enables you to manage data as a single unit. These additional streams are perfect hiding places for all type of data including VMs. ADS are covered in most forensics training courses and identified by forensic software.

In the article "How to Detect Rogue Virtual Machines on a Network," Stagner (2007) provides step-by-step instructions for using ADS to hide VMs. We will walk through that process here using a Windows Server 2003 .vhd file. This is to demonstrate how simplistic the process is and also to trigger the investigative part of your mind if you have to search for rogue VMs. The steps described below should be followed:

- Create a new virtual machine.
- Place the .vhd file into an alternate data stream.
- Point the virtual server to the .vhd file.

First, we'll explain how the ADS is created. In our example, the ADS is produced by opening a command prompt and typing: **type Windows_Server_2003.vhd > ads-test.txt:Windows_Server_2003.vhd** (Figure 7.3).

Figures 7.4 and 7.5 show the directory before and after the ADS file is created.

If you look closely at the after picture, you will notice that the .vhd file is missing. This is because once it is attached to the "ads-test.txt" file it was deleted. As an ̴estigator, upon running into a directory that is missing the .vhd file, which is a vital part of

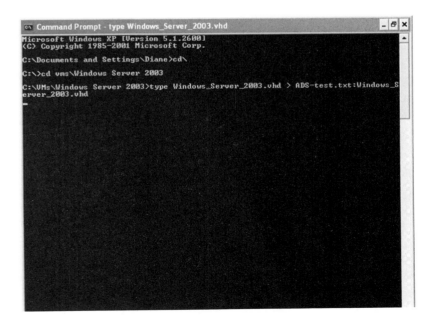

Figure 7.3 Command Used to Create ADS

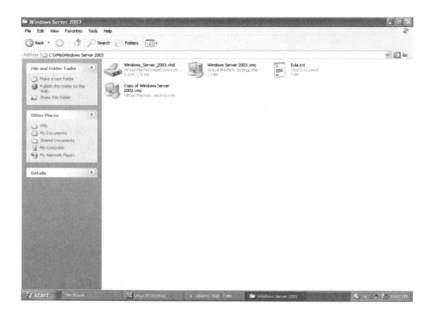

Figure 7.4 Window Server 2003 VM Directory before ADS Creation

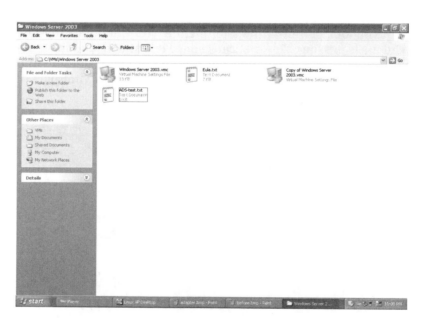

Figure 7.5 Window Server 2003 VM Directory after ADS Creation

running a VM, additional investigation is warranted. ADS can be contained in any type of file including a folder.

Once the ADS is created, the last step is modifying the configuration file (.vmc). Notice the last line. It shows that there is a file

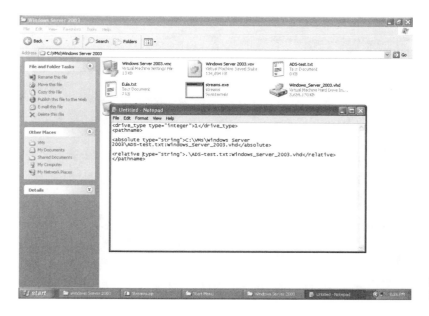

Figure 7.6 Virtual Machine Configuration File Modification

called "Windows_Server_2003.vhd" attached to an alternate data stream in the file ads-test.txt. Figure 7.6 illustrates what the .vhd path looks like in the configuration file (.vmc) when it is altered to account for the hidden data stream.

Now that the path is modified in the configuration file, the virtual machine is ready to use.

As mentioned above, most commercial forensic software will identify ADS. There are also other tools that can be used such as List Alternate Data Streams (LADS) and Streams. An example of the output from Streams is shown in Figure 7.7.

With case loads high and time being of the essence, ADS may be overlooked. Often we concentrate on keyword searches or look at user-generated documents. Since VMs can be hidden with such a simplistic process, it is important that we check for them.

As mentioned previously, searching for VMs based on extension may not lead us to all rogue VMs. Searching something that is a constant in the use of the VM may produce additional results. In Chapter 6, "Investigating Live Virtual Environments," the collection of running processes was discussed. In our ADS example, we created a Windows Server 2003 virtual server. When run, this product uses the virtual server service, which is identified as vssrvc. exe. This service creates virtual machines and provides all virtual machine functionality. It is used to project the emulated hardware into the virtual machine environment. In Windows Virtual Server 2005, the virtual server service also includes the Virtual Machine

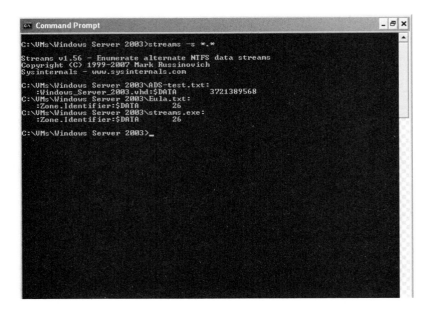

Figure 7.7 Streams Output

Remote Control (VMRC) server, which uses the VMRC Protocol to allow remote VMRC clients to interact with virtual machines. The default port used for VMRC sessions is port 5900. Any number of tools can be used to acquire running processes, such as psservices. exe. In a live investigation, the presence of vssrvc.exe without an identifiable VM will warrant further investigation.

Is It Real or Is It Memorex?

When conducting live investigations, it may be a good idea to first determine if the environment being examined is real or virtual, if for no other reason than to be prepared in the event it is questioned in court. In "Attacks on More Virtual Machine Emulators," Ferrie (2007) discusses several methods of determining if the environment is real or virtual. This is possible primarily through the fact that due to the way the hypervisor works, changes are made to the environment. For example, hardware-bound virtual machine emulators execute instructions on the physical CPU and therefore make some changes to the environment so that sharing the hardware resources between the guest and the host OSes is possible. Some of these changes are visible to applications within the guest OS, provided the applications know what those changes look like. This concept, along with Red Pill, Blue Pill, and their relevance to future use, will be explored in greater detail in Chapter 9, "Virtualization Challenges."

Scoopy Doo and Jerry are tools that detect a VMware finger-print. When both are run, the output simply states: This is/is not a virtual machine. See Figures 7.8 and 7.9 for an example of the output from each of these tools.

Snoopy Pro was written to try and answer the question: Is it possible to break out of a VM to reach the host OS or to

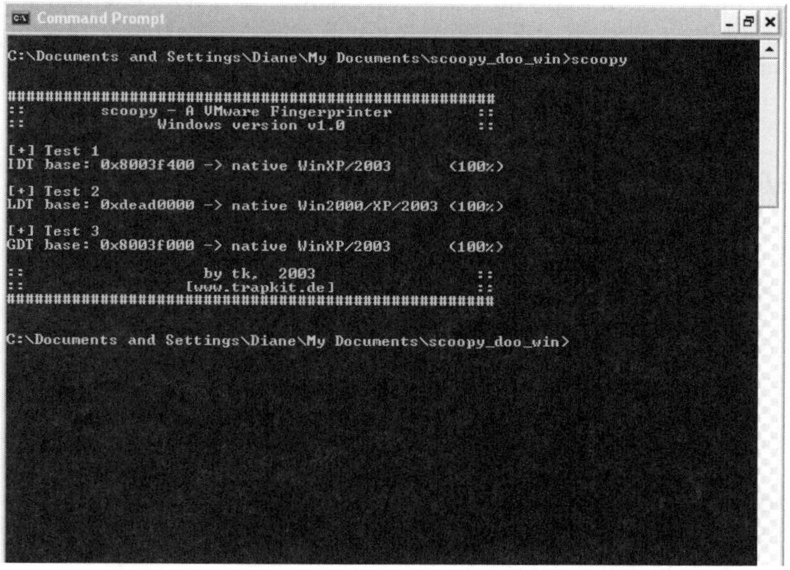

Figure 7.8 Scoopy Doo Running

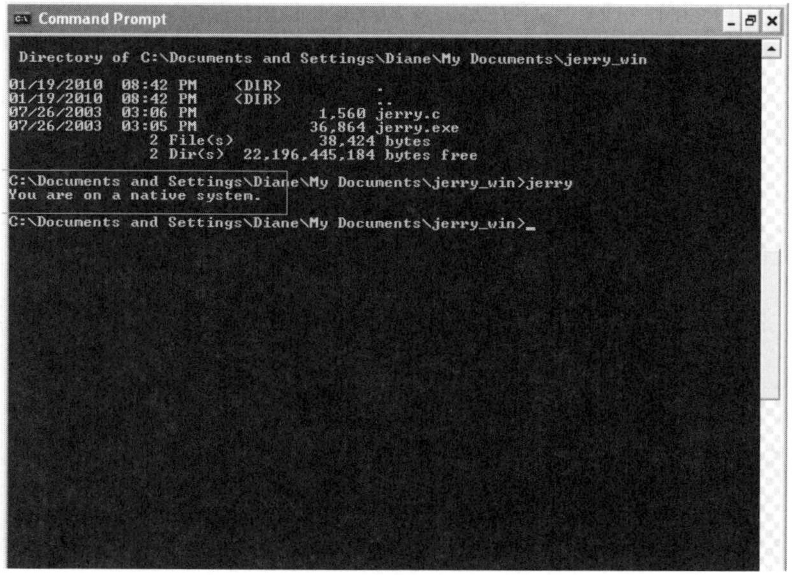

Figure 7.9 Jerry Running

manipulate other VMs? This tool analyzes virtual traffic between the device and the driver. When examining virtualized environments, it is important to reflect on what is being captured. Keep in mind that these tools are based on the environmental changes made by the hypervisor. Therefore, they may work on platforms such as Virtual PC, VMware Server, and Parallels, but they will probably not work on Bochs, DOSBox or QEMU because these are emulators and do not use hypervisors. However, because they emulate a CPU, it still may be possible to detect them through various other means such as with a CPU compatibility check function.

Virtual Machine Traces

All investigators use data carving to recover relevant tidbits of information in cases. The ability to recover deleted VMs will depend on the environment. For example, if MojoPac was deleted, it might still be able to find data intact because it is its own environment and has its own registry, documents, and so on.

In Chapter 5, "Investigating Dead Virtual Environments," we discussed some of the artifacts and remnants left behind by particular virtual environments. This section will condense that information to give the readers an overall view of the traces they might encounter, starting with directory structures.

Directories

Directories that may indicate the use of a virtual environment or emulator:

Program Files:
* VMware
* Microsoft Virtual PC
* Bochs
* DOSBox
* Portable Virtual Privacy Machine

These may be located in different directories based on the path chosen by the user upon installation.

The My Documents folder:
* My LivePC's
* My LivePC Documents
* My Shared LivePC Documents
* My Virtual Machines

Documents and Settings:
* VirtualBox

Prefetch File

Windows XP uses what is called the prefetch technique. The OS gathers information about programs the user executes and stores that information in the \Windows\Prefetch folder. Windows XP uses the information in the Prefetch folder to preload parts of those programs into memory before they are actually needed so that when the application is started again, it loads faster. The Cache Manager monitors the data being moved between the disk, RAM, and virtual memory and constructs mapping to files with a .pf extension in the \Windows\Prefetch folder. The prefetch data is passed into a layout.ini file located in the same directory as the prefetch files as shown in Figure 7.10.

The layout.ini file is used by the built-in defragmentation utility to optimize the layout of those files on the hard drive. This is why you will hardly ever see more than 130 prefetch files. It is important that an investigator realize that by default, a limited defrag operation takes place in the background every 3 days, which will affect the files specified in layout.ini. Cases of spoliation based on the defrag utility have been derailed because the investigator mistook the partial OS-induced defrag as a user-induced defrag.

This setting can be disabled by changing EnableAutoLayout to 0 in the registry key HKEY_LOCAL_MACHINE\SOFTWARE\ Microsoft\Windows\CurrentVersion\OptimalLayout. Prefetching configuration is stored in the Windows Registry at HKEY_LOCAL_ MACHINE\SYSTEM\CurrentControlSet\Control\SessionManager\

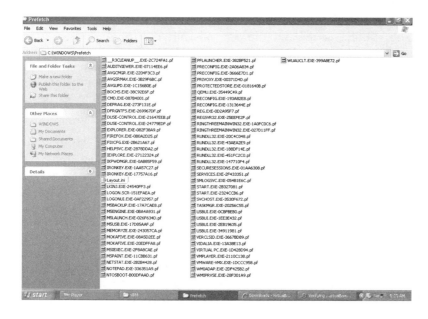

Figure 7.10 Prefetch Folder with Layout.ini File

Memory Management\PrefetchParameters. The EnablePrefetcher value can set to be one of the following:
- 0 = Disabled
- 1 = Application launch prefetching enabled
- 2 = Boot prefetching enabled
- 3 = Applaunch and boot enabled (optimal and default)

Windows Vista and Windows 7 use SuperFetch instead of prefetch. Superfetch settings are configured in the registry at the following location:

```
HKEY_LOCAL_MACHINE\SYSTEM\CurrentControlSet\Control\Session
    Manager\Memory Management\PrefetchParameters
```

Link Files

All investigators know the importance of link files. In the "Evidentiary Value of Link Files" by Weilbacher (2006) tracing remnants associated with removable media is examined along with other information that link files can provide. This is especially important when working with virtual environment cases since virtualized environments can be run from thumb drives. Some applications will leave at most a couple of actual files on the system. For example in the case of MojoPac, pvm.sys and ringthree.ico were the only two files stored on the host machine. There are many good articles on examining associations such as "The Meaning of Linkfiles in Forensic Examinations" by Parsonage (September 2008, Updated November 2009).

Registry Files

The subject of registry file analysis fills entire volumes. Carvey (2009) has done a lot of research in this area and his book *Windows Forensic Analysis* covers the registry extensively. Additionally, tools such as RegRipper offer a way to extract pertinent information quickly. Remnant information on virtual environments will be found in the NTUSER.DAT and NTUSER.LOG files and also in registry keys such as MRU and MUICache.

One issue that comes up in some of our cases is the USB to registry key correlation. Proving that a particular drive was plugged into a particular computer can be tricky. Associating a device with registry entries can be challenging, and we often encounter cases where the removable was "lost." In one current case, after reviewing a series of e-mails, it was discovered that an organization had a habit of storing proprietary information on portable hard drives. This information was inadvertently left out when the imaging environment was assessed. Upon request for this information, some of the external devices were not able to be located.

In our own experimentation with associating USB to registry activity we tried two separate approaches; one approach was successful and the other was not successful. Here is the scenario: You have three images of formatted thumb drives, the system registry files and a NTUSER.DAT file. The correlation is vital to the case. You must show that one of these three thumb drives was inserted into the machine. Mark Vosika from the University of Advancing Technology (UAT) formulated and documented the following process:

RegRipper was used to extract the registry information. Useful data found in the registry was located in the RegRipper output file System.txt, which lists the extracted results from the System registry file. Under the "mounted devices" section, the following useful data was found:

```
\??\Volume{fc39bf4c-da39-11dc-88f9-806d6172696f}
   Drive Signature = c4 bd 35 06
\??\Volume{fc39bf4d-da39-11dc-88f9-806d6172696f}
   Drive Signature = c4 bd 35 06
\??\Volume{fc39bf4e-da39-11dc-88f9-806d6172696f}
   Drive Signature = c4 bd 35 06
\DosDevices\C:
   Drive Signature = c4 bd 35 06
\DosDevices\D:
   Drive Signature = c4 bd 35 06
\DosDevices\E:
   Drive Signature = c4 bd 35 06
\??\Volume{82f02fe2-e642-11dc-bc6b-0007b8dbff17}
   Drive Signature = 78 56 34 12
\??\Volume{88e7a372-f046-11dc-89d0-806d6172696f}
   Drive Signature = 01 00 00 00
\??\Volume{31c3d5e8-fd0c-11dc-a2aa-806d6172696f}
   Drive Signature = da b0 89 7f
\??\Volume{3f40b256-ffd5-11dc-ab2b-806d6172696f}
   Drive Signature = e0 2f 37 b3
\??\Volume{3f40b257-ffd5-11dc-ab2b-806d6172696f}
   Drive Signature = e0 2f 37 b3
\DosDevices\L:
   Drive Signature = e0 2f 37 b3
```

The USB images were searched for the above drive signatures in the 0×1b8 location. The file signature from each of the USB device images was then compared to what was found in the System.txt RegRipper output file. Also found in the System.txt RegRipper output file under USBSTOR was the following:

```
USBStor
ControlSet001\Enum\USBStor
Disk&Ven_Flash&Prod_Drive_AU_USB20&Rev_8.07 [Tue Apr 1
   10:28:18 2008]
```

```
       S/N: BQENV5CR&0 [Tue Apr 1 21:07:32 2008]
         FriendlyName: Flash Drive AU_USB20 USB Device
         ParentIdPrefix: 8&252733d5&0
Disk&Ven_Memorex&Prod_TD_Classic_003B&Rev_PMAP [Fri Apr 4
     15:18:23 2008]
       S/N: 0778102104F1&0 [Fri Apr 4 15:18:16 2008]
         FriendlyName: Memorex TD Classic 003B USB Device
         ParentIdPrefix: 8&2ffa93d7&0
       S/N: 0778102B028C&0 [Tue Apr 1 21:07:32 2008]
         FriendlyName: Memorex TD Classic 003B USB Device
         ParentIdPrefix: 8&a3d19e6&0
       S/N: 0778102B05EC&0 [Tue Apr 1 21:07:32 2008]
         FriendlyName: Memorex TD Classic 003B USB Device
         ParentIdPrefix: 8&1d437750&0
       S/N: 0778102C0211&0 [Fri Apr 4 15:18:29 2008]
         FriendlyName: Memorex TD Classic 003B USB Device
         ParentIdPrefix: 8&143046d9&0
       S/N: 0778102C0441&0 [Tue Apr 1 21:07:32 2008]
         FriendlyName: Memorex TD Classic 003B USB Device
         ParentIdPrefix: 8&1b050223&0
       S/N: 0778102D041B&0 [Tue Apr 1 21:07:32 2008]
         FriendlyName: Memorex TD Classic 003B USB Device
         ParentIdPrefix: 8&6ae132f&0
Disk&Ven_SAMSUNG&Prod_HD501LJ&Rev_0-10 [Tue Apr 1 10:28:18
     2008]
       S/N: 152D203380B6&0 [Tue Apr 1 21:07:32 2008]
         FriendlyName: SAMSUNG HD501LJ USB Device
Disk&Ven_USB_2.0&Prod_Flash_Disk&Rev_1100 [Tue Apr 1
     10:28:18 2008]
       S/N: A1270000000000063&0 [Tue Apr 1 21:07:32 2008]
         FriendlyName: USB 2.0 Flash Disk USB Device
         ParentIdPrefix: 8&545ee4&0
```

The ParentIdPrefix is used to identify the drive letter that was used when the device was connected. It identifies which device was given which drive letter. Under mounteddevices in the registry, this ParentIdPrefix will be with a drive letter. The ParentIdPrefix is unique to each device. All of the S/Ns and ParentIdPrefix's were searched against the USB device images.

The next step was to get data to compare from the images of the USB media. The USB images were manually analyzed by eye using a viewer in hexadecimal (hex) and text formats. Immediately a lot of file names jumped out with the letters "chaff" and "haff." The hex value for "haff" is as follows: haff = 68 00 61 00 66 00 66. For the hex value of "haff," there were 18 hits in two files: 4 in the usb_002.000_01 USB image file and 14 in the NTUSER.DAT registry hive file. These two files were compared for a match in the 8.3 filename convention. The four hits from the usb_002.000_01 file are in the 8.3 short filename convention; this is because the file system of USB media is FAT16 file system. This is known based on a beginning text entry in the usb_002.000_01 file that states "TravelDriveFAT16" and the file usb_002_org.fdisk that also states "W95 FAT16 (LBA)." In the file NTUSER.DAT, we found 14 filenames that contained the hex value for "haff." Looking at the four short names from usb_002.000_01, we see that there are long name equivalents from the 14 hits in NTUSER. DAT, in which converted short names would be the hits from usb_002.000_01.

Although there were no coordinating matches found on the USB device images from the System.txt RegRipper output text file, the hex correlations between the NTUSER.DAT file and the files found on the USB_002 USB device lead one to believe that four files were saved or copied from the suspect's computer to the USB_002 USB device. Therefore, the USB_002 device had to have been attached to the suspect's computer.

Other Pertinent Information

Other places that will hold data on virtualized environments are as follows:
- Windows SysEvent.evt log
- User's startup folder
- Temp files
- Volatile informants such as memory, processes, and ports
- Page file
- Unique virtual hardware
- Data-carved items

Investigators use data carving to find deleted relevant data. In the case of a VM, the amount of recoverable data will be determined by the environment. If the virtual environment is similar to MojoPac, key evidence may be able to be recovered because the MojoPac environment contains many pieces, including its own registry as well as a folder for user documents. On the other hand, if a 4GB VM is deleted, it might be impossible to recover and examine. Finding any of these traces may clue an investigator into the fact that there may be additional evidence located on a removable device or actual VM stored elsewhere.

Imaging Virtual Machines

In the section "Virtual Machine Forensics" in "A Discussion of Virtual Machines Related to Forensics Analysis," Shavers (2008) asks "Why Image a VM?" There are several reasons to image VMs.

First, VMs are files contained on physical drives. If the VM itself is the only item of interest, there may not be a need to acquire the entire drive. In certain situations, it may not even be possible to image the entire drive, such as in the case of a storage area network (SAN), or an ESXi server that may be hosting multiple VMs. Live acquisition has started to become a consideration and is incredibly important in cloud OS instances and some mobile systems, especially when national jurisdiction is crossed to the physical system. On the opposite end of the spectrum, if the virtual environment is similar to MojoPac, the entire environment will have to be captured because it is a contained XP environment and has its own registry as well as a folder for user documents. As discussed in Chapter 5, "Investigating Dead Virtual Environments" and as seen in Figure 7.11, there are several files associated with a virtual machine that are needed for the VM to function.

Copying these files will allow the VM to boot and booting the VM will allow the investigator to view the environment, but it will alter the files. Forensic best practices dictate not altering the original media. Even though you are working from an image, the files may still be altered if the environment is not mounted in a way that is forensically sound. Mounting processes will be discussed in the section on "Identification and Conversion Tools."

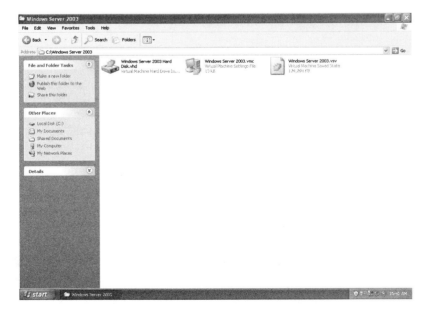

Figure 7.11 Files Associated with a Virtual Machine

The case for imaging the entire drive would be that the VM may have shared folders on the host machine. For example, MokaFive installs folders on the host machine where LivePCs can be stored. Additionally, the .lpc extension that is used is merely a pointer file. Evidence can easily be missed by not capturing the entire environment. Figure 7.12 shows the MokaFive files that are stored in a cache folder. The flat.0 file contains all pertinent information, so if it is stored on the host machine, the essential files will be missing.

According to Shavers, one method of exporting a virtual machine is to use the virtual machine's associated program. Just as the VM boots into its own actual OS, it can be booted in a forensic environment using forensic boot media, such as a forensic floppy or compact disc. The forensic boot environment allows the VM to be imaged in a forensically sound manner. Using this method, the VM is imaged without altering any file in the original VM. Most commercial forensic tools are capable of soundly dealing with VMware VMs. In EnCase, the VM can be exported and added back in as an evidence item or created as a separate case. FTK Imager can also deal with VMware VMs with relative ease. It is when there are unconventional or new environments that other methods may have to be used.

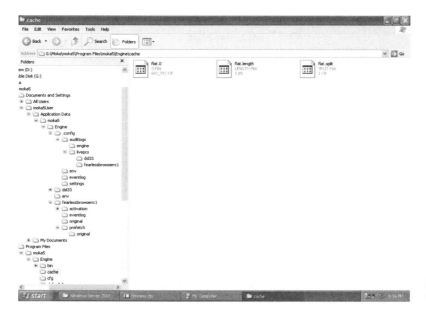

Figure 7.12 Files Associated with MokaFive

Snapshots

A VM snapshot captures the state of a VM at a particular point in time. The snapshot includes the configuration, disk data, and the current state. The purpose is to allow the user to revert to the snapshot in the event something happens to the VM to cause it not to work properly. This principle is similar to a restore point in the Windows OS. According to VMware's KB article 1015180, when using a snapshot, the configuration settings reverted include, but are not limited to previous IP addresses, DNS names, Universal Unique Identifier (UUID), and guest OS patch versions. Snapshot data files are stored as files and are usually located in the same folder as the virtual machine by default. However, if the VM was imported with snapshots, they are stored in their own folder, and if the virtual machine has no snapshots, the virtual machine snapshot setting allows the snapshots to be stored in a specified folder. The functions associated with snapshots are as follows:

- CreateSnapshot creates a new snapshot and updates the current snapshot.
- RemoveSnapshot removes a snapshot and any associated storage.
- RemoveAllSnapshots removes all snapshots.
- RevertToSnapshot "rollbacks" a virtual machine.

This concept is important for two reasons. First, snapshots, just like restore points, can contain vital information that may not show in the current state of the machine. Second, since each snapshot generates a new child disk from the last child disk and the relationship may change, there could be multiple branches in the snapshot chain. Reconstructing events may require locating all snapshots, not just the most obvious ones.

Snapshot Files

Just as with restore points, snapshot files create multiple files from which configurations can be restored. Snapshot files will initially be small (16 MB) and will grow up to the size of the original disk. Here is a listing of the files associated with snapshots.

- –delta.vmdk file – This file is also known as the redo-log file. It is a bitmap of the changes to the base VMDK. One is created for each snapshot and they are automatically deleted when the snapshot is deleted or reverted.
- .vmsd file – This file stores metadata and information about snapshots. It is stored in text format and does not cleanup completely after snapshots are taken. Once you delete a snapshot, it will still leave the fields in the file for each snapshot.

- .vmsn file – This file contains the snapshot state. It can preserve the VM's memory as part of the snapshot and is similar to the VMware suspended state (.vmss) file.

VMotion

VMware VMotion allows for the live migration of running virtual machines from one physical server to another. It is used primarily for load balancing and to perform maintenance.

Since this function allows for the dynamic movement of VMs, it is possible that there will be remnants on a machine where no VM exists because it was moved. According to VMware, VMotion technology is deployed in production by 70% of VMware customers. This concept is discussed further in Chapter 9, "Virtualization Challenges."

Identification and Conversion Tools

A virtual machine located inside a forensic image cannot be properly examined by most forensic software. Forensic software reports the virtual machine files as unknown file types. Although the virtual machine can be exported or loaded into another virtual machine, when that suspect virtual machine is loaded the file information inside the original virtual machine changes.

Some commercial forensic tools have the capability to mount virtual machine files. For example, EnCase allows a .vmdk file to be added as an evidence file for analysis as mentioned previously. In order to do this, the .vmdk file should be exported out and then added separately. Once the .vmdk file is added into the case, EnCase sees it as a hard drive of the virtual machine. Paraben has added the capability to mount a .vhd file. Other formats such as those created by MokaFive are not so easily mountable. The research into the examination of these various environments included the quest for programs that would convert a virtual image to a more universal format such as a dd file. This was done to find a way to convert the environment for mounting and examination without changing the original files. FTK Imager will open .vmdk files and acquire it to dd image. In addition to forensic software, programs such as Live View can mount a write-protected image so that no alterations are done to that dd image. This is a beginning though, and not all virtual environments are this easy to examine.

At one time, a .vmdk file was the only VM file that could easily be recognized for examination in forensic software. In order to come up with some type of process that could be used for soundly converting and mounting an image without altering the original image, we spent some time experimenting with a Microsoft .vhd file, since it was one of the most likely images that would be encountered. This experimentation process for examining a .vhd file used WinImage to convert and mount the virtual machine file. The following steps were taken:

1. Retrieved virtual disk image from target machine
2. Hashed the image for access control, chain of custody
3. Accessed disk with WinImage, extracted evidence files as necessary
4. Hashed the disk image a second time to verify that WinImage did not modify the original virtual disk
5. Loaded extracted files into forensic tool of choice for analysis

This process did not modify any of the files as the hash values matched. As vendors begin to adhere to standards, the challenge to find utilities that recognize and convert file formats should become lessened. Although now a .vhd file can be loaded through some forensics software programs, it is important to understand that experimentation may be the only recourse when the need arises to examine a format the our tools cannot interpret.

In the next few sections, we will discuss some of the tools that are available to mount or convert different formats so that the environment can be easily examined. One note here, any processes to convert and mount virtual environments must be carefully documented because their forensic soundness may be challenged.

Live View

Live View is perhaps one of the environments most often used to create a VMware virtual machine out of a raw (dd-style) disk image or physical disk. There are many good papers written on this process and Varda, from U.S. Customs and Immigration Enforcement, regularly presents on this topic at conferences. Live.View allows the forensic examiner to boot into the image or disk and see the environment just as the user did, without modifying the original image or disk.

Live View is capable of booting Microsoft OSes and some Linux OSes in the following format types:
• Full disk raw images
• Bootable partition raw images
• Physical disks (attached via a USB or FireWire bridge)
• Specialized and closed image formats using third-party image mounting software

WinImage

WinImage is disk-imaging software for creating, reading, and editing of images of FAT, NTFS, and ext2 file systems. The disk image is an exact copy of a physical disk or a partition and preserves the original structure. It can be used for the following format types:

- DMF
- VHD
- ISO (no longer supports UDF as of version 8.10)
- IMA
- IMZ
- cue

Virtual Forensic Computing

Virtual Forensic Computing (VFC) is a forensic tool used to convert physical hard disk drives and forensic image files. The original evidence is read-only and cannot be written to directly. Additionally, mounted or emulated forensic image files are opened read-only by default, as are "dd" and "img" disk image files.

VFC can boot Windows OSes.

VFC currently supports the following image formats:

- Mount Image Pro v2
- EnCase Physical Disk Emulator (PDE)
- Physical disks (IDE, SATA, USB, IEEE1394)
- UNIX-style uncompressed "dd" images
- Vogon-format uncompressed "img" images.

The mounting of VM file formats presents a couple of challenges. The major one is being able to forensically mount the VM without changing the environment. Luckily, vendors are also helping us in this area. Some of the software programs that do this include the following:

- EnCase PDE
- ProDiscover, Technology Pathways, LLC
- Forensic Replicator, Paraben
- FTK Imager

Environment to Environment Conversion

From time to time, a virtual environment may need to be converted from one format to another. For example, say that the forensic tool being used does not understand the file format of the VM that needs to be examined. Rather than use the gyrations explained in the section "Virtual Forensic Computing," tools written for this specific purpose can be used. For example, there are several tools that will convert a .vmdk file to a .vhd format.

VM File Format Conversions

VirtualBox is quite versatile and can convert .vhd and .vmdk to .vdi files.

The process is as follows:

1. Install QEMU.
2. Convert the file to a .bin. For example type the command: **qemu-img convert harddrive-name.vmdk raw-file.bin**.
3. Once the file has been converted, convert it to .vdi format using VBoxManage.

A VMware virtual appliance can be converted to work with Parallels. The process will convert IDE-based single-disk images as follows:

1. Convert the image from VMware format to a raw hard disk using the following command: **qemu-img convert appliance-harddrive-name.vmdk -O raw appliance-harddrive-name-raw.hdd**.
2. Create a virtual machine.
3. Replace "Hard Disk 1" with the hard disk image you created from the converted VMware image.

The key in both these processes is getting the VMware image into a raw hard disk image. There are a number of different VMDK types and QEMU is not currently able to convert all of them.

Vmdk2Vhd is a simple utility to convert virtual hard drive images from VMWare's VMDK format into the Microsoft's VHD format. This is a sector-by-sector copy operation from one format to the other and the source file remains unaltered. The tool is available for download from the vmToolkit Web site.

StarWind Converter is a downloadable V2V conversion tool for virtual machines. It can be used to convert .vmdk to .vhd files and .vhd to .vmdk as well as to .img file, which is a native StarWind format.

Finally, Microsoft provides its own tool in the System Center Virtual Machine Manager 2007, which provides options to convert VMware Virtual Machines to the VHD format.

Summary

In this chapter, we have discussed concepts concerning finding and imaging rogue virtual machines, acquiring virtual machine snapshots, and using conversion tools. Additionally, we also explained steps that can be used to determine if the environment is indeed real or virtual.

References

Carvey, H. (2009). *Windows forensic analysis: DVD toolkit* (2nd ed.). Burlington, MA: Syngress.

Ferrie, P. (2007). Attacks on more virtual machine emulators. *Symantic Advanced Threat Research*. Retrieved from www.symantec.com/avcenter/reference/Virtual_Machine_Threats.pdf

Parsonage, H. (September 2008, Updated November 2009). The meaning of linkfiles in forensic examinations. Retrieved from http://computerforensics.parsonage.co.uk/downloads/TheMeaningofLIFE.pdf

Shavers, B. (2008). Virtual machine forensics, a discussion of virtual machines related to forensics analysis. *Forensic Focus*. Retrieved from http:// www.forensicfocus.com.

Stagner, H. (2007). How to detect rogue virtual machines on a network. *SearchServerVirtualization.com*. Retrieved from http://searchservervirtualization.techtarget.com/tip/0,289483,sid94_gci1247530_mem1,00.html. Contributor Accessed 14.03.07.

Weilbacher, N. (2006). Evidentiary value of link files. *Forensic Focus*. Retrieved from http://www.forensicfocus.com/link-file-evidentiary-value

Wolf, C. (2007). Inventorying virtual hard disk files on a server or domain. *Virtualization Review*. Retrieved from http://virtualizationreview.com/articles/2007/05/01/inventorying-virtualhard-disk-files-on-a-server-or-domain.aspx.

Wolf, C. (2008). Rogue VMs be very afraid. *Virtualization Review*. Retrieved from http://virtualizationreview.com/articles/2008/06/01/rogue-vms–be-very-afraid.aspx Accessed 01.06.08.

Bibliography

Snapshots

Understanding virtual machine snapshots in VMware ESX, VMware's KB article 1015180, http://kb.vmware.com/selfservice/microsites/search.do?language=en_US&cmd=displayKC&externalId=1015180

Snapshots

What files make up a virtual machine? http://www.vmware.com/support/ws55/doc/ws_learning files_in_a_vm.html

Understanding virtual machine snapshots in VMware ESX. http://kb.vmware.com/selfservice/microsites/search.do?language=en_US&cmd=displayKC&externalId=1015180

VM File Format Conversions

http://www.virtualizationdaily.com/archives/73_how-to-convert-a-vmware-virtual-appliance-to-work-with-parallels.html

http://vmtoolkit.com/

http://viethak.com/2009/11/27/Convert-VMDK-to-VHD-Virtual-Disk-or-Vice-versa-Using-StarWind-Image-Converter.html

ADVANCED VIRTUALIZATION

VIRTUAL ENVIRONMENTS AND COMPLIANCE

INFORMATION IN THIS CHAPTER

- Standards
- Compliance
- Organizational Chain of Custody
- Data Retention Policies

Due to the nature of personal information, there are certain regulatory compliance requirements for many types of businesses. If the organization is required to maintain certain data for a set period of time based on regulations or policy, any information contained in virtual environments must be considered. If the organization is using virtual machines (VMs), this will need to be addressed in the security policy.

Standards

In late 2007, the Distributed Management Task Force, Inc. (DMTF) created an open standard for system virtualization management. According to Winston Bumpus, the current president of DMTF, the organization aims to "simplify and provide ease-of-use for the virtual environment by creating an industry standard for system virtualization management." The organization's role extends to ensure the success of the standard. The standard recognizes the supported virtualization management capabilities including the discovery of virtual computer systems, the management of virtual computer system lifecycles, the control of virtual resources, and the monitoring of virtual systems.

The DMTF initiated the availability of the Open Virtualization Format (OVF) standard for delivering VMs, and the new

Virtualization Management Initiative (VMAN). This standard has been discussed in previous chapters with respect to some of the virtualization market vendors' offerings and their components, so the information offered here is to basically provide an additional overview of the technologies because they have become a standard. OVF is a virtualization platform–independent. It supports a full range of current virtual hard disks and is extensible to deal with future formats. OVF is not reliant on the use of any specific host platform, virtualization platform, or guest operating system. The OVF format was developed to deal with the shortcomings of other file formats. For example, the Virtual Machine Disk Format (VMDK) encodes a single VM virtual disk without including any information about the virtual hardware of a machine. OVF provides a complete specification of the VM, including a list of required virtual disks and the required virtual hardware configuration. In addition, OVF is a portable format that allows deployment of any supporting hypervisor.

The management lifecycle of a virtual environment is addressed in DMTF's VMAN. According to the standard description provided at www.dmtf.org, VMAN's Open Virtualization Format (OVF) specification provides a standard format for packaging VMs and applications for deployment across all virtualization platforms. The VMAN initiative has provided the industry with a standardized approach to VM:

- Deployment
- Discovery and inventory
- Lifecycle management
- Creation, deletion, and modification
- Health and performance monitoring

Compliance

The rapid increase in the use of virtualization had made it almost a mainstream technology. Not only it is found in the enterprise environments, it is also found on portable devices and handhelds. As a general rule, we implement first and then figure out to secure and manage new technologies. As new regulations are passed and new technologies are implemented, we face compliance issues. This is the case with virtualization. The majority of regulations address security as a whole but not virtualization. The use of virtualization has taken the networking model that was developed by Microsoft when the Microsoft Certified System Engineer (MCSE) came into existence and totally inverted it. The concept of one role per server no longer exists in virtualization and surveying the number of machines in a data center, or networking room can no longer provide an accurate picture of the environment. It's possible to have 10 servers with 100 VMs residing on them. In addition, environments like ESXi are VM repositories, so they can hold quite few a VMs. If there is no VM tracking method in place, locating data will be difficult, and it would be impossible to determine if it had been lost or manipulated.

VMs are very flexible. They can be created, moved, and destroyed in a manner similar to a Word document. If an organization is good with classification and tracking of its physical assets, the transition to tracking virtual assets will become a bit easier.

In an article posted on August 07, 2009, by David Mortman entitled "How to find virtual machines for greater virtualization compliance," he states the real starting point in VM tracking for an organization is to become obsessed with documentation and process (Mortman, 2009). It is also recommended that in order to meet compliance needs, organizations should be extremely consistent in doing things the same way every time. This type of consistency makes virtualization compliance possible. If proper processes and documentation are in place, litigation and compliance audits will go smoother. Here is an example of how virtualized environments affect compliance. Not long ago, a forensic consultant received a call from a business partner in another city. The call went something like this:

Caller: Ms. Barrett, I'm doing a compliance audit and am having some issues I hope you can help with. I'm scanning the organization's network and cannot locate the mail server. Do you have an idea why?

Ms. Barrett: Is it up and running?

Caller: Yes. I'm absolutely sure it is.

Ms Barrett: What tool are you using to scan the network?

Caller: I'm using xxxx

Ms. Barrett: Have you found all the rest of the servers?

Caller: You know, that's the funny thing, some I find and some I don't, but right now I'm most concerned with the mail server.

Ms. Barrett: Can you ping it?

Caller: Yes.

Ms. Barrett: Is the server virtualized?

Caller: No.

Ms. Barrett: How do you know?

Caller: It's not addressed in the security policy.

Ms. Barrett: Put me on hold and go ask someone if the server is virtualized.

Caller: Well, guess what? The server is virtual. Now what?

I'll let your imagination finish the story. However, it does point out the following real issues with compliance and audits:

- Virtualization is not addressed in most security policies.
- Auditors are not trained on checking for or inquiring about virtualized environments.
- Depending on the tool used, it may or may not find VMs.

Regulatory Requirements

The earlier section addressed some compliance implications of using virtual environments. This section will provide an example of how regulatory requirements and virtualized environments intersect. Perhaps one of the best examples of this intersection is in the area of Payment Card Industry Data Security Standards (PCI DSS) compliance. This area was chosen for the following reasons:

- The PCI Security Standards Council (SSC) is international.
- There are some valuable articles written on how PCI and virtualization intersect.
- VMware has joined the PCI SSC.

First a little background on the PCI SSC. The PCI DSS is a set of comprehensive requirements for enhancing payment account data security. These standards were developed by the founding payment brands of the PCI SSC, including American Express, Discover Financial Services, JCB International, MasterCard Worldwide, and Visa Inc. International, to help facilitate the broad adoption of consistent data security measures on a global basis. PCI DSS is a group of principles and accompanying directives organized into 12 requirements in the following six categories:

- Build and Maintain a Secure Network
- Protect Cardholder Data
- Maintain a Vulnerability Management Program
- Implement Strong Access Control Measures
- Regularly Monitor and Test Networks
- Maintain an Information Security Policy

In late 2008, VMware Inc. announced that it has joined the PCI SSC to incorporate awareness of virtualization into forthcoming versions of PCI regulations because PCI DSS does not address virtualization. VMware's involvement is intended to show how certain regulations might need to be adapted to take advantage of virtualization. The company also launched the VMware Compliance Center, a Web site dedicated to educating merchants and auditors about compliance in virtualized environments. The resource includes links to relevant white papers and webcasts, some of which will be referenced in this section. There are two very good articles on PCI compliance and virtualization by Hau, Araujo, Chudgar, Hustad, and Chaubal (2009), and their most recent article, which outlines and explains in greater details the five areas mentioned here, was published in 2010.

As an example on how virtualization affects PCI DSS, we will look at a few of the categories. Under the first category, Build and Maintain a Secure Network, the requirements are to install and maintain a firewall configuration to protect cardholder data. This includes not using vendor-supplied defaults for system passwords and other security parameters. Although this statement alludes to physical firewalls, virtualization technology provides organizations the ability to implement virtual firewall technologies such as Vyatta, Kerio, and Astaro. Astaro provides virtual appliances that have been preinstalled and preconfigured for VMware environments. Vyatta provides a software-based, open-source solution that is portable to standard x86 hardware, as well as common virtualization and cloud computing platforms, and Kerio provides a firewall software appliance called *WinRoute*. The issue arises that many of these are preconfigured and if not properly documented, the virtual firewall may not provide the same level of protection as a separate physical firewall. Another issue is that all virtual appliances have the default login and password posted on the appliance download site. The default login and password are publically posted on the download site or are available when the appliance is downloaded. Due to this wide exposure, all default passwords on implementations must be changed. This includes not only the guest and host passwords but also any other related third-party components used within the virtualization infrastructure. Some of the provisions in PCI DSS appear to be adverse to virtualization, in particular PCI DSS Requirement 2.2.1, which directs merchants to implement only one primary function per server. In traditional environments, this regulation is interpreted to mean running separate, dedicated machines for servers such as Web, application, file, and database. With virtualization, the hypervisor allows multiple systems to have logical separation sharing the same underlying hardware.

Hau et al. believe it definitely possible to use virtualization and still meet the intent of the requirement, but organizations will need to carefully consider how their whole infrastructure is architected in relation to this requirement. Further, it is suggested that only bare-metal or native virtualization be considered for cardholder data environments.

Under the second category, Protect Cardholder Data, the requirements are to protect stored cardholder data and encrypt transmission of cardholder data across open, public networks. The business, legal, and regulatory requirements hold true for virtual environments, as well as nonvirtual environments, when addressing the retention time in the data retention policy. The complications related to data retention and virtual environments are discussed later in this chapter under the section "Data Retention Policies." Regarding encryption, policies and processes to properly control cryptographic keys should be implemented before the archiving and storage of VM images.

In the article "How Virtualization Affects PCI DSS: A Review of the Top Five Issues," Hau et al. (2010) discuss the top five issues and concerns that PCI Qualified Security Assessors (QSAs) have about virtualization technology. The first issue mentioned earlier is PCI DSS Requirement 2.2.1. While many PCI auditors will certify virtualized systems as compliant, not all do because the requirement is often misinterpreted. Hau et al. believe that the use of virtualization technology is not a barrier to PCI DSS compliance provided the appropriate controls are implemented to stop one virtual system from increasing the risk to cardholder data on another virtual system. There are two major concerns. The first is a data compromise as a result of guest-to-host, guest-to-guest isolation, or the direct compromise of the underlying host. The second is the segregation of networks. In virtual environments, it is important that when streamlining the execution of IT management processes through VMware vCenter Server the service console is isolated from other networks, especially the guest network. Examples of this would be live migration, provisioning, capacity management, and automated patching. In addition, the misconfiguration of virtual networks and rogue VMs must be considered where PCI compliance is concerned.

The next area we will look at is PCI DSS requirements 9.6 to 9.10. These requirements address media that might contain cardholder data. Based on how a virtual environment works, VM files can be considered virtual media and need to be protected. Unrestricted acccess to these key files allows for information disclosure, as well as unauthorized modifications. Controlled access to these files and any backups is critical from a data protection perspective.

PCI DSS requirement 10.2 relating to logging and auditing mandates that an organization must "implement automated audit trails for all system components." Logging and auditing uses valuable resources, and it is often turned off when it affects system performance. As more forensic cases are challenged, running virtual environments without any type of auditing opens the organization up to noncompliance issues and class-action lawsuits.

An organization is required to have an incident response plan in place per PCI DSS requirement 12.9. If a virtualized environment is used, the organization must take into consideration unique environmental issues such as whether to image the entire machine or just the VM at issue and how to be prepared to have all VMs residing on a server confiscated if a crime is committed in a VM on that server.

The last issue is addressed in several places in this chapter and deals with the how easily VMs can be set up, copied, stored, and deleted. Straightforward PCI DSS requirements such as patching (6.1) and change control (6.4) may require additional processes and technology to ensure compliance in the virtual environment. Hau et al. provide an excellent reminder of this: when an old or new VM is "turned on" in the cardholder data environment, it must comply with PCI DSS immediately. Template images become out-of-date almost immediately, and the convenience of snapshots can place a machine in an unpatched, noncompliant state.

Discoverability of Virtual Environment

Litigation holds and e-discovery of virtual environments add another layer of complexity to an already complex situation. Depending on whether you work in law enforcement or in the private sector, you will be involved in either preparing search warrants or assisting attorneys. The discovery of virtual environments needs to be considered. Although we have made great strides in e-discovery methodologies and products, just as in compliance issues, we may miss vital information associated with virtual environments.

Vendors are now starting to realize the ramifications of virtual environments on e-discovery and are offering methods to help track and inventory these machines.

For example, Hytrust has an appliance that sits inside the data center to segregate management traffic from ordinary users of the VMs. The appliance terminates all SSL and management sessions between the ESX servers and the clients. This ensures that ordinary users can't change the VM configuration, and the administrator can also apply fine-grained security policies to particular administrative rights to enforce separation of duties. There is also a Web-based console from which the management operations can be performed, and the appliance can grab policies from VMware's VirtualCenter management software. Another vendor who is at the forefront of e-discovery solutions to support VMware is Kazeon. Version 3.1 of the software supports VMware instances in order to track virtual instances on servers, laptops, and desktops.

One of the results of the changes to the Federal Rules of Civil Procedure (FRCP) is the increased likelihood of hefty fines for failing to produce information in legal cases. It is no longer acceptable for an organization to claim it was unaware of the existence of information or only partially produce requested data. It is also important to show that the organization did its due diligence when producing material information.

If, as an investigator, one hasn't already encountered electronic data discovery collection involving virtualization, it's only a matter of time until it happens. When a company receives an order to locate information in an e-discovery process, realizing or even being aware of information stored in old VMs is a contentious matter. The organization is liable for handing over the virtual data if it exists. The e-discovery process dictates that data is a data, regardless of where it exists. E-discovery is arduous enough, and forgetting about the data stored in VMs places the organization at even greater risk.

Much of the attorney's job in litigation is to assess the situation, to determine what needs to be collected, and then to coordinate the collection between the client and e-discovery vendor. The attorney and the client end to be forewarned when dealing with virtual environments, and there can be preservation issues and added costs. According to the article "How Virtualization Affects EDD Collection" posted on www.law.com, virtualization can affect a case in three main ways:

1. Increased costs and collections: the estimate of an electronically stored information collection is done by counting the physical computers or servers. If virtualization is used in the environment, this method can no longer be used.
2. Overlooked evidence: information contained in a VM will not respond to keyword searches. VMs are flat files that must be opened separately for examination.
3. Increased risk of collection issues and spoliation: virtualization involves separating computers and data storage from its physical hardware. The ability to roll back snapshots and move VMs makes evidence much easier to lose or destroy.

The ability to deal with these issues before they become an e-discovery nightmare with ballooning costs is dependent on being aware of the technology ramifications, asking the right questions about virtualization, and effectively communicating what is needed from the client and e-discovery vendor.

Legal and Protocol Document Language

Depending on whether you work in the law enforcement or in the private sector, you will be involved in search warrants or assisting attorneys in developing protocol documents. Virtual environments need to be considered in these documents. Newer technology methods are going to be a huge challenge in the digital evidence preservation field in order to obtain the information needed for prosecution. With the permission of the original case provider, Kelli O'Neill, special agent of the CA Department of Justice (DOJ), this section presents an example of a recent case in CA that involved cloud computing. It also includes search warrant language that is being used to deal with this type of situation. Although this is specific to cloud technology, the principles contained herein can be applied to virtual environments and will come in handy as we move to a cloud environment.

In this ongoing case, it took about 6 months to get evidence from the application service provider (ASP) who filed a motion to quash a warrant served on them.

The case background is as follows. In early 2009, agents arrived at a location with the intent to seize records pursuant to a search warrant. The Computer Forensic Investigation Team (CFIT) quickly found that the records sought were all stored electronically at an electronic service provider (ESP) in another state. The records were openly accessed by employees at the local company as part of their daily routine. The local workstations were dummy terminals and didn't contain data storage media. Since the warrant was for the local site and not the ESP, the agents attempted to get consent to print or otherwise just photocopy the records while onsite. This consent was denied and the agents left without the evidence.

To obtain the records, the case agent served a search warrant on the ESP's agent of service using California Penal Code section 1524.2, which requires an out-of-state company that provides remote computing services to the general California public to comply with the warrant. The ESP responded by filing a motion to quash the warrant stating that the ESP doesn't provide remote computing because they don't own the fiber optics that facilitate the data transfer. The ESP also claimed they didn't provide services to the general public as they only offered their services to a particular industry. DOJ then filed a motion claiming they do provide remote computing and this service is offered to the general public. DOJ went to court and CFIT testified using the ESP's own description of offered remote computing services, as claimed on their Web site. In essence, they advertised remote services to those in the industry who'd pay for it. DOJ didn't physically serve the ESP in the other state mainly due to lack of resources to travel out of state and assist in the warrant. The California DOJ would have to assist because the ESP apparently commingled client data on its servers, which raises issues such as the privacy act regulations and protected data. CFIT interviewed the chief information officer (CIO) of the target company to find out why this rather large company outsourced its IT duties among other things. Doing business this way saved the company money by allowing them to reduce internal IT staff and other costs. The CIO said their records stored at the application service provider (ASP) are accessed locally through a Citrix system, which meant all processing was done at the server level and cached on the servers at the ASP. Nothing was cached locally, and the few local workstations that had hard drives had been locked to prevent data from being copied to them.

It took the Superior Court in the county 3 months to decide on the motion, which is almost the maximum time they can take. The court ruled that the ASP provided remote computing service to the general public and denied the motion to quash the search warrant, reopening the door to secure the evidence. The ASP turned over most of the evidence but withheld a couple of thousand e-mail messages they say were protected by attorney–client privilege. DOJ asked the ASP to turnover all the e-mail messages. The ASP gave up about several hundred more and claimed no privilege for these messages. When the DOJ filed contempt of court charges against the ASP, the remaining messages were turned over to the DOJ sealed. As of the date this information was obtained, the contempt charges are still pending. The result is that it took about 7 months from the date the initial search warrant was served to secure the evidence, which is suspect. This case demonstrates that preserving the evidence, with MD5/SHA hashing onsite really protects both sides.

The new warrant language given below is being added in order to remotely seize digital evidence from a physical search warrant site. This gives the agency the ability to preserve digital evidence and prevent it from being tampered with or destroyed. The language allows agents to copy the data but it doesn't allow the agents to search it. The case agent will have to go back to court and get a second warrant or "piggyback" in order to search the data – as stated in the new language. The language only applies to third-party vendors who are in the business of providing remote computer services to the general public. This doesn't apply to in-house remote servers.

New warrant language:

Your affiant requests authorization to copy digital evidence stored on a server(s) in another location if the server can be remotely accessed from a computer(s) located at the site authorized to be searched by the approval of this court order. This authorization gives law enforcement the ability to preserve the integrity of the evidence and prevent it from being tampered with or destroyed.

Through training and experience, Computer Expert, has discovered that companies are starting to use ESPs who provide the service of storing electronic records and other data on a remote server for their customer who can access the data via a remote connection. This allows the customer to connect to the server from anywhere there is service to the Internet. In doing so, an employee at the customer company can view, alter, create, copy and print the data from the remote server as if it was at the same location as the employee. The customer typically owns and controls the data stored at the remote server while the ESP owns the server on which the data is stored.

Computer Expert told me law enforcement typically doesn't find out about the existence of the remote server until the service of the initial search warrant takes place. Law enforcement doesn't have access to a remote computer and the data on it can't be viewed without such access. Witnesses and informants who have access to the data typically don't know where it is stored.

The server maybe located in another city or state from the site of the initial service making it difficult for law enforcement to preserve the evidence. It takes hours and sometimes days to determine the location of the remote computer and gather the details containing the specificity necessary for the issuance of a second search warrant. Depending on the size of the evidence, a suspect can delete it from a system within seconds.

If your affiant obtains evidence from a remote computer he\she will note this in the property receipt for those items seized remotely. Your affiant will attempt to determine the location of the remote system and include this information in the property receipt. Your affiant agrees to return to the Court to secure further orders for search if and when the remote electronic evidence is successfully copied.

(List As Item to Be Seized: On Face of Search Warrant

All items listed in this warrant that are stored remotely on a server(s) at a third party electronic server provider. If seized, your affiant will return with a second warrant request to search these items.)

The new language goes in the affidavit as an extension of the existing computer expert information.

Here is some additional information for forensic examiners, as well as sworn and nonsworn investigative staff, regarding the use of the above language.

1. If the records are stored outside the United States, there exists a risk of violating a foreign jurisdictions computer crime laws

subjecting the affiant to arrest – it goes without saying we won't use the language in this situation without first discussing the issue with case DAG (DOJ prosecutor) and only if the affiant won't be arrested when visiting that foreign country.

2. The case agent must attempt to determine if the suspect company is storing evidence at an ESP prior to using this language only if he or she can do so without jeopardizing the investigation.

3. If the case agent determines there is evidence stored remotely at an ESP prior to the service of the warrant, then the language can't be used. There is no need to use the language if we know who the provider is prior to the warrant service as we can simultaneously serve this company with a warrant and seize the evidence that way.

So practically speaking this means the team can

- copy and preserve the data onsite by printing it or by obtaining an electronic copy of it. MD5/SHA hashing should be used to preserve data.

- record all the seized data on a property receipt with other computer evidence, including the location of the remote third-party server if possible.

- provide a report on how CFIT accessed the data and copied it.

Disclaimer: The above listed language is not meant to be legal advice. It is meant to be offered as an example of what one agency did to deal with a new and upcoming technology that affects the ability to collect evidence.

Organizational Chain of Custody

Forensics analysis involves establishing a clear chain of custody over the evidence. This is the documentation of all transfers of evidence from one person to another, showing the date, time, and reason for transfer and the signatures of both parties involved in the transfer. It tells how the evidence made it from the crime scene to the courtroom, including documentation of how the evidence was collected, preserved, and analyzed. This requires careful collection and preservation of all the evidences, including the detailed logging of investigative access and the scope of the investigation. After the data is collected, it must be secured in such a manner that you can state with certainty that the evidence could not have been accessed or modified during your custodial term. Is the chain of custody different for VMs than it is for physical machines?

Hard drives, USB memory sticks, and cell phones are tagged and bagged, and then the information on these devices is copied onto another system for analysis. Establishing a "chain of custody" for virtual environments involves being able to see where VMs are running and managing them properly to quell any legal concerns. In the article entitled "Data center virtualization: Four steps to compliance," four steps were outlined and recommended to CIOs in order to make them aware of legal risks involved with virtualization (Special to SearchCIO-Midmarket.com, 2008). We will discuss two of the recommendations that involve chain of custody. First, track your VMs. The chain of custody includes which machine a VM is installed on, what data is associated with that VM, who is in control of the machine, and what controls are in place.

Second, keep your assets separate when using off-site hosting. This is critical to avoid potential liability for security exposures, including improper access.

So, what happens when virtualization and compliance collide and the matter ends up in court?

Well, it could turn out like the case we went over earlier. It is highly unlikely that a commercial contract for hosted or outsourced services will address the potential need for the service provider to cooperate in testifying in lawsuits. Any contract with a third-party custodian of data should include a service provider's commitment to cooperate in the courtroom.

Acquisition

Finding and imaging a VM was covered in Chapter 7, "Finding and Imaging Virtual Environments." The only caveat to discuss here is that VMs may not be fully understood, and the soundness of methods used to acquire and mount the data may be questioned in a court of law. For example, if a VM image is booted, the original image is no longer intact because some files were written over with new data. This theory was also presented in "Computer Forensic Analysis in a Virtual Environment" by Bem and Huebner (2007). In their paper, they expressed that an image that is known to be considerably changed would be immediately challenged in a court of law as flawed. Even though a computer expert could argue that the changes were not relevant to the evidence being presented, it is unlikely that it would be accepted by the court.

VM Snapshots versus Full Machine Imaging

Evidence is most commonly found in files that are stored on hard drives and storage devices and media, so there may be instances where you don't necessarily want or need the entire operating system. In the case of criminals who are not technically savvy, perhaps you only want user-created files. Files such as address books and database files may prove criminal association, pictures can produce evidence of pedophile activity, e-mail or documents may contain communications between criminals, and spreadsheets often contain drug deal lists. In these types of cases, it may be more efficient to copy only the directories or files that are pertinent to your case rather than the entire drive contents.

In the case of VMs, you can acquire an image of the entire physical machine, the VM you are interested in, or the most current snapshot. When you create a snapshot, all changes made on the initial virtual disk image are not actually made on the image itself. They are written to a new disk file that copies only changed, written blocks that are contained in the snapshot image. This is similar to differential backups. Only the changes are written. A snapshot image grows as the data on the virtual disk image changes. When a snapshot is taken, a series of REDO virtual disk files is created. VMware uses these to monitor and apply changes to the underlying virtual disk that is in use. The REDO files are generated when the machine is first started after a snapshot has been taken. Mounting and modifying via the REDO files will leave the original cloned image unaltered.

Mounting Virtual Machines

In Chapter 7 "Finding and Imaging Virtual Environments," under the section on conversion tools, an experimental process for forensically examining a .vhd file using WinImage to convert and mount the VM file was described. The goal of the experimentation was to show that this process did not modify any of the files as the hash values matched. The problem with merely taking an image of a VM to examine is that as soon the VM is booted, the image itself had been altered. While some investigators are of the opinion that changing the VM system files won't matter as long as it's documented in the report, a better method would be one that does not alter the files. As vendors begin to adhere to standards, the challenge to find utilities that recognize and convert file formats should become lessened.

Data Retention Policies

In virtualization, there is the ability to roll back or delete a bad or defective machine. With the FRCP governing data retention, will VMs need to be included in an organization's data retention policy? As investigators find ways to examine VMs, will the processes be questioned as to the original evidence file?

When an organization has long-term employees who are storing data in e-mail for basically years on end, that's a cost problem and a litigation risk problem. For example, in a recent case, a long-term employee never deleted any e-mail. The employee had been employed at the organization for 14 years. Upon reviewing the amount of data being stored and subject to discovery, the organization implemented a data retention policy. Data retention policies serve to make sure that users are aware of statutory and legal obligations to keep data. When electronic documents are reviewed, basically a search is run and both parties will agree on certain filters such as dates and other parameters like "protected" information that cannot be disclosed. When an organization has a good data retention policy that is enforced, the amount of data to sift through can be reduced significantly.

Litigation holds can be quite costly. The process of reviewing electronic documents can literally cost millions of dollars because attorneys have to review the data to ensure that nothing constituting privileged, confidential, proprietary information is produced.

Data retention policies are based on federal or state laws, regulations, or organizational needs. When a litigation hold is issued, process should be in place that protects the data that must be retained, that discards unnecessary data, and that ensures that the organization is not leaving itself open to unwarranted expense and risk. The cost of sifting through large volumes of data is enormous, and it may become more enormous with the use of VMs.

An organization should also be utilizing data deduplication. Virtual environments present issues in discovery matters and are compounded by redundant data issues. Often, IT will use multiple VMs to establish the system availability and scalability that is characteristic of a large data center. This practice of utilizing multiple VMs, each dedicated to running a particular application, generates a large amount of duplicate, discoverable data.

Virtual Machine Sprawl

We already discussed about how easy it is to create and deploy VMs. This rapid deployment creates what is termed *VM sprawl*. VM sprawl, just like any other sprawl, is an increased, outward spreading of VMs over time. This is due to the ease-of-use of VMs. VM sprawl can be described as the rapid creation of VMs without sufficient oversight. The main concerns with VM sprawl are as follows:

* Unnecessary taxation of the infrastructure
* Unnecessary licensing costs
* Noncompliance to policies

One of the best examples of this is a data center. In a data center, there are a large number of machines that are underutilized. As new VMs are created, they seem to magically multiply overnight. Before you know it, there are thousands of VMs. When policies and processes were originally designed, virtualization didn't exist in the capacity it exists now, so there is no oversight and control on deployment. Compounding this issue are users that create their own VMs without adhering to organizational security policy or requirements.

VMs take up no actual physical space, so they often stay around long past their usefulness, but there is usually no mechanism to check the network for old or unused VMs. As discussed in the previous sections, most organizations are faced with regulations on how information is accessed, protected, and stored. Because of the portability of VMs, it's possible that a VM that holds Personally Identifiable Information (PII) is accidentally put on the same server as a VM that is used for testing, or worse put on a Web server. VMs should be segmented by the sensitivity of the information they contain, and a policy should be in place that specifies that hardware is not shared for test environments and sensitive data. However, this situation is often not addressed.

VM sprawl can easily lead to software licensing violations and complicate maintenance. Every VM requires operating system and application licensing. With the ease of copying VMs, an organization can fall out of compliance quite quickly.

The Dynamic Movement of VMs

Organizations are beginning to grapple with the fact that there is really no good way of knowing concrete information about VMs, including where they are located, what applications they are running, and when they are created. Technologies such as VMware's VMotion and VApp make it possible to create flexible systems that can dynamically adapt to changing business conditions. As discussed earlier, complying with regulations may be unattainable if an organization does not have a structured, well-defined process to track all VMs. Chain of custody for VMs is important for many of the reasons already discussed. Due to the inherent differences between the physical environments, organizations have been accustomed, and the virtual environments they are now dealing with, traditional approaches often don't work. Standard processes to collect and maintain lifecycle information about VMs don't really fit into the usual inventory tracking systems, and the network discovery tools may or may not find VMs. The flexibility of VMs also allows the option to change a VM from being a virtual resource to a physical resource and vice versa. In an article entitled "Virtual Machines You Have to See Them to Manage Them," Kusnetzky (2008) explains that "not only is the fundamental data model of traditional tools flawed in these ways, the architecture is equally inappropriate. Fat agents in each virtual machine could be the end of any performance gains made by virtualization. And log files are often not sufficient for generating real-time insight into the environment. The challenge of monitoring virtual environments has many new dimensions of complexity."

Another issue with the dynamic movement of VMs is where the tracking responsibility lies. Tracking constant movement of resources presents a huge challenge for system management. Vendors have begun to address this issue, and by the time this book goes to print, the offerings will surely have increased. One example of this technology is Fortisphere's vRadar, a component for its Virtual Service Manager platform that was showcased at the Gartner Data Center Conference in Las Vegas held in December 2009.

According to Fortisphere's CEO Siki Giunta, vRadar keeps track of the relationship between a particular VM and the applications that run on top of it and the rest of the physical IT infrastructure. vRadar works by embedding agent software into each guest operating system running on top of the VM, which in turn communicates information about its status back to the Fortisphere console.

Many organizations have not embraced the next generation of virtualization because they are still struggling with challenges associated with managing VM software as it moves around the enterprise.

Backup and Data Recovery

Backups and data recovery are necessary for disaster recovery, business continuity, and regulatory compliance. This extends to VMs as well. VMware has a backup and recovery solution for VMs that provides
- full-image backup of VMs
- full and incremental recovery of VMs and individual files and directories

One of the main components of the backup and recovery solution is the deduplicated destination storage. It's nice to see that data deduplication is addressed. The vCenter Server interface contains options relating to the selection of VMs to be protected, backup job scheduling, data retention policies, and the selection of destination disks. One of the main points regarding backups is that the backup files should be protected just like a regular server backup. Policies for the backup of VMs should be addressed right along with regular backups.

Restored VMs can add to the VM confusion. Here's an example: Symantec NetBackup allows IT administrators to dynamically restore the backup of a VM running a version of Windows Server to either its native ESX Server state, using VMDK and other Virtual Machine File System (VMFS) files, or as a logical Windows system with New Technology File System (NTFS)-formatted files. This ability, while great for immediate resolution to a hardware failure, also means that a stolen backup can run on any number of platforms.

Summary

In this chapter, we have discussed the issues that face investigators from a legal standpoint, including standards, compliance, chain of custody, and data retention policies.

We also discussed some of the methods that can be used to mitigate these issues.

References

Barrett, A. (2008). VMware makes the case for PCI DSS compliance. *SearchServerVirtualization.com*. Retrieved from http://searchservervirtualization.techtarget.com/news/article/0,289142,sid94_gci1338681,00.html. Accessed 12.11.08.

Bem, D., & Huebner, E. (2007, Fall). Computer forensic analysis in a virtual environment. *International Journal of Digital Evidence, 6*(2), www.ijde.org.

Fegreus, J. (2009). Automating D2D backup of virtual machines. *InfoStor*. Retrevied from http://www.infostor.com/index/articles/display/articles/infostor/backup-and_recovery/disk-based-backup/lab-review__automating.html. Accessed 01.10.09.

Hau, W., Araujo, R., Chudgar, V., Hustad, R., & Chaubal, C. (2009). How virtualization affects PCI DSS Part 1: Mapping PCI requirements and virtualization. *VMware*. Retrieved from http://www.vmware.com/files/pdf/technology/mapping_pci_req_part1_wp.pdf

Hau, W., Araujo, R., Chudgar, V., Hustad, R., & Chaubal, C. (2010). How virtualization affects PCI DSS Part 2: a review of the top five issues. *VMware*. Retrieved from http://www.vmware.com/files/pdf/technology/review_top5_issues_wp.pdf

Kusnetzky, D. (2007). Virtual machines you have to see them to manage them. *Kusnetsky group*. Retrieved from http://www.virtual-strategy.com/Dan-Kusnetzky/Virtual-Machines-You-Have-to-See-Them-to-Manage-Them.html

Miller, R. (2008). Virtual machines can be an e-discovery nightmare. *Fierce Content Management*. Retrieved from http://www.fiercecontentmanagement.com/story/virtual-machines-can-be-e-discovery-nightmare/2008-09-11

Mortman, D. (2009). How to find virtual machines for greater virtualization compliance. *Information Security Magazine*. Retrieved from http://searchsecurity.techtarget.com/tip/0,289483,sid14_gci1359272,00.html. Accessed 07.08.09.

Shread, P. (2008, September 10). Virtual machines pose e-discovery risk, vendor says. *EnterpriseStorageForum*. Retrieved from http://www.enterprisestorageforum.com/ article.php/3770706.

Bibliography

Standards

Distributed Management Task Force, Inc. DMTF Creates Open Standard for System Virtualization Management. http://www.dmtf.org/newsroom/pr/view?item_key=70d5d3ba78d39488626f838397a3d1e9812e5d40

Discoverability of Virtual Environments

How Virtualization Affects EDD Collection (Law.com)

Virtual Machine Sprawl

VM Sprawl – prevention rather than cure. http://www.techworld.com/virtualisation/news/index.cfm?newsID=115876&pagtype. Accessed 17.05.09.

Organizational Chain of Custody

Data center virtualization: Four steps to compliance, Special to SearchCIO-Midmarket.com, http://searchcompliance.techtarget.com/tip/0,289483,sid195_gci1340735_mem1,00.html. Accessed 11.06.08.

VIRTUALIZATION CHALLENGES

INFORMATION IN THIS CHAPTER

- Data Centers
- Security Considerations
- Malware and Virtualization
- Red Pill, Blue Pill, No Pill
- Additional Challenges
- Virtualization Drawbacks

Virtual environments come with special challenges. Some of the challenges covered in this chapter include data centers, security considerations, storage virtualization, malware, and the drawbacks associated with the use of virtual environments.

Data Centers

A data center, sometimes called a *server farm* or *cluster*, can present special challenges to forensic investigators. The computing environment contained within a modern data center is the perfect environment for virtualization. A machine in a data center may hold 30 to 50 virtual machines (VMs). The equipment typically housed in a data center can include the following:

- Systems with 16+ CPUs/cores per server
- 64-bit addressing schemes
- Considerable amounts of physical memory
- Power-aware CPUs, servers, and racks
- Converged input/output (I/O) fabrics
- Shared high-speed interface to network and storage
- Network-based, virtualized storage
- Stateless servers with flexible I/O connections

Storage Area Networks, Direct Attached Storage, and Network Attached Storage

As organizations become more fluid, data centers provide a repository for the rapid configuration of IT resources. VMs are more attractive because the restart and provisioning times are greatly reduced. There are several options available for storing the large amounts of data in a data center. In order to understand what challenges this environment presents, it is important to understand some of the basic concepts of network storage and the various type of storage methods an investigator might encounter.

Storage can be physically connected to a single host machine. This is considered a direct-attached storage (DAS) system. The most simplistic example is a hard disk in a desktop computer or server. The main advantage of this is that response time is usually fast because the storage system is dedicated to one host. DAS systems can be made up of internal or external drives with the following connection types:

- Small Computer Storage Interface (SCSI)
- Parallel ATA (PATA) otherwise called *integrated drive electronics* (IDE)
- Serial ATA (SATA)
- Universal Serial Bus (USB)
- FireWire
- External Serial ATA (eSATA)

This storage method is economical, but it only provides storage for the attached system.

As servers are added to a network and the amount of data increases, more and more drives need to be added to individual servers to accommodate the additional data. In order to eliminate the need to constantly add storage capability to individual machines, a shared storage technology called *network attached storage* (NAS) can be used. A NAS is a storage system that shares network bandwidth with the standard server and the user traffic. NAS systems are easy to operate and maintain. The box usually comes ready to plug-in, and the hardware has some management functions along with the sharing capability. One of the main issues with a NAS system is the limitations of the network speed for accessing data. On a side note, although these units are used in environments investigators will examine, many of us use storage technology simply due to the sheer volume of data we process. In our experimentation, we did not find the particular NAS purchased suitable for processing forensic cases. We purchased several units with the intention of using them to

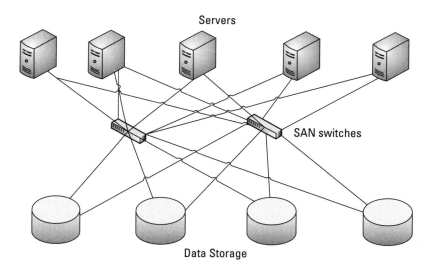

Servers

SAN switches

Data Storage

Figure 9.1 SAN Components

store images for use with Forensic Toolkit (FTK). The speed was extremely slow. The issue did not have to be with our network speed, but a problem with the way the box itself handled data. This problem could be inherent to the particular manufacturer.

With DAS, sharing data and resources may not be conducive to productivity, and with NAS systems, network performance can be slow. A storage area network, or SAN, is an architecture method of attaching remote storage to a server in such a way that the storage appears to be logically attached to the server. In a SAN, separate storage disks are grouped and consolidated in an array so that servers can access the array as though it were a local storage device. A SAN is comprised of components such as disk arrays and servers. Servers and storage are connected by a series of fiber-optic cables called a *SAN fabric*, as shown in Figure 9.1.

A SAN fabric has multiple connections that reduce downtime and help meet high-availability requirements. It also improves security by separating storage processes from normal network traffic. Due to the advantages of SANs, the virtualization of data storage has become popular.

Cluster File Systems

In a SAN file system, the storage is carved into individual chunks and allocated to different hosts. A block-level metadata manager controls access to the SAN devices. A cluster file system is a distributed file system. It is a cluster of servers that are combined to provide service to the clients where the file system software

Physical Drive

Storage Block	Storage Block	Storage Block	Storage Block	Storage Block	Storage Block
Storage Block	Storage Block	Storage Block	Storage Block	Storage Block	Storage Block
Storage Block	Storage Block	Storage Block	Storage Block	Storage Block	Storage Block
Storage Block	Storage Block	Storage Block	Storage Block	Storage Block	Storage Block
Storage Block	Storage Block	Storage Block	Storage Block	Storage Block	Storage Block
Storage Block	Storage Block	Storage Block	Storage Block	Storage Block	Storage Block
Storage Block	Storage Block	Storage Block	Storage Block	Storage Block	Storage Block
Storage Block	Storage Block	Storage Block	Storage Block	Storage Block	Storage Block
Storage Block	Storage Block	Storage Block	Storage Block	Storage Block	Storage Block
Storage Block	Storage Block	Storage Block	Storage Block	Storage Block	Storage Block
Storage Block	Storage Block	Storage Block	Storage Block	Storage Block	Storage Block
Storage Block	Storage Block	Storage Block	Storage Block	Storage Block	Storage Block
Storage Block	Storage Block	Storage Block	Storage Block	Storage Block	Storage Block
Storage Block	Storage Block	Storage Block	Storage Block	Storage Block	Storage Block

Figure 9.2 SAN Storage Blocks

handles storage requests. The storage space on each drive is logically divided into storage blocks, as shown in Figure 9.2, allowing individual drives and drive array storage units to be treated as part of a larger group.

The storage blocks are managed as a single virtual storage device called a *storage pool*. Managing storage this way allows storage space to be assigned as a group of storage blocks spanning different physical drives in that pool. This concept is considered virtual storage because it hides the underlying physical infrastructure of the storage. It abstracts the way a server sees storage from the way drives actually read and write.

VM File System

Depending on the technology, proprietary file systems may be used with this type of environment. For example, if using VMware ESX Server, a partition can be created and formatted with VMware's Virtual Machine File System (VMFS). VMFS is a distributed, clustered file system. VMware's white paper (2006), "Virtualization: Architectural Considerations and Other Evaluation Criteria," describes VMFS as a specialized file system that acts as a storage virtualization router from the perspective of the VM. It is a cluster file system that is used for multiple installations of

VMware ESX Server and is part of VMware Infrastructure 3. A clustered file system is a disk resource mounted as a local disk to multiple computers at the same time.

VMFS has many advantages including the following:

- Administrative oversight not required when creating new VMs
- Volume size can be adjusted without interrupting network operations
- ESX Servers can be added or removed from a VMFS volume without affecting other hosts
- The file and block sizes can be adjusted
- Can be used on Internet SCSI (iSCSI) or fiber-channel storage systems

Unlike Microsoft's Cluster Server, VMFS allows simultaneous access to the drives across multiple servers. VMFS has one primary distinction from some of the other cluster file systems, which is described in "Breaking down the vStorage Virtual Machine File System (VMFS)" by Vanover (2010). He explains that VMFS runs on each host cooperatively and directly manages the file system namespace to regulate access to files by clients. There is no server or software that inherently controls access to the file system. Also referenced is VMware Knowledge Base article 1001618, updated: Aug 14, 2009 that details some useful information about free space in the event VMFS had to be examined. There are hidden indexes and descriptors of the files on the file system, which cannot be deleted. These hidden files cause some free space to be missing from a newly created VMFS data store. From previous discussion, you know that in a cluster file system, all space is organized in collections of resources. In VFMS3, there are four resource types managed: file system blocks, sub-blocks, pointer blocks, and file descriptors. These are managed by the following system or VMFS metadata files:

- .fdc.sf – file descriptor system file
- .sbc.sf – sub-block system file
- .fbb.sf – file block system file
- .pbc.sf – pointer block system file
- .vh.sf – volume header system file

Vmkfstools is used to manipulate VMFS volumes and virtual disks. The data makeup of VMFS volumes is different from other file systems because it has a mixed block size. In order to be more efficient, VMFS uses a method to handle different file sizes that consists of file blocks and sub-blocks. The primary file blocks are selected when the volume is formatted. Sub-blocks are smaller allocations within the file system used to reduce internal fragmentation. Each VMFS3 volume will have 64KB sub-blocks carved out of the primary blocks. Figure 9.3 shows a VMFS volume formatted

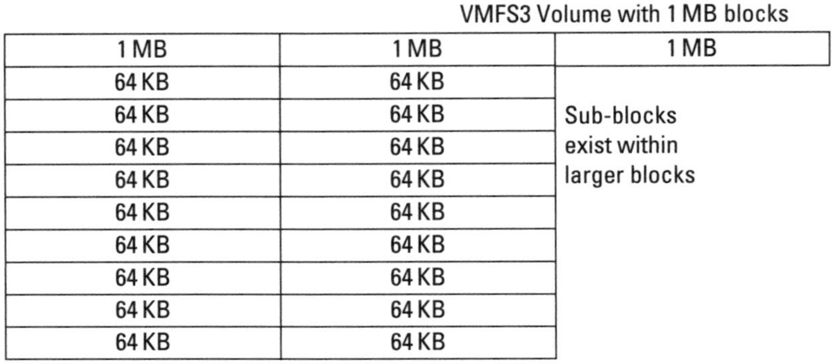

VMFS3 Volume with 1 MB blocks

1 MB	1 MB	1 MB
64 KB	64 KB	
64 KB	64 KB	Sub-blocks
64 KB	64 KB	exist within
64 KB	64 KB	larger blocks
64 KB	64 KB	
64 KB	64 KB	
64 KB	64 KB	
64 KB	64 KB	
64 KB	64 KB	

Figure 9.3 VMFS Mixed Block

with the 1 MB block size with several 64 KB blocks that accommodate the smaller files.

IBM's General Parallel File System

IBM General Parallel File System (GPFS) is used in scientific supercomputers and commercial applications requiring high-speed access to large volumes of data. It is capable of managing petabytes of data and billions of files.

Hadoop Distributed File System

The Hadoop Distributed File System (HDFS) is a distributed file system designed to run on hardware based on open standards or what is called *commodity hardware*. This means the system is capable of running different operating systems (OSes) such as Windows or Linux without requiring special drivers. HDFS has significant differences from other distributed file systems. It is not designed for user interaction. It is used for batch processing of applications that need streaming access to their datasets. The emphasis is on high throughput of data access rather than low latency of data access.

Lustre

In October 2007, Sun Microsystems acquired Cluster File Systems, Inc., including the Lustre file system. Lustre is an open-source object-based, distributed file system used in large-scale cluster computing. It is designed to enable I/O performance scaling and suitable where very high I/O bandwidth is required. A merging of the words Linux and cluster make up Lustre's name. It can support clusters of tens of thousands of nodes and petabytes of storage capacity.

Red Hat Global File System

Red Hat Global File System is supported for use with Red Hat Enterprise Linux (RHEL) OSes. It is an open-source cluster file system and volume manager for RHEL Servers attached to a SAN and is commonly used when Oracle databases are clustered using Oracle's Real Application Clusters (RACs) software.

Analysis of Cluster File Systems

Analysis of a cluster file system can be a bit tricky. Our forensic tools are made for analysis on individual computers, not huge data stores. The technology used to maximize efficiency may not be understood by our tools. A VM residing on a cluster file system can easily be acquired, and although efforts to capture the file system data may be successful, the underlying blocks may not be able to be analyzed by current tools. Hankeln (2008) posted a video documenting his process to extract data such as .iso, .vmdk, and .vmem files from a DELL Server with a RAID of SCSI disks formatted with VMFS that can be found on the Web site http://sanbarrow.com/latest-video-esxi-exe.html. The question an investigator needs to answer when dealing with cluster file systems is "What is really needed?" If the underlying file system is needed, you'll have to do some homework on dealing with these systems and how to read your image once it is acquired. Forensic analysis of VMFS is still developing.

VM Defragmentation

VMs are defragmented just like regular OSes. Defragmenting a VM that has an active snapshot will modify disk blocks and cause the snapshot file to grow rapidly. Due to the nature of the mixed block structure of VMFS, the data stores do fragment nearly as much as traditional file systems.

Security Considerations

Virtual environments present some of the same security challenges that physical environments do as well as challenges that are unique to the environment. This includes physically securing the files, malware infestation, and hypervisor security concerns.

Technical Guidance

VM infrastructures have been implemented by government agencies, corporations, and academic institutions. This widespread use has garnered the need for VM security configuration benchmarks and standards. There are two vendor-neutral guides available, which are as follows:

- The Center for Internet Security (CIS) has developed a commercial guide.
- Defense Information Systems Agency (DISA) has created a guide for U.S. government entities.

The "CIS Level 1 Benchmark for Virtual Machines" (2007) provides a consensus of best practices recommendations for hardening VMs with technical controls and configuration settings. The documentation assures that the minimum due care is always reflected in the recommended settings. The "Security Technical Implementation Guide (STIG)" (2001) is a series of individual sections covering a wide variety of topics. There are a few sections on VMs and virtual environments. Both of these are living documents and are updated on a regular basis. For example, in late October 2009, STIG was updated for Citrix XenApp. This documentation can provide guidance and insight to audits as well as administrators.

VM Threats

The CIS security benchmark report identifies several potential virtualization security threats but as the use of virtualization increases, other threats appear. The security of VMs is a concern because many VMs are hosted on one machine. Threats to a virtual environment consist of the following:

- Attacks on the physical machine
- Attacks on a VM
- Attacks on the hypervisor
- Denial of service (DoS)

For example, comingling VMs containing sensitive data with VMs that are used for general purpose or testing can compromise the VMs containing sensitive data if they're not configured correctly. Other security issues unique to VM environments are as follows:

- Virtual network adapters are enabled.
- Machines with different security contexts are tied to a single physical adapter.
- Patch levels between OSes may vary.
- Programs within VMs escape and affect the host.
- VMs can cause a DoS on the host by hogging resources.
- Shared clipboards can allow infection of the host machine and other VMs.
- VM logs are not secured.
- Uncontrolled external modification to VMs.
- Unsecured VM files allow theft of information.

There are many potential threats to the physical server, the VMs, and the hypervisor. At DefCon 15, Capelis (2007) presented on security issues in VMs and possible attack vectors including shared hardware attacks, covert channels, shared networking, and live migration. In 2007, this type of attack was proof of concept, but today, it is a reality. In December 2009, a Zeus botnet command and control center was discovered on a public cloud computing infrastructure. Investigation into the incident revealed that a VM Web server was exploited and was being used as a botnet control point.

Hypervisors

In addition to the threat of VM infection, hypervisor infection may be possible. This method to seize the host OS and gain control of its VMs is detailed in what is called the *blue pill*. This is based on the idea that the design of virtualization itself leaves a security flaw that can compromise the hypervisor and all the VMs running on the machine. Blue pill concepts along with red pill concepts will be discussed later in this chapter. Remember from Chapter 1, "How Virtualization Happens," that in paravirtualization, hypercalls are used. The hypercalls may not be checked by the hypervisor as to origin of the hypercall, leaving open the possibility of buffer overflows. Additionally, according to Cargile (2009), hypervisors can bypass the guest OS interface for remote setting changes. Just about every security reporting Web site posted information about Microsoft's Xbox 360 Privilege Escalation Vulnerability. The following is the report that was posted to www.securityfocus.com:

```
BugTraq ID: 22745
Remote: No
Date Published: 2007-02-27
Relevant URL: http://www.securityfocus.com/bid/22745
Summary:
The Microsoft Xbox 360 is prone to local privilege
   escalation vulnerability.
```

A local attacker may execute arbitrary code in "hypervisor" mode to completely compromise a vulnerable Xbox 360 gaming system.

Although the Xbox is not used in a corporate environment and Microsoft has since published a document on how to secure the hypervisor, it's possible that future hypervisor attacks may be successful. Due to the changes being made by vendors, hypervisor vulnerabilities may typically be exploited from malware that compromises a VM as opposed to direct hypervisor attacks.

The final concern is the fear of a VM escaping, whereby a VM breaks out of its isolation and maliciously interacts with the hypervisor. In an August 2008 presentation to the Arizona Security Practitioners Forum (AZSPF), Randell from VMware stated that there are currently no known hypervisor attack vectors that have lead to VM escape. As attacks on virtual environments become more common, the chances of having to investigate an environment where a VM flaw or incorrect configuration was exploited will increase.

Virtual Appliances

Virtual appliances are convenient and readily available. Taking a look at VMware's appliance marketplace, it is apparent that many of the appliances are provided by other contributors, and there are many versions of the same appliance. It is possibly that an appliance infected with malware can easily infect an entire network. Malware is discussed later in this chapter. Default logins and passwords associated with virtual appliances were discussed in Chapter 8, "Virtual Environments and Compliance." With virtual appliances, there is always the possibility of the appliance containing a backdoor.

The VM

We have made great strides in packing a lot of data on small devices. In early February 2010, the Kingston DataTraveler310 became available in the United States. It holds 256 GB of data. At a price of $1100.00, it won't be flying off the shelves, but to someone wanting to steal valuable data, it may be a small price to pay to be able to put that much data in a pocket and walk out the door unnoticed. As mentioned in previous chapters, because a VM is stored as single file, anyone with the appropriate access can easily copy the file. In "How to Steal a Virtual Machine and Its Data in 3 Easy Steps," Siebert (2010) sums up how to steal a VM as "Snap it, copy it, mount it." He goes on to walk through the process. In summary, the first step is to snapshot the VM. The second step is to copy the VM configuration file (.vmx) and the virtual disk file (.vmdk) and delete the snapshot. The final step is to mount and import the copied virtual disk. Although the steps are a bit more detailed, the article demonstrates how simple it is to take a VM that contains proprietary information if proper access controls are not put in place. Additionally, the file containing the in-memory contents of the

VM (.vmem) could be used to determine privileged account names and passwords.

Networking

Using virtual environments should be included in the network topology. As the use of VMs enables server consolidation, the principles of trusted zones should be applied as they are in the existing security infrastructure. In Chapter 8, "Virtual Environments and Compliance," we looked at implementing virtualization in a payment card industry (PCI) environment. There are many areas that require segregation and protection of data. In any physical environment, there are trust zones. According to a VMware white paper titled "Network Segmentation in Virtualized Environments," a trust zone is loosely defined as a network segment within which data flows relatively freely, whereas data flowing in and out of the trust zone is subject to stronger restrictions. Examples of trust zones include the following:

- Demilitarized zones (DMZs)
- PCI cardholder data environment
- Site-specific zones such as segmentation according to department or function
- Application-defined zones such as the three tiers of a Web application

In a virtual environment, trust zones are often crossed because one server holds many VMs and a trained administrator may merely look for a server that has space to host the VM, thereby putting it in a vulnerable position. In addition, there is a chance that the VM virtual network interface card (NIC) is accidentally placed in the wrong trust zone. As more and more organizations move to virtualization and consolidate physical servers, the virtual aspect of security needs to be addressed. VMs need to be secured in the same manner as physical machines. The network topology should include mapping out which virtual servers will reside on which physical servers and then establishing the level of trust that is required for each system. In addition, administrators should be trained in how to configure, secure, and place VMs in the proper trust zone.

Malware and Virtualization

The infection of VMs has been a topic of discussion since virtualization began its resurgence into the market. Various papers, presentations, and theoretical suppositions have been made in this area. The next few sections will discuss some of those topics along with the implications.

Detection

In a physical environment, in addition to installing antivirus on the machines, intrusion protection and detection systems (IPS/IDS) can be installed on the network. The dynamic nature of the virtualized environments presents new challenges for these systems. Remember that VMs are fluid files, and it can be difficult to maintain consistent security in this type of environment. The dynamic nature of the virtualized environments can result in VMs being introduced to the production environment without any security measures in place.

At VMworld 2008, VMware introduced a product called *VMsafe*. The premise behind the product is to give vendors a way to develop security products to protect applications running in VMs through application program interfaces (APIs). The intent of VMsafe technology is to prevent threats and attacks such as viruses, trojans, and keyloggers from ever reaching a VM. At the time of the announcement, 20 security vendors embraced VMsafe technology and committed to building products to enhance the security of VMs.

Based on the list of vendors that committed to VMware's VMsafe program, we can expect to see a wide range of security functions including antivirus, encryption, firewall, IDS/IPS, and system integrity. This would make it possible to finely tune VM monitoring and stop previously undetectable viruses, rootkits, and malware. In May 2009, VMware released Virtual Disk Development Kit (VDDK) 1.1, which is a disk API that allows other programs to access a VM's hard disk in a manner similar to VMware's Consolidated Backup solution. As of December 2009, there have been very few vendors, if any, that have released a product to market that uses the VMsafe program.

Based on this, it seems that the market is moving toward developing a tool that can help in the detection of malware in VMs.

Red Pill, Blue Pill, No Pill

You take the blue pill, the story ends, you wake up in your bed and believe whatever you want to believe. You take the red pill, you stay in Wonderland, and I show you how deep the rabbit hole goes.

This iconic line from the movie *The Matrix* was the inspiration for this portion of the chapter where we'll discuss red pills, blue pills, no pills, and other concepts. The purpose is to help an investigator understand a bit more about the inner workings of virtualization technology and how it might be possible to exploit it.

Blue Pill

A "blue pill" is the codename for a very controversial rootkit, which was researched and presented by Polish security specialist Rutkowska in 2006. A blue pill is a special type of malware that utilizes the virtualization techniques of certain CPUs to execute as a hypervisor. It induces as a virtual platform on which the entire OS runs. It is capable of examining the entire state of the machine and allowing the perpetrator full privilege while the OS thinks it is running directly on physical hardware. The basic idea behind the blue pill is that a piece of malware that also was a VM monitor (VMM) could be created, take over the host OS and be undetected by remaining within the VMM. There are some issues with this theory, including the following:

1. Having a VMM take over a host OS would be very difficult.
2. The malware would have to prevent the OS from being able to detect that it was now a VM.

Red Pill and No Pill

A "red pill" is the opposite of the blue pill in that red pill techniques help the OS to detect the presence of a hypervisor. The red pill is a small piece of code that, when run on a VM, focuses on detecting VM usage without looking for file system artifacts based on relocation of sensitive data structures. In short, it's able to determine if it is running in a virtual system or a real, physical system. This theory is based CPU instruction sets and how they are handled when a hypervisor is involved and takes advantage of a CPU instruction that usually does not need to be called from ring 3. In a VM, this instruction returns a pointer to a different location than when running natively. In virtualized environments, there are two OSes. In a normal environment, there are sensitive data structures that are associated with *an* OS. In other words, there is no accommodation for two OSes. There is only a single interrupt descriptor table (IDT) register, but there are at least two OSes running concurrently, so the VMM relocates the registers for the guest OS so that it will not conflict with the host's OS. A single-machine language instruction store interrupt descriptor table (SIDT) is run in user mode that takes the location of the interrupt descriptor table register (IDTR) and stores it in memory. Rutkowska's research shows that on VMware, the relocated address of the IDT is at address 0×ff*XXXXXX*, whereas on Virtual PC, it is at 0×e8*XXXXXX*. This was tested on VMware Workstation 4 and Virtual PC 2004, both running on a Windows XP host OS (Rutkowska, 2004).

The no-pill variation by Offensive Computing took red pill's SIDT-CPU instruction and replaced it with store global descriptor table (SGDT). In "Attacks on More Virtual Machine Emulators," Ferrie (2007) discusses this concept and furthers the research. VMware makes use of the local descriptor table (LDT), which is not otherwise used by Windows, so he found a simple detection method for VMware to check for a nonzero LDT base on Windows OSes. Ferrie also found that the red pill and no pill methods for detecting VMware are unreliable on machines with multiple CPUs. Ferrie determined that the Scoopy Doo method uses the same basic idea as the red pill method, but it compares the IDT base value to specific hard-coded values in order to identify VMware specifically. Scoopy runs SIDT, SGDT, and SLDT. While the Scoopy Doo method is less likely to trigger false-positives as to the red pill method, there is still a chance that some false-positives will occur (Ferrie, 2007.).

In 2009, Charette posted "How not to detect virtualization" in which he conducted testing in how to detect virtualization from within a user-mode application, based on the red pill and no pill theories with the following specifications:

• Takes place within a user-mode application
• Must work from within Linux (specifically, Ubuntu 9.10)
• Must work with all of the popular consumer virtualization products (VMware Player, VirtualBox, and so on)
  Here are his findings:
  Using these methods, two things have happened that render this test useless:

1. Virtualization products have got better at doing what they do.
2. The data returned by the CPU instruction is actually a per-CPU or per-core table vector. This means that even in nonvirtualized environments, if you have multiple cores or CPUs, this test now returns false-positives. For example, on a quad-core system running natively, and assuming even distribution across all cores, 75% of the time this test will tell you it is running in a virtual environment.

This concurs with Ferrie's research in regard to the use of these methods with multiple core CPUs.

Other Rootkits

The discussion in this section would not be complete without discussing two other VM rootkits, Vitriol and SibVirt. In "SubVirt: Implementing Malware with Virtual Machines," King et al. (2006)

discuss a type of malware, called a *VM-based rootkit* (VMBR). This rootkit installs a VMM underneath an existing OS and moves the original OS into a VM. This is a principle similar to blue pill. Their proof of concept implemented VMBRs on both Windows XP and Linux, and we implemented four example malicious services using the VMBR platform. They also used what they learned to explore ways to defend against this type of rootkit. The initial step is access with privileges to modify the system boot sequence. Next, the VMBR is stored somewhere on the hard drive. King et al. stored the VMBR state in the beginning of the first active disk partition in their target Windows XP system. Then the rootkit can insert itself beneath the existing system, by manipulating the system boot sequence. This will allow it to load before the target OS and applications. After loading VMBR, it boots the target OS using the VMM. Then, it can run malicious services.

Vitriol is a hardware VM rootkit for Mac OS X using Intel VT-x on Intel Core Duo/Solo processors. "Hardware Virtualization Rootkits" was presented by Goldsmith, Rauch, Ptacek, Snyder, and Zovi at Black Hat in 2006. This presentation details a hardware-based rootkit that targeted the Intel VT-x technology on the Core Duo and Solo processor technology. They discovered that the entire OS-visible state of the processor is swapped in and out of memory. In addition, VMs can have direct memory and device access (Goldsmith et al., 2006). They combined this with the fact that the processor operates in two different modes, but does not have a hardware bit or register that indicates that the processor is running in VMX nonroot mode to provide a demonstration on how these factors would allow a rootkit to be installed. At the time of this presentation, there were issues with being able to recreate this in an environment with multiple cores, which is the same issue many of the other exploit methods developed ran into.

Other Methods of Finding VMs

Some simpler methods of locating VMs by malware programs are to look for VM tools and VM-specific hardware. VM tools leave a large footprint including running processes and services and registry keys. Some instances of the phatbot malicious code look for these items. Malware may also look for specific virtualized hardware such as network and audio adapters. So despite the methods that have been developed to detect and insert malware in VMs, the ever-changing world of technology and virtualization had made many of them obsolete. Remember in Chapter 7, "Finding and Imaging Virtual Environments," we discussed methods used to detect if an environment is real or virtual. Two of the tools used were Scoopy Doo and Jerry, which are software based. Scoopy

Doo's method of detection was discussed in the "Red Pill No Pill" section. The Doo tool by Tobias Klein, who was also the author of Scoopy, looks for virtualized hardware. The Linux version checks for the string "VMware" associated with I/O, ports, and SCSI in the virtual/proc directory and looks for kernel messages or boot messages mention VMware-specific hardware. The Windows version checks the following registry keys for VMware associations:

```
HKEY_LOCAL_MACHINE\SYSTEM\ControlSet001\Control\Class\
    {4D36E968-E325-11CE-BFC1-08002BE10318}\0000\DriverDesc
HKEY_LOCAL_MACHINE\SYSTEM\ControlSet001\Control\Class\
    {4D36E968-E325-11CE-BFC1-08002BE10318}\0000\ProviderName
HKEY_LOCAL_MACHINE\HARDWARE\DEVICEMAP\Scsi\Scsi Port 0\
    Scsi Bus 0\Target Id 0\Logical Unit Id 0\Identifier
HKEY_LOCAL_MACHINE\HARDWARE\DEVICEMAP\Scsi\Scsi Port 1\
    Scsi Bus 0\Target Id 0\Logical Unit Id 0\Identifier
```

Another method to detect VMs is to analyze the processor for VM behavioral characteristics. Two VME processor anomalies are used to identify VMEs: looking for support for nonstandard VME machine language instructions and identifying a guest-to-host communication channel (Liston & Skoudis, 2006). VMDetect, Jerry, and checkvm are all tools that use this techniques as well as various malware. The methods are described in detail in "On the Cutting Edge: Thwarting Virtual Machine Detection," by Liston and Skoudis. Realize that like the rest of the methods described, they were developed in 2006. As one can see, 2006 was a busy year for research into VMs and how they work. Since then, processor and VM technology have changed immensely, and these methods may not be successful in locating VMs.

Additional Challenges

Encryption

As of January 2010, there is no native encryption of .vmdk files when using VMware's vSphere. However, when Workstation 7 was released, in late 2009, .vmdk file encryption was an option. This may be a sign of things to come with other VMware products. This does not mean that as an investigator you will not run into an encrypted VM, it merely means that built-in encryption capabilities are just starting to become mainstream. Users and administrators have options available to encrypt virtual products from VirtualBox to VMware storage volumes (VMFS). The options available can include the following:

- An encrypted hard drive solution such as TrueCrypt or PointSec

- Encrypt the individual files
- Use hard drives that come with built-in encryption

For example, in 2008, Seagate announced a data encryption technology on their Momentus laptop hard drives that can encrypt drives without the need of software or custom installation. At that time, DELL was interested in using the technology, which provides different levels of security based on whether the use is a home environment or corporate environment. In order to activate Advanced Encryption Standard (AES) encryption, the home user installs the drive and enters a BIOS password. Encryption is becoming more common and with it comes the challenge of being able to access data on an encrypted drive. This is another case for live acquisitions. VMs are no different than physical machines in this respect. VMs can be placed on a TrueCrypt hidden volume just as any other data can. Vendors that provide virtual solutions may already provide an encryption method. For example, InstallFree converts a Windows machine into an encrypted VM file.

Solid-State Drives

Solid-state drives (SSDs) are becoming more typical in investigations. If you have not run into one yet, you will. They are mostly found in netbooks, which are popular due to their size and cost. But with the price for SSDs dropping and the number of suppliers increasing, it is possible that entire databases are going to be running in-memory. In December 2009, Seagate released the Pulsar, a 2.5-inch on-server drive. Other vendors that entered the SSD enterprise solutions market before Seagate include STEC with its fiber-channel interface ZeusIOPS product and Intel with its X25 product. In addition, Western Digital is planning to move into the enterprise SSD space. Many drive manufactures, both large and small, are coming out with new techniques to improve the read and write performances of SSDs, making them more attractive.

When examining netbooks, there are some items to keep in mind. First, not all live CDs will boot on an Eee PC. The investigator may have to try several different disks in order to get the machine to boot. In shops where all acquisitions are done by actually removing the hard drive from the machine, depending on the model, it may take longer to disassemble the netbook and remove the drive than it does to actually image the drive. Reassembly can also require a bit of time. The read accuracy decreases after a certain number of reads possibly making carving difficult. The internal data structure is not well understood and may contain hidden data useful in forensics.

"Data Recovery and Information about Solid State Devices and NAND Flash Memory" is a presentation from DefCon16 in the summer of 2008 (Moulton, 2008). It is a five part, hour-long, YouTube video that details about 2 years of research about how these devices work: www.youtube.com/view_play_list?p=C337FACBF12BDCE2

New File Systems and Disk Types

As technology evolves, new file systems are developed and implemented. Earlier in this chapter, we explored VMFS. With the advent of Vista SP1, Microsoft released exFAT support for desktop and server OSes. It was originally used for embedded devices in Windows Embedded CE 6.0 and is designed for removable drives. It's important to understand new file systems and how they work. More importantly, it is imperative to know whether the tool you are using can understand the file system you are feeding it. As of December 2009, some of the commercial tools used for analysis support the exFAT file system.

In addition to new technologies such as SSDs, which we discussed previously, there may be a technology specific to a particular vendor that is not hardware related. For example, VMware ESX VMs use three disk types for file storage: raw, thick, and thin.

- Raw disks have direct access to a logical unit number (LUN) on a SAN.
- Thick disks are set physical space allocations and may have not been cleared of previous data.
- Thin disks are useful for conserving disk space on a VMFS volume.

Compression and Data Deduplication

The amount of data any organization store grow exponentially as VMs are created and implemented. When using SAN technology, most larger organizations will implement real-time compression and deduplication in an effort to reduce the amount of primary storage required. The data deduplication process identifies and finds redundant blocks of data across a volume and then stores only one copy of that block. Data deduplication can significantly reduce the amount of data that needs to be acquired as well as examined.

Real-time compression compresses and decompresses all data regardless of how much commonality there is between blocks. Although deduplication removes duplicate data, in dealing with certain types of data, such as databases, compression will produce better storage efficiency than deduplication. When compression is used, the investigator may encounter an in-line compression appliance such as the one offered by Peribit, which is a rack-mounted hardware appliance.

Virtualization Drawbacks

Some of the drawbacks associated with virtual environments are listed below. These have all been discussed in Chapter 8, "Advanced Virtualization" and are here merely to provide a list for investigators to be aware of as they investigate these environments.

- Server sprawl – Server sprawl is a situation in which multiple, underutilized servers take up more space and consume more resources than can be justified by their workload.
- Tackling server sprawl – Server sprawl may be confined to a single server room, but it can, in some cases, be spread across multiple facilities in widespread geographical locations, especially in cases where one company has acquired another one or where two companies have merged.
- Potential conflicts from resource sharing – In a complex virtual environment, even in a not so complex one, resources have to be shared between hypervisors and this can sometimes lead to performance-slowing conflicts or even system crashes.
- Software provisioning – It is the process of preparing and equipping a network to allow it to provide software services to its users. Much like resource sharing, there are finite resources for a specific number of users and sometimes demand outweighs supply.
- Nonstandardization of protocols, formats, and programming interfaces – Different protocols and interfaces create additional workload for a virtual environment, and this can lead to reduced performance, data corruption, or outright incompatibility in extreme cases.
- Software licensing and auditing – Virtualization can have an immediate and direct effect on software licensing schemes that are based on a traditional client-server environment, which if not managed properly could lead to licensing violations.
- Security – Security in a virtual environment can add new problems to existing ones. Aside from adding an additional OS, which must also be patched and maintained, traditional intrusion detection systems don't work on virtual servers and malware can be spread among virtual servers.

Summary

In this chapter, we have discussed data center technologies and how they relate to virtual environments. This includes storage and storage considerations such as DAS, NAS, and SAN technologies and VMFS. We covered security considerations such as trusted zones, hypervisors, and networking components. Malware and rootkit threats to the virtual environment along with the concepts behind many of these threats were also discussed. Finally, we covered some of the drawbacks associated with using virtual environments.

References

Capelis, D. J. (2007). Virtualization: Enough holes to work Vegas. *Defcon 15*, Las Vegas. Retrieved from http://www.dc414.org/download/confs/defcon15/Speakers/Capelis/dc-15-%20capelis.pdf

Cargile, A. (2009). Hypervisor security concerns. *The Coffee Desk*. Retrieved from http://thecoffeedesk.com/news/index.php/2009/12/01/hypervisor-security-concerns/

Charette, S. (2009). How not to detect virtualization. Retrieved from http://charette.no-ip.com:81/programming/2009-12-30_Virtualization/

Kirch, J. (Ed.). (2007). Virtual machine security guidelines (version 1). *The Center for Internet Security*. Retrieved from http://www.cisecurity.org/tools2/vm/CIS_VM_Benchmark_v1.0.pdf

Ferrie, P. (2007). Attacks on more virtual machine emulators. *Symantic Advanced Threat Research*. Retrieved from www.symantec.com/avcenter/reference/Virtual_Machine_Threats.pdf

Hankeln video. (2008). Retrieved from http://sanbarrow.com/latest-videoesxi-exe.html.

King, S. T., Chen, P. M., Wang, Y.-M., Verbowski, C., Wang, H. J., & Lorch, J. R. (2006). SubVirt: implementing malware with virtual machines. Retrieved from http://portal.acm.org/citation.cfm?id=1130383

Liston, T., & Skoudis, E. (2006). On the cutting edge: Thwarting virtual machine. *IntelGuardians*. Retrieved from http://handlers.sans.org/tliston/ThwartingVMDetection_Liston_Skoudis.pdf

Moulton, S. (2008, August). Data recovery and information about solid state devices and NAND flash memory. Video posted to www.youtube.com/view_play_list?p=C337FACBF12BDCE2

Rutkowska, J. (2004, November). Red Pill... or how to detect VMM using (almost) one CPU instruction. Retrieved from http://invisiblethings.org/papers/redpill.html

Siebert, E. (2010, January 7). How to steal a virtual machine and its data in 3 easy steps. *SearchVMware.com*. Retrieved from http://searchvmware.techtarget.com/news/article/0,289142,sid179_gci1378347,00.html

STIG Security Technical Implementation Guides. (2001). Information Assurance Support Environment. Retrieved from http://iase.disa.mil/stigs/stig/index.html

Vanover, R. (2010). Breaking down the vStorage Virtual Machine File System (VMFS). *SearchVMware.com*. Retrieved from http://searchvmware.techtarget.com/tip/0,289483,sid179_gci1368383_mem1,00.html

VMware. (2006). Virtualization: architectural considerations and other evaluation criteria. http://www.vmware.com/pdf/virtualization_considerations.pdf

Bibliography

VM File System

VMware knowledge base. Some space missing from a new VMFS data store due to hidden files. http://kb.vmware.com/selfservice/microsites/search.do?language=en_US&cmd=displayKC&externalId=1001618

Install and Configure ESX server. http://virtualizationinformation.com/docs/Notes%20on%20VI%203.pdf

Analysis of Cluster File Systems

VM Defragmentation

Defragmenting virtual machine files. http://itknowledgeexchange.techtarget.com/virtualization-pro/defragmenting-virtual-machine-disk-files/

Hypervisors

VMware, Randell. August 2008 presentation to the Arizona Security Practitioners Forum (AZSPF)

Xen Wiki Hypercall formal definition

Security

Haletky, E. (2009). *VMware vSphere and Virtual Infrastructure Security*. Prentice Hall.

Networking

Network segmentation in virtualized environments. VMware white paper. http://www.vmware.com/files/pdf/network_segmentation.pdf

CLOUD COMPUTING AND THE FORENSIC CHALLENGES

Cloud computing and all the various flavors and uses of this technology, such as Desktops-as-a-Service (DaaS) and streaming operating systems (OSes), are like the other virtualization methods we've discussed so far in this book and have huge potential for dramatically simplified information technology (IT) infrastructure with greater security and more cost-effective IT management and utilization.

The uses of cloud computing, DaaS, and streaming OSes are promising, but when you get past the marketing brochures, there are still considerable challenges. Some of them are technical; for example, performance challenges to those users who are distributed across a country or the globe. Some desktop virtualization products do use networking protocols designed for wide area networks, but even they have two big challenges: bandwidth and latency. Bandwidth will obviously limit the amount of data that can be transmitted, as well as limiting the number of users who can access the virtualized environment. Latency prevents applications from performing as though they were local to a traditional desktop. Then, there are the social challenges: the various comfort levels associated with the idea of outsourcing all networking operations and how it affects day-to-day operations in an organization. For some, it is the perfect solution, and for others, it looms as a legal and liability nightmare.

In the following sections, we'll take a closer look at how cloud computing, Platform-as-a-Service (PaaS), and streaming OSes work, and what their implications are for the IT world and forensic investigations.

What Is Cloud Computing?

Cloud computing has two distinct meanings. The first, and probably the most common meaning, is simply the use of a commercial service delivered over the Internet, in real time, from storage to Web applications. The second refers to the actual architecture of cloud computing and the necessary technology to deliver cloud services. These technologies can be combined in a variety of ways depending on the service being delivered. The term *cloud* computing came from the cloud symbol that is commonly used to represent the Internet in network diagrams. Cloud computing has become one of the new hot things in the IT community over the past couple of years, yet the concepts of cloud computing can be traced back to the modern computer's mainframe ancestors where multiple users were given small slices of the computer time to run whatever program they needed to run. It is a paradigm shift that, like the graphical user interface on a common desktop, abstracts the details of what's going on in the background from users who no longer need knowledge of, or expertise in, or even direct control over the technology infrastructure they are using. It is an interesting transition that is merely another indicator of how prevalent computers are in every facet of modern life.

A cloud service has several distinct characteristics that differentiate it from traditional hosting, which are as follows:

1. Cloud computing is very flexible. It is an on-demand self-service that is sold based on the needs of the user, usually in minute-by-minute or hour-by-hour increments. As with all successful services, it is designed to fit the needs of the users and adjust with them. As this book has outlined so far, virtualization is maturing rapidly, and like many other technologies used today, there is a convergence of functionality. Cloud computing is the blending of virtualization, distributed computing, and prevalent high-speed bandwidth. The last big motivator for cloud computing has been the weak economy of 2008 to 2009, which has created practical interest in this method of computing due to reduced budgets.

2. The cloud can be public. A public cloud is a service that is sold to anyone over the Internet. The largest and most recognized public cloud provider is Amazon Web Services (AWS). Public cloud computing providers offer virtual servers with assigned Internet Protocol (IP) addresses and chunks of storage space based on the user's needs.

3. The cloud can also be private. A private cloud is often a proprietary network that provides hosted services in the same way a public cloud does, only to a limited number of users.

4. Cloud computing has broad network access. Its capabilities and resources need to be available over a network and accessible through standard computing platforms whether it be a PC, smartphone, or PDA.

5. Cloud computing is resource pooling. A cloud environment, whether public or private, uses a pooled base of resources to serve multiple customers or users using the "multitenant" model with different physical and virtual resources assigned and reassigned based on user demand. This pooling of resources also creates a location-independent environment where the user has no control or knowledge over the exact physical location of the resources that are being provided but may be able to specify a location on a higher, logical level, such as by state, region, or data center.

Multitenancy

This is not a formal characteristic of cloud computing, but it is an important element to understand and be aware of. From a provider's perspective, multitenancy is the design approach to enable scalability, availability, management, segmentation/isolation, and operational efficiency by leveraging the shared infrastructure across many different users.

Cloud Computing Services

There are many types of cloud computing services that are available today; below is a list of the ones you are likely to encounter.

Infrastructure-as-a-Service

Infrastructure-as-a-Service (IaaS) is the delivery of computer infrastructure in a hosted service model over the Internet. This method of cloud computing allows the client to literally outsource everything that would normally be in a typical IT department. Data center space, servers, networking equipment, and software can all be purchased as a service. IaaS follows the same model as power and water; you're billed for how much you use, so it falls under the category of "utility computing."

IaaS implementations typically have the following:

- Internet connectivity: the foundational service for the other services
- Computer networking: including dedicated IP addresses, firewalls, load balancing, and so on
- Clustered servers or grid computing: a lot of computing resources often from different domains whose resources are pooled for a specific purpose
- Hardware virtualization: the virtualization of a computer or OS

Platform-as-a-Service

PaaS is the delivery of a computing platform, often an OS with associated services, over the Internet without downloads or installation. Often, PaaS systems are development platforms designed to operate specifically in the cloud environment. GoogleApps is an example of PaaS.

PaaS implementations typically have the following:

- Integrated development environment services: there are many variations of PaaS offerings with the most all-inclusive having an integrated development environment with all the necessary source code, version controls, and audit capabilities.
- Interface creation tools
- Web and database integration

Desktops-as-a-Service

DaaS is the technology that delivers virtual desktop images to end-user desktops as a subscription service. The intent of DaaS is to attempt to leverage the best of PCs while removing the inefficiencies in a corporate environment. One of the earliest developers of this concept was Deskstone, and in 2009, IBM announced the availability of the industry's first public desktop cloud service.

DaaS works by leveraging both machine virtualization and remote computing technologies. While corporate PCs have become a fixture in any IT department, they are required to deliver more and more critical applications and services to their users.

The DaaS model addresses some of the bigger challenges associated with the management of physical PCs in the modern work environment:

- IMAC: while it is also a line of computers from Apple, in this instance IMAC refers to Install-Move-Add-Change. While many PC management functions have been automated, there are still some that require an actual person to carry out, such as moving a PC or upgrading its components.

- Underutilization: the average x86 server is used to about 10 to 15 percent of capacity, and the average PC utilization is less than 5 percent.
- Cost: PCs depreciate in value about 50 percent per year.
- Security: PCs and laptops are getting smaller and therefore more portable thus making the data they carry far easier to steal.

The DaaS model also addresses other limitations of physical machines. Modern business has continued to evolve thanks to the communication advances in the 1990s. Telecommuting has become commonplace in many industries, and the expectation of employees to be able to work at anytime from anywhere has put a much greater demand on IT departments for flexibility and reliability. The factors of mobility, availability, and the separation of personal and business computing are all reasons behind the focus and development of DaaS. DaaS offers many of the same benefits as traditional virtual machine (VM) technologies such as easier desktop deployment, improved security and compliance, and customizable systems based on the user.

However, there are also significant challenges with this technology that have yet to allow for its wide-scale adoption. Some of these include the outright complexity of some of the desktop solutions that require the utilization of numerous software tools. Cost structures and operational complexity also rank as big challenges to the DaaS solution. It's these problems that create the interesting and difficult transition phase that exists now between enabling a PC to accept a network-delivered service and outsourcing the entire infrastructure to a service provider.

Software-as-a-Service

Software-as-a-Service (SaaS) is the delivery of a licensed application to customers over the Internet for use as a service on demand. A SaaS vendor will host an application and allow the customer to download the application for a set period of time, after which the application becomes inactive. This model is useful for individuals and businesses to have the right to access a certain application without having to purchase a full license. This model creates an on-demand licensing environment, which allows for all the benefits of the full application without the large up-front costs and maintenance associated with traditional software purchases.

SaaS architectures are classified into one of four levels:

- Custom: at this level, each user has his or her own customized version of the application that runs on the host servers.
- Configurable: at this level, users can separate instances out of the same application rather than being constrained to just their own version of the application.

- Configurable, Multitenant-efficient: this builds on the previous level by allowing a single application to serve all users.
- Scalable, Configurable, Multitenant-efficient: this level adds scalability to the previous level allowing for load balancing and the increasing or decreasing of system capacity based on user demand.

Other Cloud Computing Services

This section includes brief descriptions of other cloud computing services.

Storage-as-a-Service is the capability of using storage that exists at a remote site but appears as a local, logical storage to any application that needs it. This is one of the most basic components of cloud computing.

Database-as-a-Service is the capability of using the services of a remotely hosted database. This includes the capability to share data with others as well as the appearance that the database is local. There are many different models of this service, but the real value of this type of cloud computing is being capable of using high-end database technology that would typically cost thousands of dollars in hardware and software license fees.

Information-as-a-Service is the capability of consuming any type of remotely hosted information through a well-defined interface such as an application program interface (API). Some examples of this kind of cloud computing is stock price information and address lookup.

Process-as-a-Service is a remote resource that can bind several different resources together. An example of this would be services and data, hosted in the same or different clouds, brought together to create a business process. This allows for the creation of meta-applications that span several systems and leverage key services and information, combining them into a new sequence to meet a specific customer or organizational need. Since processes are easier to adjust than applications, this approach provides a great deal of agility to those who need this kind of process engine.

Integration-as-a-Service is the capability of delivering a complete integration stack from a cloud environment. Essentially this provides many of the same functions as other enterprise application integration technology, except they are delivered as a service.

Security-as-a-Service is the capability of delivering core security services remotely. At present, many of the typical cloud security services are very basic, but more sophisticated services are becoming available.

Management-as-a-Service is an on-demand cloud service that provides the capability of managing other cloud services.

Typically this service allows for the management of topology, resource utilization, and virtualization.

Testing-as-a-Service is the capability of testing both local and cloud applications using testing software and services that are hosted in the cloud. This system may see a lot of use in the future, as it is capable of testing other cloud applications and Web sites.

In the following section, we'll step out of the cloud environment for a bit to discuss three other virtualization methods that are in use today. While these technologies can certainly be used in a cloud environment, it is not a requirement. The virtualization methods we're going to look at are streaming OSes, application streaming, and virtual applications.

Streaming Operating Systems

Full streaming of an OS is also a new approach to desktop virtualization that is making its way into the mainstream IT community. A streaming OS provides the same benefit as a virtualized desktop but with more use of the desktop hardware in a traditional manner. With a streaming OS, an end user downloads a complete package, OS, and applications. This gives distributed users the advantages of a full operating system with the benefits of customization, security, as well as patches and updates. The trade-off with this architecture is similar to that of other virtualization models: the greater the distance, the slower the performance.

Some good uses of streaming OSes are as follows:

- Diskless workstations with streaming OSes that are used for sensitive or classified work environments. With this model, there is no need for lockdown protocols or secure storage for hard drives. The diskless client system increases security, and the network storage aspect allows for indefinite scalability.
- OS streaming could be used quite effectively in an education environment where configuration and maintenance costs can be prohibitive.
- OS streaming, much like a virtual desktop environment, can make the introduction of a new OS much easier. Users can be offered choices allowing for the selection of which OS they want to use based on their needs at that time.

Application Streaming

The easiest way to think of application streaming is as a form of "on-demand" software delivery. The reason behind this approach to virtualization is that most applications require only a small fraction of their total program code to run. Much like progressive video or audio downloads from YouTube or Pandora, application streaming is designed to be completely transparent to the end user.

The way this works is the server sends the client enough information to launch the application, which is often as little as 10 percent of the total application. The rest is then streamed to the client in the background while the user is working. Application streaming uses the Real-Time Streaming Protocol and is often used in conjunction with desktop virtualization.

Application streaming is a great advantage for IT administrators, as they can now give users a license to an application only when they need it. The users are streamed the application while they are using it, and then, it is uninstalled once they are finished.

Some additional advantages of application streaming are as follows:
- Easier OS migrations
- Quicker application deployment
- Central management of applications
- Full-featured desktop applications as opposed to Web based
- Optimized software licenses

Virtual Applications

Application virtualization is a general term that describes software that improves the portability, manageability, and compatibility of applications by abstracting them from the underlying OS on which they are executed. A fully virtualized application is not installed in the usual way, but it is still executed as if it is. The application operates as though it is directly interfacing with the original OS and all the resources managed by it, when in reality it is not. Application virtualization is different from platform virtualization in that with platform virtualization the whole OS is virtualized as opposed to only specific applications.

Benefits and Limitations of Virtual Applications
Benefits
- Application are allowed to run in environments that do not suit the native application.
- In some cases, virtual applications can protect the OS from poorly written code.
- Incompatible applications are capable of running side by side.

- Security and stability are improved by isolating the application from the OS.
- Virtual applications use fewer resources than a VM.

Limitations

- Not all applications can be virtualized, specifically those applications that still require heavy OS integration.

Cloud Computing, Virtualization, and Security

Cloud services at the infrastructure, platform, or software level often go hand-in-hand with virtualization in order to create economies of scale. However, combining these technologies does create some additional security concerns. We have discussed several types of virtualization so far in this book, but for this section, we will be focusing on the virtualized OS and some of the specific security risks associated with it, which are compartmentalization, network security, and centralization. We'll look at each in turn:

- Compartmentalization: specifically, if VM technology is being used in cloud services, it is very important to ensure that appropriate compartmentalization of virtual environments is happening and that the VM systems themselves are being hardened.
- Network security: since VMs communicate over hardware that simulates a network environment, standard network security controls have no capability of seeing this traffic and cannot perform monitoring functions. Network security needs to take on a new form in the virtual environment.
- Centralization: while centralizing services and storage has security benefits to be sure, in this instance, there is now the problem of centralizing risk that increases the consequences of a breach. Another concern with this kind of centralization is the different levels of sensitivity and security that each of the VMs may need. In cloud environments, typically the lowest common level of security is the standard in a multitenant environment, which can quickly lead to insufficient security for VMs requiring more.

Some questions to consider when looking at virtualization from a cloud provider include the following:

- What types of virtualization do they use, if any?
- What security controls are in place on the VM beyond just hypervisor isolation?
- What security controls are in place external to the VM?

- What is the integrity of the VM image being offered by the cloud provider?
- What reporting mechanisms are in place providing evidence of isolation?

Cloud Computing and Forensics

This section looks at cloud computing from two important distinctions. The first is conducting a forensic investigation "on" the cloud environment, a daunting challenge under the best of circumstances. The section afterwards discusses using a cloud environment "for" a forensic investigation.

Conducting a Forensic Investigation on a Cloud Environment

Cloud computing will have a considerable impact on how digital forensics is approached and conducted, that much is certain. What has yet to be fully realized is what these impacts will look like. Currently there are a number of obstacles to conducting a forensic investigation "in" the cloud, much less "on" the cloud. Factors like the law, court-approved methods, standard operating procedures for investigators, the involvement of a third party – the cloud provider – and a list of others stand in the way of a modern digital forensics investigator conducting a successful investigation in a cloud environment. Part of the problem is simply the old rules of investigation don't apply. A perfect example of this is the differences between traditional hard drive forensics and mobile forensics. An investigator has to treat mobile devices very differently than he or she would treat a seized hard drive, as one is live and active, and the other is not, and watching the transition within the industry has been a gradual process with a lot of frustration and ruined evidence along the way. Cloud computing will be no different.

Gartner warns that "Investigating inappropriate or illegal activity may be impossible in cloud computing. Cloud services are especially difficult to investigate, because logging and data for multiple customers may be co-located and may also be spread across an ever-changing set of hosts and data centers. If you cannot get a contractual commitment to support specific forms of investigation – along with evidence that the vendor has already successfully supported such activities – then your only safe assumption is that investigation and discovery requests will be impossible." While this is a dire warning, there are options available to the investigator, just not as many (at present) as are available with traditional digital forensic investigations. In the next section, we'll look at how to prepare for incident responses in a cloud environment.

Incident Response

The nature and architecture of cloud computing creates some new difficulties in determining who to contact in the event of an intrusion, security incident, data breach, or any other event that requires a response and investigation. Established incident response procedure and techniques can be used, with some modification, to address the changes that result from shared reporting responsibilities.

One of the biggest problems for the cloud computing customer is that many applications that are deployed in the cloud environment are not always designed with security and data integrity in mind. As with noncloud applications that lack security and integrity features, this may result in vulnerabilities on the applications being deployed in the cloud, thus creating security incidents. Significant risks to cloud operations can also arise from flaws in the cloud architecture, errors made during system hardening procedures, and other oversights.

Organizations will need to have a strong understanding of the incident response strategy for the cloud provider they intend to use. This incident response strategy should address identification and notification and have options for correcting problems associated with unauthorized access to data. Another point to be aware of is that application data management and access can have different meanings and fall under different regulations based on where the data is located, specifically in different states or countries. This added complication makes incident identification very challenging in this environment.

Here is a list of recommendations in order to be more prepared for incident responses within the cloud:

- Customers need to clearly communicate and define to cloud providers what they consider incidents as opposed to suspicious events.
- Customers should have prearranged lines of communication to the cloud provider's incident response team.
- Customers should ensure that the cloud provider's incident detection and analysis tools are compatible with their own systems. Proprietary formats can become huge time wasters in an investigation, particularly if it is a joint investigation with legal or government entities.

- Customers should look for cloud providers that can deliver snapshots of the customer's entire virtual environment for offline analysis.
- Any sensitive data that would violate a regulation in the event of a breach should be encrypted.
- Choose multitenant incident response tools. Currently there are application-level firewalls, proxies, and other logging tools that assist in incident response in the cloud.

Conducting a Forensic Investigation in a Cloud Environment

Cloud computing holds some interesting promise for the actual process of conducting a forensic investigation. By leveraging the inherent capabilities of cloud computing and IaaS providers, computer forensics becomes an "on-demand" service allowing for as much storage and processor power as needed to conduct an investigation. Dedicated forensic servers can remain in standby in the cloud, offline, until need arises for them. For a large case, with often an accompanying short deadline, this could be a saving grace for both law enforcement organizations and private companies, large and small.

An additional benefit of the cloud environment, assuming it is done properly of course, is in the preservation of documents for electronic discovery cases. Documents could be backed up into the cloud for investigators to use without having to disrupt normal business. And naturally the cloud resources could be used for sorting, searching, and hashing the evidence data. An easy real-world example of this already exists with the AWS, which can automatically provide a MD5 hash of every file that is on the system.

Some additional benefits of conducting forensics in a cloud environment are as follows:

- Reduce evidence acquisition time: if a server in the cloud is compromised, it can be cloned and made immediately available to a cloud forensics server.
- Reduce service downtime: due to the hardware abstraction in the cloud, specialized hardware will not have to be obtained in order to continue the acquisition of the evidence in some situations.
- Reduce evidence transfer time: the clouds distributed file system allows for making fast bit-for-bit copies.
- Reduce forensic image verification time: some cloud environments use a cryptographic checksum or hash that can drastically reduce the time required to hash files offline.

- Decrease time to access protected documents: the pooling of CPU power available in the cloud can make decryption much faster.
- Virtually unlimited log storage: cloud storage solutions will make the need for estimating how much disk space is needed for logging unnecessary, allowing for a considerable amount of log data to be kept and used during an investigation.
- Improve log indexing and searches: along with unlimited storage, logs can be indexed and searched effectively in real time with cloud resources.

While cloud computing presents some interesting opportunities for forensic investigations, the technology will have to be thoroughly vetted every step of the way. Reliability, best evidence, and other factors will need to be examined with great care, and standard forensic practices in this environment will have to be accepted in court before this method is widely used.

Summary

In this chapter, we have discussed the fundamentals of cloud computing, the specific distinctions that comprise a cloud environment, and the numerous services available. We have discussed the characteristics and distinctions of streaming OSes, application streaming, and virtual appliances. We also discussed security challenges associated with cloud computing, as well as how to conduct forensics on and in the cloud environment.

Bibliography

What Is Cloud Computing?

InfoWorld.com InfoClipz: Cloud Computing. April 2009.

Cloud Computing Services

Beckman, M. (2009, September). Cloud computing deep dive. *InfoWorld*.

Cloud Computing, Virtualization, and Security

Amoah, S. Cloud computing and network forensics in the eyes of computer forensic examiner. *Decision Group*. 02/2010.
Navetta, D. Legal implications of cloud computing. *LLRX.com*. September 12, 2009.
Security guidance for critical areas of focus in cloud computing. *Cloud Security Alliance*. December 2009.

VISIONS OF THE FUTURE: VIRTUALIZATION AND CLOUD COMPUTING

In this book, we've looked closely at all elements and variations of virtualization as they exist today. In this chapter, we will look forward and outline some of the trends that are emerging to shape virtualization and cloud computing in the future. When looking at trends and the future, it's always best to remember that there is an art to the science and that predictions are at best "trajectories," a general direction in which something is moving as opposed to hard and fast information.

Virtualization and cloud computing are not in the foreground on the grand stage of technology that we'll see enter our lives in the twenty-first century; however, they do have their part to play and looking at where these technologies are going does have value as it puts present events into context and creates a framework for where things are going. By exploring these trends, we uncover the positive opportunities and the negative factors with the intent of giving investigators valuable insight into the future. In addition, exploring the trends in virtualization and cloud computing will remove some of the sting that comes with the ever-quickening pace of change and the necessary absorption of new and complex information that comes our way.

Future of Virtualization

As virtualization continues to evolve with ever-increasing demands for flexibility and performance as well as full hardware utilization, we will start to see new innovations in how the hypervisor is developed and deployed. These ideas are in their early stages, and there is a great deal of development and support that will have to go into this, but they are coming.

Hardware Hypervisors

The use of a hardware hypervisor has interesting potential and could increase performance and security in a number of ways. This concept is being looked at a couple of different ways in the virtualization community.

In Chapter 1, "How Virtualization Happens," we discussed the flash-based hypervisor and its potential benefits. While economics, politics, and free-market competition will certainly have their slowing effects, there are strong indicators that hypervisors will start moving from the software level down into the hardware level. Currently, the next-generation hypervisor is being designed around the idea that it will be embedded within a server motherboard and will have the capacity to boot any client operating system (OS). Moving the hypervisor down from the software to the hardware level creates an environment where potentially any OS that is compatible with the hardware can be virtualized. Done properly, this type of virtualization could considerably improve performance and improve security, which in turn would create more options and uses for virtualization.

Virtual Machines Will Be Used for Antiforensics

With the ready availability of portable virtual machines that can be configured with a wide array of tools and applications, they can also be considered "throwaway" or "disposable" to avoid detection or recovery. From this perspective, the virtual machine can be considered as an antiforensics tool if the intent of the user is to avoid forensic detection. Virtualization by its very design assumes the hardware management duties of the OS. Add to this the growing number of applications that are moving to the Web that now assume the application management duties from the OS, and you have a very interesting set of conditions that, over time, could lead to the creation of a truly disposable OS that is created from a combination of hypervisor functions and Web applications that operates for a single session and is then dismantled completely when shut down.

Mobiles and Virtualization

Virtualization will also begin moving into the mobile arena. Currently, cell phone companies are investigating the applicability of providing multiple phone environments on the same hardware. In the future, you could choose your handset and then specify whether you wanted Blackberry OS, Windows Mobile, or both. One such example that exists today is called *Dalvik*. It is a virtual machine that runs the Java platform on Android mobile devices. It runs applications, which have been converted into a compact executable format suitable for systems that are constrained in terms of memory and processor speed. It has some specific characteristics that differentiate it from other standard virtual machines; specifically, it has been slimmed down to use less space and takes advantage of the mobile architecture so that a single device can run multiple instances of the VM efficiently.

This type of virtualization will also help the phone run with fewer chips. Typical mobile phones today require a baseband processor, which allows the phone to communicate; an applications processor, which runs applications like e-mail; and a multimedia chip, which of course takes care of graphics, audio, and video. However, using a virtualized phone two processors can accomplish what used to take three.

VMware Mobile Virtualization Platform

Another platform that comes from VMware is the VMware Mobile Virtualization Platform or MVP. VMware MVP is a thin software hypervisor that will be embedded on mobile phones, decoupling the applications and data from the underlying hardware. It will be optimized to run efficiently on low-power and memory-limited mobile phones. A small piece of code, roughly 20 KB, will run on the mobile device virtualizing the resources of the device and allowing other OSes to run on the virtualized hardware. As expected, there are some overhead and performance hits that occur when virtualizing hardware on a mobile device. However, as mobiles continue to get faster these effects will become less noticeable compared to the advantage of being able to choose which OS you want to run on your mobile device.

Home/Work Convergence on the Same Device

The popularity of mobile devices and their productivity benefits in the workplace is self-evident. However, there are side-effects. Employees, tired of carrying two, or more, mobiles are beginning to pressure their companies to support their employee-owned mobile devices. Naturally, this creates a number of new issues ranging from managing a wide variety of devices to security concerns, and it will certainly create some interesting forensic cases with more interesting legal ramifications.

As mentioned in the section "VMware Mobile Virtualization Platform," a mobile virtual platform, deployed properly, could allow for work-related and personal businesses to be conducted independently yet on the same device creating "secure personas" for the mobile-phone owner depending on the situation they are in. In time, this type of virtualization could become an important part of a purchasing decision – specifically the ease at which each persona can be backed up and migrated to a new device. Additionally, virtualization software would enable a mobile-phone maker, or third-party developer, to add features regardless of the OS.

The Evolving Cloud

Cloud computing services, much like virtualization technology, will continue to evolve in a number of interesting ways. One of the first that will likely be addressed will be a more robust legal framework around cloud computing. Another will be the creation and use of data-flow tools that will allow security and forensics professionals to track where and how data moves around a cloud environment – this in and of itself may create a whole new subdiscipline within digital forensics. In the next section, we'll explore these aspects of cloud evolution as well as several others.

Trends in Cloud Computing

With the growing commercial popularity of cloud computing environments, there are a number of trends that are emerging as a result of it. For individuals and small companies, cloud computing has been of great benefit for some time. In the mid-1990's, there were a number of free e-mail services that cropped up such as Rocketmail, Hotmail, and many others. With time, these services were either absorbed or expanded, becoming photo-storage sites, social networking sites, and so on, in addition to e-mail sites. These technologies use cloud computing to work.

As industry and market competition have demanded an "always on, accessible from anywhere" mentality, the use of cloud computing for commercial purposes on a large scale was inevitable – this fact and Moore's Law churning ever forward creating faster and cheaper computers at a rate that most individuals and organizations have no need to keep pace with. The days of buying the next hardware upgrade for a small increase in computing power is largely over – computers, while technically obsolete, can still perform effectively and efficiently for years without being an obvious dinosaur in the computer world. This was not the case in the 1990s when useful functionality ended in a much shorter period of time.

Cloud computing has entered the market now as a solid service with a number of important trends to consider. The first is that companies and large organizations are building their own private clouds. One of the easiest examples is IBM's "Blue Cloud" project, which is as way for a company as large and dispersed as IBM to have all the advantages of a cloud computing environment while addressing the security, and legal liability, concerns that would otherwise stop a company like IBM from using a public cloud. This trend also leads into another trend, in which large, private clouds will become part-time cloud computing vendors. Even "Blue Cloud" runs with excess capacity some of, if not all of, the time this excess computing power could easily be leased out to other customers. Amazon has already done this with its S3 and Elastic Compute initiatives. As more and more private clouds are created, there's nothing to say that any company from Wal-Mart to General Dynamics couldn't do the same thing.

The next trend is that cloud computing will change the skills that are required by IT workers. Since the very nature of cloud computing is abstraction, many technological implementation functions that are common in traditional client/server environments will change or dissolve all together. Rather than managing new integrations and development projects, the shift will likely focus on getting the most business value out of new technologies.

Another trend that will likely take root is the idea of blending professional services with cloud services. As it stands now, cloud computing is another vector for paying for hardware and software with very little interaction with a live human on the other end. The next evolutions of cloud computing will see the usual computing services with human thinking and interaction included in the mix. This trend will also see cloud computing services becoming much more customizable. While every standard requires a "best practices" approach, the "one size fits all" model applies less and less every year to computing needs and some of the very specialized software that is used today. A natural progression of a maturing cloud computing environment, particularly if it is coupled with a live human consulting capability, will allow for applications to become more customizable by the end user.

The biggest trend, which in many ways encompasses all the other trends that were just discussed, is that cloud computing will unleash a wave of innovation. The very real obstacles of energy costs, space requirements, and IT infrastructure investment costs will be dramatically reduced or disappear as companies are able to tap into as much or as little computing power as they need anywhere in the world. Just like the technology visionaries of the past predicted the hard drive but could never have predicted the iPod, so it is today with cloud computing. The raw materials are there but have yet to be fully explored and innovated on. This will happen, but over time and based on necessity and market drivers.

More Robust Legal Procedures Will Be Developed

One of the simple, unpleasant realities of cloud computing is that there will be tremendous financial pressure on organizations to take advantage of the pricing and efficiency of cloud computing. Failure to fully understand the issues of cloud computing arrangements will create some serious legal issues. Currently, the big legal issues surrounding cloud computing are as follows:

- Trans-border data flow and the legal obligations in multiple jurisdictions
- "Reasonable security" under the law
- Evidence and e-discovery

In time, and certainly with some mistakes along the way, attorneys and organizations will begin to develop more robust legal procedures and contracts that will allow for the benefits of cloud computing without the risks that exist today.

One potential catalyst for this change, and many others for that matter, is the Cyber Security Act of 2009. In a nutshell, this Act is designed to federalize critical infrastructure security. Currently, there is a lot of controversy over this Act as this bill will shift power from private entities to the federal government. One of the bigger sticking points is the provision giving the President full authority to shut down Internet traffic in an emergency and disconnect critical infrastructure systems on national security grounds. While this bill is far bigger than just cloud computing, I anticipate a side effect will be to further focus people's attention on cyber-related issues and create an environment where new laws are addressed and passed at a much faster pace.

Data-Flow Tools Will Evolve

Data-flow tools have existed for some time and are used for a variety of different functions. In the cloud computing realm, new tools will be developed that will have the following characteristics:

- Real-time
- Online
- Follow the "Push" model
- Low latency
- Data-driven as opposed to demand-driven

As we have seen the new "real-time Web" evolve based on a data-driven, real-time, Push model, it is likely we will see these type of techniques adapted and used for monitoring and managing data-flow in the cloud. In time, data-flow analysis could become a speciality unto itself and become a useful tool in carrying out incident response activities and forensic investigations within a cloud environment.

The Home Entrepreneur

In a recent BusinessWeek article, it was shown that more than half of all the businesses in the United States are run in a person's home, not in traditional office space. While there are a number of factors behind this trend, one of the main factors is the recession, which has forced companies to lower costs by outsourcing business to contractors. While the concept of "working from home" is not a new one, this resurging trend of home-based knowledge workers is helping facilitate new services to accommodate them, and one of them is cloud computing. In the near-term, largely due to economic necessity, cloud computing services will be used, hopefully leading to considerable improvements in infrastructure as well as a more stable balance between risk and liability.

The iPad, Tablet, and Slate

When the iPod was introduced, it quickly replaced the Walkman as the standard for portable music players. It also changed the way people used and defined "phones" as it was no longer just a phone but a multifunction platform with one of its functions being voice communications. Since the iPhone's release in 2007, it has spawned a number of similar devices such as the Palm Pre and the Droid.

Now the iPad, in spite of its interesting reception into the marketplace, is likely to be another game changer in time. With the netbook now comfortably part of the consumer culture, there will certainly be design changes to compete with the iPad and its descendants. It will also be interesting to see how Google, Palm, and possibly even Amazon formally respond to the iPad. Google in particular will be interesting to watch since it has its own tablet concept already, and it already has a significant cloud computing presence and service that can present a significant challenge to Apple.

There is also nothing to stop Amazon from reinventing the Kindle and enabling it to access Amazon cloud services. While this is speculation to be sure, it brings up some interesting questions and ideas about how the markets will move and what effects that will have on work and play. The consumer market will dictate how this progresses, but it's not difficult to imagine that the success of the iPad, and the new cloud services that will arise out of its proliferation into the market, will create new and interesting ways for users to take advantage of the cloud environment.

Autonomic Computing

Civilization advances by extending the number of important operations which we can perform without thinking about them.
Alfred North Whitehead

As cloud computing continues to develop and more and more clouds are ultimately joined together, a method of managing the complexity that will arise will have to be implemented. One proposed solution from IBM is to design the systems to regulate themselves much in the same way our autonomic nervous system regulates and protects the human body. This model of computing is called *autonomic computing*. Some components are currently available, but complete autonomic systems do not yet exist. IBM believes, due to the development of raw computing power paired with the exponential growth of computer devices, that the increasing system complexity is reaching a level beyond human ability to manage and secure. The intent behind autonomic computing in the short term is a reduced dependence on human intervention to maintain complex systems.

The challenges ahead for autonomic computing lie in creating the open standards and new technologies needed for systems to interact effectively, protect themselves, and "heal" themselves with a minimum of administrator support. While truly autonomic systems are still years away, autonomic functionality will appear in servers, storage, and software. This functionality will likely be used in virtualization and cloud computing as both technologies will be framed around managing their increasing complexities.

Summary

In this chapter, we discussed some emerging trends and technologies relating to virtualization and the evolution of cloud computing. While trend speculation isn't meant to be perfectly accurate, it does provide a likely preview of things to come, and thus what to watch and plan for. As security professionals and forensic investigators, we are perpetually overworked and underfunded, which makes any informational advantage very beneficial.

Bibliography

Future of Virtualization

Coates, J., & Jarrat, J. (1989). *What futurists believe*. Mt. Airy, MD: Lomond Publication, Inc.

Stokes, J. (2009, May 6). The future of virtualization: a view from the front lines. *ars technica*. Retrieved from http://arstechnica.com/business/news/2009/05/the-future-of-virtualization-a-view-from-the-front-lines.ars

Mobiles and Virtualization

Kharif, O. (2008, April 9). Virtualization goes mobile. *BusinessWeek Online*. Retrieved from http://www.businessweek.com/technology/content/apr2008/tc20080421_235517.htm?chan=technology_technology%2Bindex%2Bpage_top%2Bst.

VMWare Mobile Virtualization Platform. (n.d.). Retrieved from http://www.vmware.com/products/mobile/

The Evolving Cloud

Tozzi, J. (2009, October 23). The rise of the Homepreneur. Retrieved from http://www.businessweek.com/smallbiz/content/oct2009/sb20091023_263258.htm

NetworkWorld Asia Staff. (2009, September 4). Mobile phone virtualization to really enable workers and IT staff. *NetworkWorldAsia*. Retrieved from http://www.networksasia.net/content/mobile-phone-virtualization-really-enable-workers-and-it-staff

Goldman, D. (2010, February 4). Tablet wars: Google looks to take on Apple iPad. *CNNMoney.com*. Retrieved from http://money.cnn.com/2010/02/04/technology/apple_ipad_google_chrome/index.htm

Mark, R. (2010, February 4). House Passes Cyber-Security Act. *eWeek.com*. Retrieved from http://www.eweek.com/c/a/Government-IT/House-Passes-Cybersecurity-Act-682741/

Shankland, S. (2009, October 20). Gartner: Brace yourself for cloud computing. *CNET news*. Retrieved from http://news.cnet.com/8301-30685_3-10378782-264.html

Autonomic Computing

IBM. (2005, June). An architectural blueprint for autonomic computing. Retrieved from http://www-03.ibm.com/autonomic/pdfs/AC%20Blueprint%20 White%20Paper%20V7.pdf

Horn, P. (2001, October 15). How autonomic computing will reshape IT. *CNET news*. Retrieved from http://news.cnet.com/2010-1071-281578.html.

APPENDIX: PERFORMING PHYSICAL-TO-VIRTUAL AND VIRTUAL-TO-VIRTUAL MIGRATIONS

INFORMATION IN THIS CHAPTER

- Hyper-V Migrations
- Migration Scenarios
- Migrating Physical-to-Virtual
- Migrating Virtual-to-Virtual

In this chapter, we discuss a function of Hyper-V that will likely become one of the most heavily used in your new "dynamic data center." Whether you perform a migration simply to retire outdated hardware, consolidate workloads, or create mirror-like test environments, you'll learn quickly that migrating servers into and among the virtual server farm is something that will be done quite often in the overall migration to your dynamic data center. In this chapter, we will discuss exactly what a migration is and when to best perform one; benefits are not always gained through a migration from a physical server to a virtual server. We will also step you through actual migrations, both from a physical server to a virtual server and a virtual server to a new virtual server.

Hyper-V Migrations

Migrating servers is not new; IS professionals have been migrating servers from one piece of hardware to another for years. Let's face it; we're not quite to the point of hardware lifecycles matching up with software life cycles, so there's a really good chance that the brand-new enterprise application you're implementing today will outlive the server platform it's being deployed on; anybody supporting legacy applications knows this well. The introduction of virtualization to the mainstream began to change the rules. Of course, nobody wants to jump right in and be the first to move revenue-generating powerhouse applications to a virtual environment, no matter how hard our inner geek is screaming to do so. So starting in the late

1990s, IS professionals began to use virtual environments for testing – not just for applications, but for the virtualization technology itself. In its infancy, virtualization technology simply did not allow for migrating existing platforms into the virtual world; as a result, over the years we all became very fluent at building virtual servers and workstations from scratch. Of course, this process evolved into creating templates or pre-staging copies of virtual operating systems that could be implemented within minutes. It was only a matter of time before the technology would catch up to the desire to import an existing physical server platform into the virtual world. We are now on the cusp of flawless migrations of physical server platforms into the virtual world, and doing so seamlessly while the server is in use by end users, without impacting performance.

In the brave new world of using virtualization to support frontline production operations, the upper echelon of management is looking to their own engineers and trusted vendors to provide the confidence and the expertise needed to begin moving more toward not only data center virtualization but also a truly dynamic data center environment. You should expect hesitation in the discussions to implement production supporting virtualization; there's a mind-set obstacle that many managers need to overcome when it comes to the use of virtualization. Managers comment on preferring a "real" server over a virtual platform. For some, it's as simple as preferring to have a solid object to visualize in their mind, whereas for others, it's simply having skepticism about the technology itself. Regardless of the reasoning, your design should be written in a way to accommodate and address all concerns. That said, as mentioned elsewhere in this book, your approach needs to be focused on accomplishing your goals in a feasible, appropriate way. Don't virtualize for the sake of virtualizing.

Microsoft calls out some specific best practices when migrating specialized server platforms. Familiarize yourself with these best practices thoroughly before attempting to migrate any of the specialty servers discussed in the following section.

Microsoft Exchange Server

Virtualizing Exchange has been a topic of great controversy ever since virtualization first came on the scene. In the early years of virtualization, it was recommended *not* to run Exchange in a virtual environment because of the limitations of the infant technology. In the years since, virtualization has matured in a way that has removed many, if not all, of those limitations. Unfortunately, the recommendations of the past have remained as a worry in today's discussions surrounding the partnership of virtualization and Exchange. The truth is, Microsoft fully supports the virtualization of Microsoft Exchange today. As with any other environment, you must be sure that you configure your virtual platform to properly support Exchange, but there are no limitations within Microsoft's Hyper-V technology that should cause any concern in your discussions to virtualize Exchange.

There are some key items that Microsoft has called out that IS professionals should be aware of when designing their virtual Exchange environments.

- The software platform should be Windows Server 2008, or any third-party vendor virtualization platform that has been validated by Microsoft's Windows Server Virtualization Validation Program. This program can be found in www.windowsservercatalog.com/svvp.aspx?svvppage=svvp.htm. The Validation Program includes some of the most well-known vendors of both hardware and software. This Web site will help you to identify those who have been validated by Microsoft to provide platforms capable of running all flavors of the Microsoft servers.

- If you're planning to virtualize your Exchange environment, you must use Exchange Server 2007 with Service Pack 1 or later. Earlier Exchange versions are not fully supported on a virtual platform. The use of the unified messaging role is not supported if your Exchange Server is running within a virtual platform. It's important to note that the base Exchange 2007 system requirement without the use of virtualization is Windows 2003, but the use of this operating system as a host for Exchange 2007 is not supported in the virtualization world. We mention this because some may consider building Exchange 2007 in a nonvirtual environment with the plan to migrate the complete operating system into Hyper-V at a later date. If you plan to do this, you must build your environment using Windows 2008 or later.

- Exchange 2007 on a virtual platform supports all of the most common forms of storage. These include Virtual Hard Disks (VHD), Small Computer System Interface (SCSI), and Internet SCSI (iSCSI) storage. If you plan to use SCSI or iSCSI, you must configure it to be presented as block-level storage within the hardware virtualization software, and it must be dedicated to the Exchange guest machine. Exchange 2007 does not support the use of network-attached storage, but if the storage is attached at the host level, the guest will see it as local storage. Should you plan to use SCSI or iSCSI in your virtual Exchange environment, Hyper-V only supports VHDs up to 2,040 GB in size, and virtual IDE drives up to 127 GB; plan accordingly.

- Microsoft supports the use of both cluster continuous replication (CCR) and single copy clusters (SCC) within Exchange running in a virtual environment so long as there are no hypervisor-based clustering or migration technologies in use. An example of these technologies would be Quick Migration for Hyper-V and VMotion for VMware. Likewise, Microsoft does support the use of hypervisor clustering and

Note

Unified messaging is the *only* Exchange 2007 server role that is not supported in virtualization; all other server roles are fully supported.

Note

If you plan to use a third-party hypervisor, you should plan to check with the vendor to see what their SCSI, iSCSI, and virtual IDE drive size limitations are prior to designing your new Exchange environment.

migration so long as CCR and SCC are not in use within the Exchange environment.

- One of the biggest advantages of virtualization is the ability to take snapshots of your virtual environment as part of a backup or disaster recovery plan. In the Exchange world, this can be problematic because this kind of technology is not "application aware." This means that the snapshot technology is not capable of taking into account the way the application actually uses and processes its data. Because of the way Exchange processes data, Microsoft does not support the use of any kind of snapshot technology with your virtual Exchange Server. However, it should be noted that in the case of Exchange, the other benefits of virtualization tend to outweigh the inability to use snapshot technology.

- When you are configuring the virtual processors for your Exchange host, it's important to understand that Exchange running in a virtual environment does not support a ratio of greater than 2:1. Hypervisors provide the ability to share the logical processors of the host server to the guest machines. For example, a dual-processor system using quad-core processors contains a total of eight logical processors in the host. You may have some virtual servers that end up using less processor power than others, so the full processor may not be needed by that server. Depending on the virtual servers, this may allow you to have much more than eight virtual servers configured to have two processors each. However, in the Exchange world, Microsoft would not support the allocation of more than 16 virtual processors across all of the guest machines running on the server, or a total of four quad processor Exchange servers.

Microsoft SQL Server

The structured query language (SQL) performance team has published a document related to the use of SQL 2008 in a Hyper-V environment. A few of the key items are listed in this section, but it's strongly suggested that you download and review this document in its entirety prior to implementing SQL in a Hyper-V environment. To download this SQL team's document, go to http://download.microsoft.com/download/d/9/4/d948f981-926e-40fa-a026-5bfcf076d9b9/SQL2008inHyperV2008.docx.

Use a synthetic network adapter provided by the Hyper-V integration tools instead of a legacy network adapter when configuring networking for the virtual machine.

Avoid emulated devices for SQL Server deployments when possible. These devices can result in significantly more CPU overhead when compared to synthetic devices.

SQL Server is input/output (I/O) intensive, so it's recommended that you use the pass-through disk option as opposed to the fixed-size virtual hard disks (VHDs). Dynamic VHDs are not recommended for performance reasons.

In the SQL team's document, they used locally attached storage on the Hyper-V server. Many virtual hosts are connected to shared storage using fiber channel, iSCSI, or NFS. Selecting the proper storage connection will greatly impact the I/O performance of the virtual SQL Server.

Microsoft SharePoint Technologies

Microsoft fully supports the use of SharePoint servers and technologies within the Hyper-V environment. A great deal of information can be found at TechNet (http://technet.microsoft.com/en-us/library/cc816955.aspx), but some of the key items are included in the following list:

- Any Hyper-V virtual server must meet the requirements of the physical server (for example, CPUs, memory, and disk I/O) that you are going to run as a Hyper-V guest. As with all virtual technologies, there is an overhead cost on the host computer for each virtual machine.

- Do not use the Hyper-V snapshot feature on virtual servers that are connected to a SharePoint Products and Technologies server farm. This is because the timer services and the search applications might become unsynchronized during the snapshot process and once the snapshot is finished, errors or inconsistencies can arise. Detach any server from the farm before taking a snapshot of that server.

- Do not use more virtual CPUs than there are physical CPUs on the Hyper-V host computer. Although Hyper-V will allow you to allocate more virtual CPUs than the number of physical CPUs, this causes performance issues because the hypervisor software has to swap out CPU contexts.

Finally, before we jump into some scenarios and examples of how to migrate your servers, there are some key points that *must* be understood by IS professionals in order to establish accurate expectations.

1. Do not expect every migration from physical-to-virtual to be smooth, or quick. Most migrations will take longer than a vendor may lead you to believe. This is not because you're doing it wrong, it's simply the nature of converting an established server from running on dedicated hardware to running under a virtualized platform.

2. Virtualize properly. Having the capacity to virtualize your entire data center doesn't mean that you should blindly plan to migrate all of your servers. Do your homework and check twice when creating your design.

3. Ease the pain. Discuss with your peers and management the truth and the myths associated with virtualization, because if you leave room for skepticism and doubt, both will grow in a negative way.

4. Migrate methodically. Start with smaller, less critical servers and perfect your techniques before tackling the core business application server. Allow time after each round of migration to test and stabilize the environment. Too much change at once can lower client satisfaction and acceptance. Taking the migration in manageable chunks will allow management and other stakeholders to become comfortable with their choice to virtualize.

Migrating into virtualization is a big step for any organization, but it's much safer, and more controllable than a lot of other technologies. The biggest fear about virtualization is typically based on the misunderstanding of the technology. Learn it thoroughly and present it honestly, and you'll soon look past the fears and forward to the benefits. Migrations are nondestructive to the source machine. If the new virtual machine does not work or fails to migrate, the source can be turned back on to restore access to the data or the services. It is a good practice to power down the migrated server and let it sit in place for at least a day or two before disconnecting and reallocating it.

Migration Scenarios

Hyper-V is a great tool for demonstration, testing, QA, and production environments. Many IS professionals have known for years that the use of a virtualization platform on a laptop is a great way to present proposed designs and implementations without the need for a full collection of multiple servers and workstations. There are a growing number of situations where using Hyper-V can be beneficial, but before we jump into some of those scenarios, there are some key considerations of which you should be aware.

Microsoft recommends a minimum of two network adapters on the server or workstation you plan to use as a Hyper-V host. If you plan to use iSCSI, you should bump your minimum network adapter count to three. Common practice would be to use one network adapter for the host, the second network adapter for the iSCSI connection, and the third network adapter exclusively for the hosted environments to communicate with the network. But you can get creative when needed. The following are a two examples of how you can manage your network adapter usage.

- Four adapters, no iSCSI – In this example, one adapter is assigned to the host partition, and the remaining three adapters are used for virtual networking. Storage is either attached directly or provided through fiber. This setup allows for the creation of three separate virtual switches.

- Four adapters, with iSCSI – In this example, one adapter is assigned to the host partition, one adapter is assigned to the iSCSI connection, and the remaining two adapters are used for virtual networking. This setup allows for the testing and use of multiple virtual environments on a single virtual switch.

Server consolidation is often the first thing to come to mind when people begin to discuss the use of server virtualization. The reduction

Note

It's important to remember that Hyper-V does *not* provide support for the use of wireless networks. This will rarely be noticed on a true server hardware platform, but as mentioned previously, a lot of IS professionals prefer to use laptops running full virtual environments for demonstrations and testing design concepts. Hyper-V also does *not* support the use of "sleep" or "hibernation." Neither should be a problem, but it is something to keep in mind in your configuration steps for the laptop.

of 20 hardware servers into a single hardware server is a pretty big incentive. There are still licensing costs associated with the software being used within the virtual servers, but the cost savings related to the reduction in hardware is hard to ignore. Using the advanced Windows Server 2008 licenses will allow different numbers of virtual machines to be run on the same physical host. Using Windows Server 2008 Data Center licenses for a two-processor server to achieve our 20 to 1 consolidation, you can save the cost of about 14 Windows Server licenses. Just remember that in the big picture, server consolidation should be seen as a nice side benefit to using server virtualization, and not the primary focus. Should the focus be to simply reduce the number of hardware servers, chances are key items and considerations will be missed, resulting in future regrets. Done properly, server consolidation can result in a much lower total cost of ownership not only for server hardware but also for power consumption and cooling costs. Consolidating servers into a virtual environment also allows for benefits not always initially envisioned, such as infrastructure optimization, more efficient asset utilization, and flexibility.

Business continuity and disaster recovery are issues that a lot of companies are just now beginning to take a serious look at when it comes to the use of virtualization. The elimination of previous technology limitations is allowing for the use of virtualization in a broad spectrum across the enterprise data center. This is a great plan, but as with anything, it needs to be researched thoroughly for your company. Every company is different in the way it embraces new technology; there's not just the implementation of new technology to consider, but the mind-set of those who manage it and those who must be confident enough to sign off on the cost required.

Migrating Physical-to-Virtual

As discussed previously, there are many reasons to migrate a physical server to a virtual platform. In this section, we'll walk you through the step-by-step process of migrating a physical server using the System Center Virtual Machine Manager. We'll also touch on a new tool called Disk2vhd that was released by Microsoft while this book was being written, which will allow you to perform a physical migration in alternate ways.

Physical-to-Virtual – System Center Virtual Machine Manager 2008 (VMM2008)

Before performing a physical-to-virtual migration using Virtual Machine Manager 2008 (VMM2008), be sure that the server you are planning to migrate is a member of the same domain as your VMM2008 server.

1. Launch the System Center Virtual Machine Manager by browsing to **Start | All | Programs | Microsoft System Center | Virtual Machine Manager**. Doing so will display the splash screen seen in Figure A.1.
2. With the VMM console up and running, browse to **Actions | Virtual Machine Manager | Convert Physical Server** from the toolbar. Figure A.2 provides an example of this step.
3. The completion of step 2 will begin the Migration Wizard. All of the steps in this process allow for modification of the default process. Do not make changes you don't fully understand or it could result in a failed migration. The first screen of the Wizard is the "Select Source" window, displayed in Figure A.3.
4. You have a few options: you can enter the host name of the server, the IP address of the server, or you can browse for the server. For our example, we chose to browse for the server. Clicking the **Browse** button brings up the typical "browse for" Wizard used for locating computers, users, and user groups. As you can see in Figure A.4, we entered the host name of the server we planned to migrate, and then clicked **OK**.
5. Figure A.5 shows our Select Source window with the server selected. You'll need to enter the credentials of an account that has administrative rights on the server to be migrated. Once the credentials have been entered, press the **Next** button.

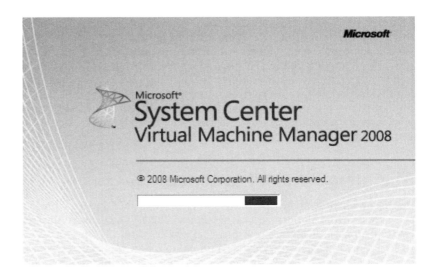

Figure A.1 VMM2008 Splash Screen

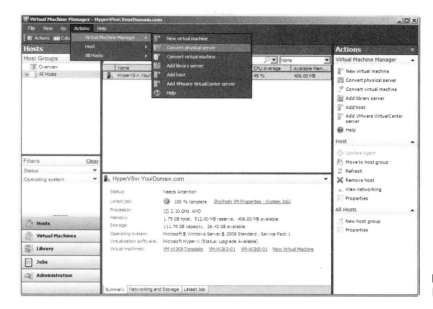

Figure A.2 Launching Physical-to-Virtual Migration

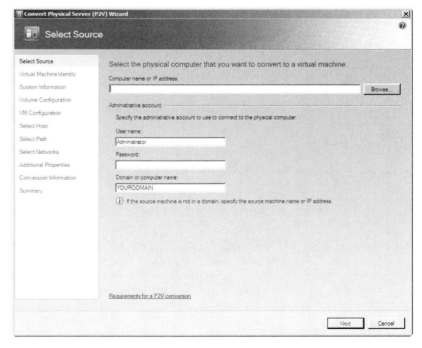

Figure A.3 Select Source

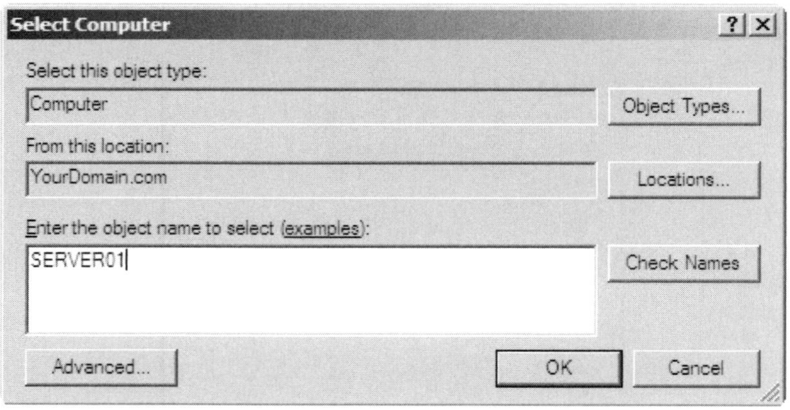

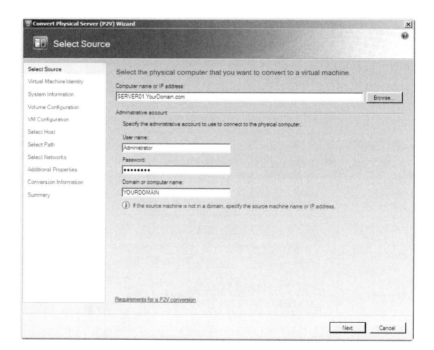

Figure A.4 Select Computer

Figure A.5 Populated Select Source

6. The next window in the Wizard is the Virtual Machine Identity window (see Figure A.6). For our example, we're going to continue to use the same name as the physical server; however, you may want to consider changing server names slightly as they get migrated so that you can more easily manage them, such as adding a "V" to the beginning of the name. With the virtual machine name entered, click **Next** to continue.

7. The next window in the Wizard is the System Information window (see Figure A.7). This step performs a remote scan of the target

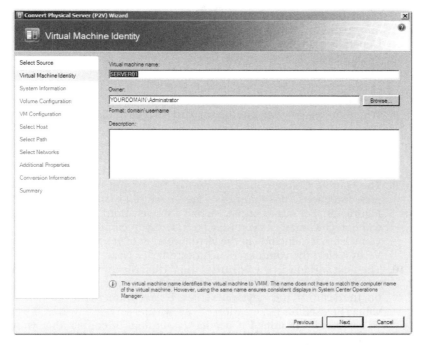

Figure A.6 Virtual Machine Identity

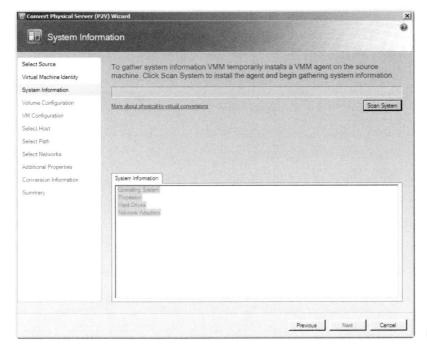

Figure A.7 System Information

server in order to validate connectivity and gather some of the basic information required to create the virtual framework for the server. Depending on the network speed and the attributes of the server being migrated, this step can take a little time. For our example, we migrated a basic Windows 2008 Standard Server on the same local network as our VMM console, and it took about 3 minutes to complete this step. Click **Next** to begin the scan.

8. When the system scan completes, you can see in Figure A.8 that the Wizard will display some of the basic information about the server being migrated. If any of the information displayed is unexpected, verify that you are migrating the proper server before moving forward. Otherwise, click **Next** to continue.

9. The Volume Configuration window of the Wizard will allow you to pick and choose the volumes of the server you wish to migrate (see Figure A.9). For our example, we had a single volume, but the Wizard will detect as many as you may have, and you can deselect any that you wish *not* to include in the virtual version of your physical server. Verify\Select the volumes to include and click **Next**.

10. The next window in the Wizard is the Virtual Machine Configuration window (see Figure A.10). This window will be prepopulated based on the scan of the physical server. It's recommended that these values be used for the creation of your virtual server; however, these values can be modified if needed (assuming, of course, that your Hyper-V environment has the available resources). Verify\Modify the selections and click **Next** to continue.

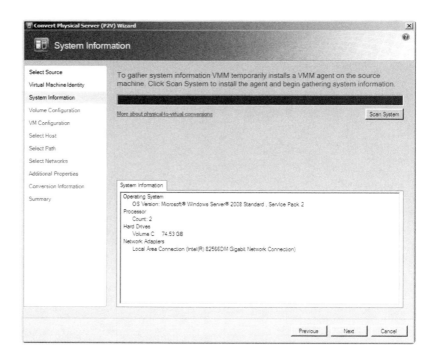

Figure A.8 System Information Scan Complete

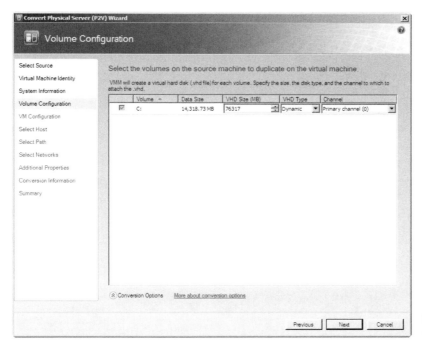

Figure A.9 Volume Configuration

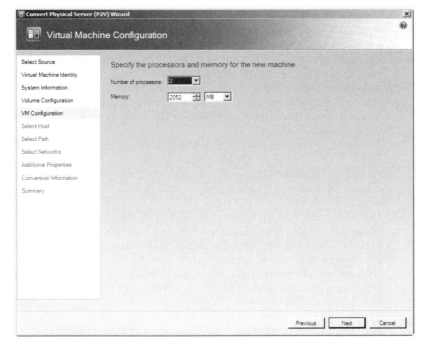

Figure A.10 Virtual Machine Configuration

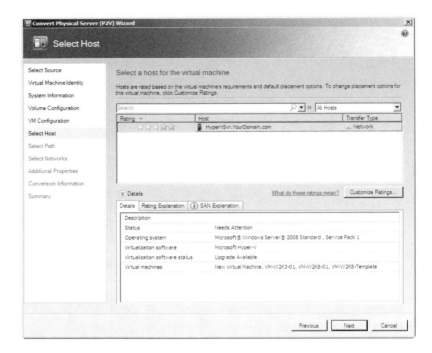

Figure A.11 Select Host

11. The Select Host window of the Wizard allows you to choose the Hyper-V host that your virtual server will be added to (see Figure A.11). For our example, we only have a single host, but most production environments will have multiple Hyper-V hosts for the sake of redundancy. This step also gives you a "rating" based on the available resources of your target host compared to the configurations you just defined for your virtual server. Select your host and click **Next** to continue.

12. The next step allows you to modify the default path of the VHD file you are about to create. Verify\Modify this selection and click **Next** to continue (see Figure A.12).

13. The Select Networks option is the next window in the Wizard (see Figure A.13). This selection allows you to choose the network adapters or configurations you have available on the Hyper-V host you've chosen to create the virtual server on. Select an option and click **Next** to continue.

14. The Additional Properties window of the Wizard allows you to modify the way Hyper-V manages your new virtual server, such as automatically booting the server as soon as the Hyper-V environment is available and how to treat the virtual server in the event that the Hyper-V server encounters problems. Choose the selections that best apply to your virtual server and click **Next** to continue (see Figure A.14).

15. At this point, you have entered all of the information and configured all of the settings required to migrate your physical server into a virtual

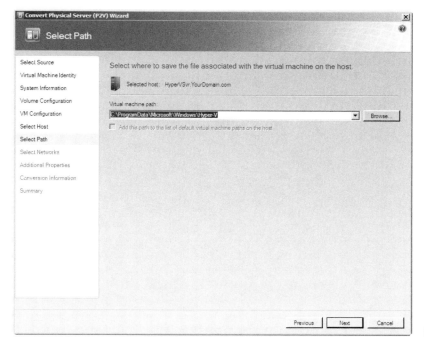

Figure A.12 Select Path

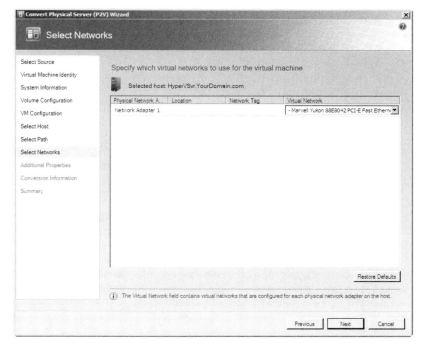

Figure A.13 Select Networks

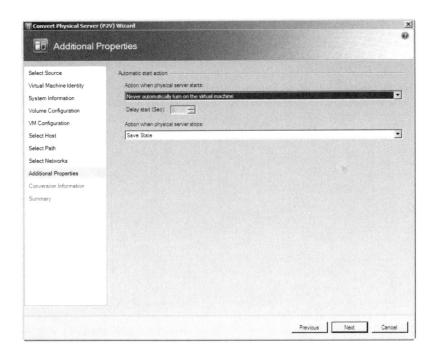

Figure A.14 Additional Properties

server. The next window is the Conversion Information window. This step will inform you of any issues that have been detected and will need to be corrected before continuing. Assuming no issues have been detected, click the **Next** button to continue (see Figure A.15).

16. The Summary window displays all of the key information related to the migration itself. Review this information and click **Create** to begin the migration (see Figure A.16).

17. Once the **Create** button is clicked in step 16, the Job Status window will become active. This window displays a great deal of information related to the migration process (see Figure A.17). Again, depending on the server you're migrating and your network environment, this step may take a great deal of time. For our example, the migration of a basic 2008 Standard Server took just under an hour and a half.

18. Once the migration is complete, the job status will change from a numerical percentage, to a message of Completed. At this time, you can view the logs of the migration on all three tabs at the bottom of the screen: Summary, Details, and Change Tracking. Figures A.18, A.19, and A.20 provide an example of the data collected during our server migration.

With your new server completely migrated, you will now be able to see it in the Hyper-V console. At this point, the server is completely virtualized and capable of being managed like any other virtual server. Figure A.21 shows our server fully migrated and running within the Hyper-V console.

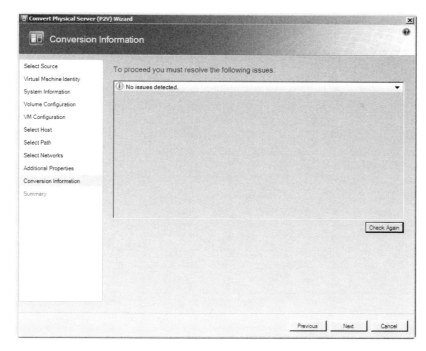

Figure A.15 Conversion Information

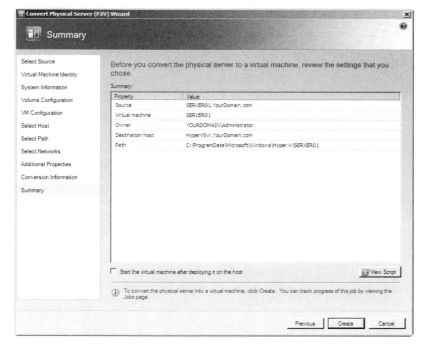

Figure A.16 Summary

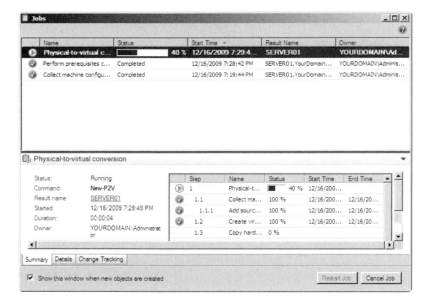

Figure A.17 Job Status

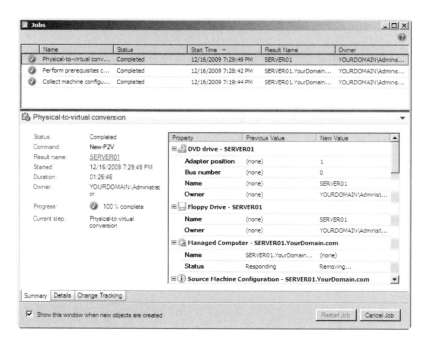

Figure A.18 Completed Status – Summary

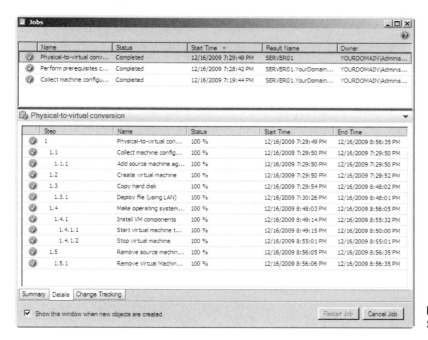

Figure A.19 Completed Status – Details

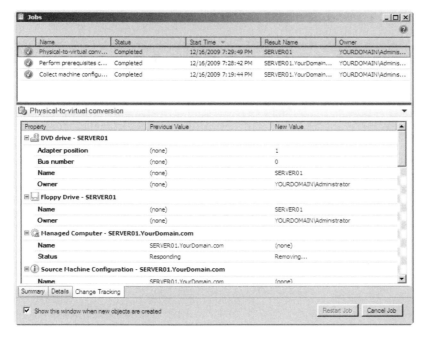

Figure A.20 Completed Status – Change Tracking

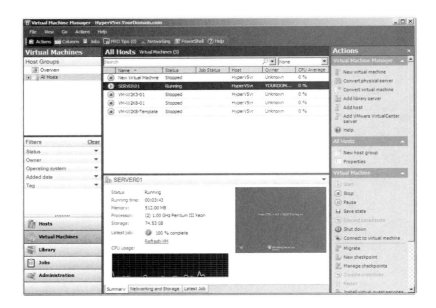

Figure A.21 Virtual Server

Physical-to-Virtual – Disk2vhd

As of the writing of this book, Microsoft released a new tool called Disk2vhd. (For more information go to http://technet.microsoft.com/en-us/sysinternals/ee656415.aspx). Most IS professionals are familiar with Sysinternals tools. Over the years, we have grown to love the valuable tools that it includes. Disk2vhd will be no different. A great tool that gets right to point, it will help many an IS professional tasked with migrating physical servers to the virtual world. Disk2vhd allows an IS professional to create a virtual hard disk of a physical server that you can then take and import into a Virtual PC or Hyper-V session.

Once you create the VHD, you can create a new VM with the attributes you prefer and then add the newly created VHD to the VM's configuration as an IDE disk(s). In its current version, Disk2vhd does not make anything other than IDE virtual hard disks. This is an ideal tool to use for legacy servers that may not be a member of the same domain as your SCVMM console or Hyper-V environment. It can also be useful when you have a large number of servers to virtualize and multiple engineers to assist in the process. Each one can move from server-to-server and create VHDs independently of the SCVMM console.

Note

When you are working with Virtual PC, it's very important to remember that Virtual PC supports a maximum virtual disk size of 127 GB. So if you create a VHD larger than this limit, it will not be accessible from Virtual PC.

Note

Microsoft does not support attaching VHDs to the same system they were created from. So, if you create VHD from the system drive of Server A and then attach it to an instance of Virtual PC running on Server A, it will fail to boot.

As with most of the Sysinternals tools, Disk2vhd includes command-line options to allow for the scripting of VHD creation. Below is the usage syntax and an example:

- Usage: disk2vhd <[drive: [drive:]…]|[*]> <vhdfile>
- Example: disk2vhd * c:\vhd\snapshot.vhd

We downloaded a copy of Disk2vhd and ran a quick test on my laptop. Here are the screenshots we collected from this test. The test itself was run on a laptop with a Core 2 Duo 2.20 GHz CPU and 4 GB of RAM. The operating system is Windows 7, and the entire process took about 20 minutes. Obviously, the length of the process will vary depending on the system being used.

In step one, we launched a command window and entered the Disk2vhd command; for our example, we are creating the VHD file on the root of an external drive mapped to U:\.

Launching the application displays a license agreement prompt. Clicking **Agree** allows the process to continue.

Clicking **Agree** opens the Disk2vhd console. It's fairly basic and straightforward, but that's what we liked about it. It's more of a graphical user interface confirmation of the command you entered. Clicking the **Create** button will launch the process. The window stays active for as long as the VHD creation is running.

Once the process is complete, the window goes away and you are done. This process turned our 60 GB HDD with 23 GB of used space into a 14 GB VHD file that we can now use to create a VM in Virtual PC or Hyper-V.

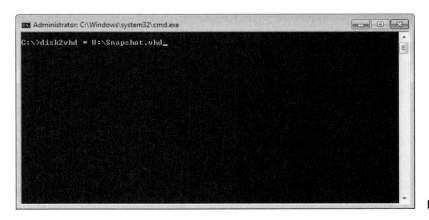

Figure A.22 Disk2vhd Command

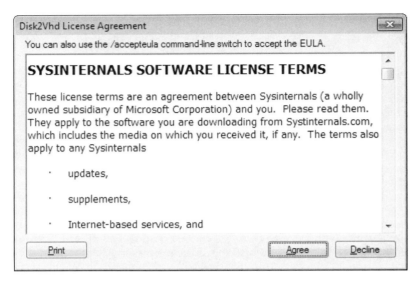

Figure A.23 Disk2vhd License Agreement

Figure A.24 Disk2vhd Confirmation and Progress Window

Migrating Virtual-to-Virtual

Some of you may be wondering why this section is even here, thinking that migrating virtual-to-virtual doesn't seem to make a whole lot of sense. Well for those of you who are a little confused over this section, think outside of the Microsoft world … ah yes, it quickly makes sense.

You need to have the ability to migrate your virtual servers between different vendors. For example, you may be a Microsoft shop looking at VMware or vice-versa. If you were unable to migrate your huge number of virtual servers from one platform to another, you might choose to stay away from that vendor altogether, so all of the big players in the virtualization world play nicely in this respect. You can migrate your virtual servers between VMware and Hyper-V all day long without issue. This is especially assuring when you begin to look into disaster recovery options and alternatives. For example, you may use VMware in your data center, while the facility you need to access for disaster recovery services uses Hyper-V. It's OK. Each of the vendors have their own built-in wizards that allow you to perform a migration from one environment to another. You may want to contact your vendor prior to migrating an especially vital server or an older legacy server just to see if there are any extra steps you should follow, but for standard servers, migrating between vendors in fairly simple.

Summary

In this chapter, we discussed the reasons why and the methods to use when migrating a physical server to a virtual environment. The points mentioned in this chapter must be used as a guideline only. The same server may be a perfect candidate in one data center, and not even a consideration in another. Remember that your data center consists of more than a bunch of hard drives and memory, your data center supports your company, and you must be capable of supporting your data center. Virtualization is no longer in its infancy, it is becoming the method of choice for deploying new servers to the enterprise.

A tool that you may want to consider using in your planning is the Microsoft Assessment and Planning Toolkit. Designed precisely for the purpose of identifying potential virtualization candidates, the toolkit allows you to run a query against your production environment without the need of installing any agent software on your existing devices. The toolkit may also help to identify previously unmanaged devices both virtual and physical.

There are many gains that can come from the use of virtualization, but remember not to virtualize simply for the sake of virtualizing. You must have a solid plan built upon thorough investigation and research in both the technology itself, and how you're company in particular might benefit from the use of it.

Design your virtualization plan in a way that includes both short-term and long-term goals. The best short-term plans can easily crumble if they do not take into account future growth.

GLOSSARY

A

ACE A VMware product that provides a way to secure and manage virtual machines (VMs).

Active upgrade An upgrade that enables a new version of an application to be added to an App-V Management Server or streaming server without affecting users currently running the application.

AMD-V AMD's implementation of virtualization hardware assist.

Application Source Root Reference to a registry key that allows an override of the OSD CODEBASE for the Hypertext Reference element (for example, the source location). This registry value enables an administrator or electronic software distribution (ESD) system to ensure that application loading is performed according to a planned topology management scheme.

Application Virtualization drive The default virtual application client drive (Q:\) from which sequenced applications are run.

Application Virtualization reporting Virtual application information gathered for data analysis. Data is collected for assembly of custom views and interpretation.

AutoLoad configuration parameter A client runtime policy configuration parameter that enables the secondary feature block of a virtualized application to be streamed to the client automatically in the background.

B

Bare-metal hypervisor Virtualization platform that runs directly on the hardware and does not require a separate host operating system (OS). Examples are Hyper-V, ESX Server, and Citrix XenServer.

Binary translation A virtualization technique pioneered by VMware in the late 1990s for the x86 architecture in which the instruction stream is inspected and nonvirtualizable machine instructions are replaced with "safe" code. Contrast with hardware assist.

Binding A process by which software components and layers are linked together. When a network component is installed, the binding relationships and dependencies for the components are established.

Blue Pill The codename for a controversial rootkit based on x86 virtualization technology.

Branch a package To upgrade an existing sequenced application package and run it side by side with the original sequenced application package.

Boot Camp virtual machine Using an existing Boot Camp installation as a VM. Contrast with normal VM.

Bubble computing Computes in a contained and well-managed environment. It combines the concepts of enterprise-level management, application services hosting, and cloud computing where everything is hosted remotely.

C

Checkpoint A snapshot of a VM that enables an administrator to roll the VM back to its state at the moment the checkpoint was created.

Child operating system Another term for the guest OS that runs in a VM on top of the parent or host OS.

Cloning Virtualization permits the fast creation of running systems. The conventional installation of OSes and applications can take some time. With cloning, copies of a VM can be created in a single installation and configuration process. It simplifies and accelerates the distribution of standardized computing environments to employees or the creation of a base configuration for testing.

Cloud computing A consumption and delivery model for information technology (IT) services based on the Internet. It typically involves the use of dynamically scalable and often virtualized resources.

Compact To reduce the size of a dynamically expanding virtual hard disk by removing unused space from the .vhd file.

Connection Broker In Virtual Desktop Infrastructure, a software or hardware solution for VM management, network connection and session tracking, and access rights management.

Console window The window on the host that allows you to interact with the guest.

Converter With a Converter, physical computers can be converted into VMs.

Copy-On-Write (COW) disk Part of a snapshot and keeps track of disk changes since the snapshot was taken.

D

Desktop virtualization Using VMs to serve a number of desktop environment needs such as running multiple OSes simultaneously on the same hardware, hosting multiple virtual desktop environments on a single server, and simplifying management of multiple desktop environments.

Differencing Virtual Hard Disk A virtual hard disk that stores the changes to an associated parent virtual hard disk for the purpose of keeping the parent intact. Changes continue to accumulate in the differencing disk until it is merged to the parent disk.

Disaster recovery In virtual environments, it is the setup of new systems and the recovery of OSes without the need for special hardware, patches, and firmware.

Dynamic Suite Composition An application virtualization feature that enables a virtual application package to allow dependent plug-ins to use the virtual environment. This feature enables plug-ins and middleware packages to behave and interact with each other in the same way as if they were installed locally on a machine.

Dynamically Expanding Virtual Hard Disk A virtual hard disk that grows in size each time it is modified.

E

ESXi A free VMware virtualization software product aimed at businesses and enterprise.

F

File-based disk A virtual disk in which the contents are stored in a file or multiple files for split disks.

Fixed-size Virtual Hard Disk A virtual hard disk with a fixed size that is determined and for which all space is allocated when the disk is created. The size of the disk does not change when data is added or deleted.

Fullscreen A view mode where the guest display takes up an entire physical monitor (or more). Contrast with single-window and unity.

Fully virtual A VM that completely emulates all hardware devices.

Fusion A VMware hosted virtualization software product. Runs on Mac OS X hosts. The proper name is *VMware Fusion*.

G

Grab To direct input (that is, keyboard and mouse) to a VM, for example, by clicking in a console window. Contrast with ungrab.

Grid computing The combining of computer resources from multiple administrative domains applied to a common task, usually applied to scientific or technical problems that require a tremendous number of processing cycles.

Guest clustering Clustering of VMs within the same node or across different nodes.

Guest operating system The OS running on a VM. There can be multiple guests per physical machine but only one per VM.

H

Hardware virtualization When the VM manager is part of the circuits of the hardware instead of within a software hypervisor.

High availability A tool capable of restarting VMs automatically on another server if a server fails. The tools also monitor the capacity of a server and choose an optimal server for the VM to run on.

Host The OS that has direct control of the hardware.

Host–Guest File System VMware's name for the guest-visible aspect of a shared folder.

Hypervisor Also called *virtual machine monitor*. A software application that allows several instances of one or of several different OSes to run on a single machine. It controls the CPU and all hardware resources and provides every OS instance with the required resources.

I

Importer A companion program for Fusion 1.x that translates other VMs to a format that Fusion understands.

Installation directory The directory where the installer for the application virtualization sequencer places its files.

Integration Services A collection of services and software drivers that maximize performance and provide a better user experience within a VM.

J

JeOS Pronounced "juice", this is short for Just Enough Operating System. It is a type of software appliance with a customized OS designed to precisely fit the needs of a particular application.

L

Live backup The capability to backup a VM without a perceived interruption in service.

Live migration The capability to move a VM from one node to another node without a perceived interruption in service.

M

Multitenancy A cloud computing term describing a software architecture where a single instance of the software runs on a server, serving multiple client organizations, or tenants.

O

Operating system virtualization The virtualization of an OS permitting the creation of several virtual instances of an OS on a physical system.

P

Paravirtualization A guest OS that has been modified to execute the corresponding instructions of the hypervisor directly within a VM so that no performance loss arises from the emulation of the complete hardware.

Parent partition The partition that manages the VMs.

Physical computer A hardware-based computer that you can physically touch and move as opposed to a software-based VM.

Physical-to-virtual (P2V) migration The process of decoupling and migrating a physical computer's OS, applications, and data to a VM guest.

R

Raw disk A virtual disk where the contents are stored directly on a partition on the physical machine.

S

Saved state A manner of storing a VM so that it can be quickly resumed.

Shared folder A specific method for accessing the host file system from the guest that does not require a network connection.

Snapshot A snapshot conserves the state of a VM so that it can be moved back any time to an earlier, stable system state.

Soft ungrab An "automatic ungrab" such as when your mouse leaves the console window to interact with the host OS.

U

Ungrab To direct keyboard and mouse input away from a VM.

Unity A viewing mode within VMware whereby applications running on the guest OS appear as application windows on the host OS desktop as if they were running on the host OS.

Utility computing The packaging of computing resources that are metered as a service similar to a traditional public utility.

V

Virtual appliance A VM with a fully preinstalled and preconfigured OS image, usually hosting a single application.

Virtual application An application packaged to run in a self-contained, virtual environment without installing the application locally.

Virtual file system The abstraction layer within a virtual environment that allows client applications to access different types of file systems in a standardized way.

Virtual floppy disk A file-based version of a physical floppy disk used in virtual environments.

Virtual hard disk The storage area for a VM. It can reside on any type of storage the host OS can access such as external devices, storage area networks, and network-attached storage.

Virtual machine A software version of a physical computer that operates and executes programs like a physical machine.

Virtual machine configuration The configuration of the resources assigned to a VM such as memory, processors, disks, and network adapters.

Virtual machine monitor See hypervisor.

Virtual network A virtual version of a physical network switch that can be configured to provide access to local or external network resources for one or more VMs.

Virtual switch See virtual network.

Virtual symmetric multiprocessing The process of using multiple cores in one VM.

X

Xen A free software virtualization solution used to manage virtual environments with guest OSes.

INDEX

Page numbers followed by *f* indicates a figure and *t* indicates a table.